THE DAVID GLENN HUNT
MEMORIAL LIBRARY
GALVESTON COMMUNITY COLLEGE
GALVESTON, TEXAS

# The Proustian Vision

# The Proustian Vision

BY MILTON HINDUS

*Columbia University Press, New York, 1954*

*Library of Congress Catalog Card Number: 53-11068*

PUBLISHED IN GREAT BRITAIN, CANADA, INDIA, AND PAKISTAN
BY GEOFFREY CUMBERLEGE, OXFORD UNIVERSITY PRESS
LONDON, TORONTO, BOMBAY, AND KARACHI

MANUFACTURED IN THE UNITED STATES OF AMERICA

FOR LUDWIG LEWISOHN

*the artist, the teacher, and the friend*

# Preface

In the tradition of punning upon Proust's own titles which has been so popular with his critics and commentators (*Du côté de chez Proust* by François Mauriac, *A la recherche de Marcel Proust* by André Maurois, *Du côté de chez Proust* by Benjamin Crémieux) I was a little tempted to call my study *Remembrance of Things Proust.* That is what my book will be found to be. It is *my* Proust that I am trying to project here. This book is personal in its nature, selective in its approach, loosely informal in its method, and makes no pretence to finality or completeness in the treatment of its subject. The reader acquainted with other Proustian criticism will perhaps miss from my own discussion some long familiar landmarks and references. He will, on the other hand, find emphasis given to certain subordinate figures slighted elsewhere.

My subject is an outstanding example of what might be called the Monastic Movement in Modern Literature. Of this movement, Joyce is the twin pillar with Proust, and cells of the monastery are occupied by such fascinating personalities as Kafka, Italo Svevo, and Pound. The original monastic movement, as we know, performed some notable services for the world, though there were occasional lapses from the ideal which it represented—lapses thoroughly explored by writers from Boccaccio and Rabelais to the Marquis de Sade and

Robert Browning. Not everyone who entered a cloister had the qualities to become a saint, and not everyone who contributes to the littlest magazines or publishes esoteric volumes is necessarily a genius. But much of the genius in our time has made its unheralded appearance in hermetic forms and in unlikely places difficult of access. Our best writers have often come to resemble anchorites (even when, like Joyce, they are of the Nietzschean rather than of any Orthodox persuasion) who have retreated into hermitages far removed from the confusing competition of the noisy market place and the fickle pressures of a directionless mass. The solitudes which Proust entered have become mythical.

We are too near to say with certainty what the consequences of this movement will be, but one thing seems clear even now to the most sensitive readers. Autonomous isolation was for many great artists in our time the only alternative to the still more frightening possibilities of completely hostile alienation and hopeless divorce from society. They were not wrong, in other words, in taking the road of separation. In saving themselves, they have also saved a portion of us. Their faith has been justified by their works, and though we sometimes lack the courage to follow in their footsteps all the way, we have been permanently humbled by their example.

## Acknowledgments

CONDENSED versions of my chapters on Proust's sociology, psychology, and ethics have been printed in various magazines over a number of years. Grateful acknowledgment is due to *The New Republic* in which my article "Proust and Society" appeared on December 8, 1941; to the *University of New Mexico Quarterly Review* in which the article "The Pattern of Proustian Love" appeared in the Winter of 1951; and to *The Chicago Jewish Forum: a National Quarterly* in which "Proust's Ethics and the Jews" appeared in the Fall of 1952.

I wish to thank Random House for its permission to use the quotations which are made in this book from the American edition of Proust. The translations from *Jean Santeuil,* which has not yet been published in this country, are my own.

I am indebted to Brandeis University for a generous grant out of the Research Fund of the University, and I should also like to record my appreciation of the helpful criticisms of my manuscript made by Dr. Joseph Cheskis, Professor of Romance Languages and Chairman of the School of Humanities at Brandeis University.

I remember gratefully those students of mine at The College of The University of Chicago, at The New School for Social Research, as well as at Brandeis University, who have listened to the ideas of this book as these were presented to them in various courses. Mention should also be made of The Edgar Allan Poe Society in New York and of The College English Association before which I presented some of my materials.

The help of my wife throughout deserves something better than a banal formula. This help, in the form of many concrete and practical suggestions, has been so constantly real to me that it should puzzle me at this time to be asked to point out the places in the text where I introduced modifications or changes because of her comments.

M. H.

# Contents

INTRODUCTION 3

THE AESTHETICS OF PROUST 33

THE PHILOSOPHY OF PROUST 78

THE PSYCHOLOGY OF PROUST 122

THE SOCIOLOGY OF PROUST 165

THE ETHICS OF PROUST 205

CONCLUSION 252

SELECTED BIBLIOGRAPHY 279

INDEX 283

*This fiction, however, is in so far different*
*from other fictions that it includes profound ideas*
*and great mysteries, removes great doubts, and reveals*
*the most important truths.*

MAIMONIDES, *The Guide for the Perplexed*
Part III, Chapter xxii

# The Proustian Vision

# *Introduction*

IN THE YEAR 1952, thirty years after the death of Proust, one of his earlier works, the existence of which had for some time been suspected but not confirmed, was finally published in its entirety by Gallimard in Paris for the inspection of the critical public. By critical public, I mean naturally a public of critics, for the public in general can hardly be expected to show more than a perfunctory and polite interest in the work of a master which is only a suggestion of a masterwork.[1] But the more specialized Proustian public will not only be curious about this new, three-volume, one-thousand-page work, but will doubtless, after examining it, be perfectly delighted.

As a result of the discovery of *Jean Santeuil*, there is now a bridge to cover the gap between *Les Plaisirs et les jours* and *A la recherche du temps perdu*. There had been till now an astonishing, unaccountable leap from the immaturity of the first work to the mastery of the last. With nothing to stand in between them, the differences were an obvious invitation to romantic conjectures, for not only did it seem that the writer had managed to raise himself by his own bootstraps into greatness, but that he had done so all at once. *Jean*

[1] This conjecture was subsequently confirmed by André Maurois, *Letter from Paris* in *The New York Times Book Review* of December 14, 1952: "*Jean Santeuil* by Marcel Proust, a novel discovered after the author's death, has aroused much interest in the literary world but not among the general public."

*Santeuil* supplies the necessary link, and we now see the development from the earlier to the later Proust as a gradual, evolutionary process, much less exciting and dramatic but also much more natural. The long foreground of Proust's accomplishment is at last securely established.

It is instructive to look at the evolution of Proust's faculties as a creative artist in terms of the categories of Aristotle's *Poetics*. Aristotle called the management of *plot* the most important element in dramatic composition, and he subordinated to it the ability to create character, the command over language, and the other elements that enter into literary composition. The philosopher said, furthermore (and it is one of his amazingly fruitful observations), that it may be observed among the dramatists that mastery with regard to the drawing of character precedes mastery with regard to the satisfactory management of the plot, which generally awaits the growth of the writer's abilities. This fine distinction is fully confirmed by the development which we find in Proust, it seems to me. The principal difference between *Jean Santeuil* and *A la recherche du temps perdu* lies in the management of the plot found in the latter work and entirely absent from the former.

So far as the ability to animate his characters is concerned, Proust's talents must certainly be judged notable in the earlier work. What is absent there is the ability to put his characters into any real and long-drawn-out relations with each other. It is the pattern of these interrelationships that creates the conviction of the passage of time in the later novel, and with the passage of time the changes which the characters undergo. *Jean Santeuil,* on the other hand, can only by the widest latitude of criticism and with the utmost courtesy of definition be called a novel at all. It lacks entirely that organic unity and logic which seem inherent in the concept of this literary form. The difference is not such as exists between the episodic type of story and one with a more tightly knit development, because even in the episodic type the writer must create a coherent sense of movement or progress in the steps of his fable. *Jean Santeuil* does not manage to convey this movement to the reader. It is nothing more than a bundle of charming sketches revolving for the most part around the same characters. These characters do not seem to be going anywhere in particular. We are *told* that they grow old, for example, but we do not really believe it, because the author has not as yet the skill to create the illusion by imitating the slow and subtle changes by which age shows itself.

This skill of the full-fledged novelist Proust was to achieve in a pre-eminent degree later on. The delicate functioning of the connective tissues in his masterpiece is something to consider, and this smoothes over the deep changes in character, so that they carry conviction to the reader and are accepted without difficulty. Proust's gifts in *Jean Santeuil* are still mostly hidden in the cocoon, and the result is a work which possesses about as much organic connectedness as a bag full of beautiful marbles. The chapters individually are filled with lovely impressions, but we fail to see why any one of them should precede or follow any other. As a book, it is without beginning, middle, or end. Its sequences seem to be entirely fortuitous. Necessity here is not a compelling and unbreakable chain but only the slenderest of threads.

In his later life, Proust used to refer to his "architectural labors" ("travaux d'architecte") upon *A la recherche du temps perdu.* The phrase is instructive. What Aristotle means by the term plot is indeed the work of an "architect" of literary form. In the earlier work there is little evidence of long-range, planned construction, and successful articulation of separate parts. Everything seems largely improvised, and though a plan seems to lurk somewhere in the back of the author's mind as a potentiality of his material, it is all pretty vague, indefinite, and unrealized.

What we have then in *Jean Santeuil* is a gathering of the writer's forces and a marshaling of his materials, which are as yet not subjected to the proper discipline and order. The experienced reader of Proust will take pleasure in discovering the germs of many later developments in his work. As a trivial example, in the description of the novelist C. in *Jean Santeuil*—"Occasionally he would remove his pince-nez, wipe his forehead, and run his hand through his reddish hair which was just beginning to be touched with gray" [2]—the reader of *Remembrance of Things Past* is reminded of Swann's hair and of one of his most characteristic gestures. When Proust tells us that Jean regularly attended the courtroom sessions of the trial of Zola which grew out of the Dreyfus Case and that he took sandwiches along with him, we recall the transposition of this into a similar anecdote told about the character Bloch in the later novel. Sometimes both a minor character and incident are lifted bodily from the earlier composition. This is the case with the Bonapartist Prince de Borodino, whose name and traits remain unchanged in both books. Jean's memory of a happier time in love is reawakened by a theme of music in the same way as Swann's is. And Jean's cross-examination of his mistress becomes Swann's of Odette with little change. When Mme Cresmeyer does not open a message which is delivered to her on the eve of a great party in her house because she suspects

[2] *Jean Santeuil* (Paris, 1952), I, 43.

that it may be an announcement of the death of a close relative which would force her to postpone the party, we recognize, beneath a change of both sex and social station, one of the striking features in the character of the Duc de Guermantes. Bergotte, with whom we are familiar in the later work as a great writer, turns up in the earlier as a painter. And Gilberte's well-known agate is here too, though Gilberte herself is not. Present also is a premonition of one of the most powerful scenes involving the jealousy of Swann—the scene in which he believes that he has at last surprised the perfidious Odette in a room at night with her guilty lover, only to find at the last moment, after intolerable suspense, that he has mistaken the lighted shutters of another house on the same street for those of the windows of her room.

All these scenes and characters are virtually unchanged, and yet the forceful effect which they have in the later book is lacking in the earlier one. The force is lacking because the arrangement of materials in the two books is different. This seems to be clear proof that the power of a character or an episode is not inherent in itself alone but is dependent on its precise place in the composition of which it is a part. No better argument exists for the importance of form in art. I remember once hearing a dance critic say that art without form would be like soup on a flat plate—"there just wouldn't be any soup." Something of the kind may be said of *Jean Santeuil.* There are many nourishing qualities in this earlier book of Proust, but he has not yet devised the receptacle from which the reader might imbibe its effect with pleasure.

A legitimate extension of Aristotle's remarks about plot and character and the degree of maturity in the writer necessary to mastering each one is that some of the other elements of composition which he mentions—thought and diction—may be mastered by the writer even before he has solved the problems of character and plot. Certainly this proves to be so with Proust whose *Les Plaisirs et les jours,* earlier in date of composition than either *Jean Santeuil* or *A la recherche du temps perdu,* is inferior to both of these with regard to characterization and storytelling. Only a certain sweetness of style, a music of words, and an aphoristic ability are to be found in all the works of Proust from first to last. He visibly mounts from one rung of the ladder of composition to the next, beginning with a harmonious style and proceeding from mastery of character drawing to the command of plot construction. Style is his native endowment. It is his starting point. Everything else comes to him slowly through hard work.

### THE RELATIONSHIP BETWEEN PROUST'S WORK AND HIS LIFE

I shall have little to say about Proust's life except as a knowledge of his life is intimately connected with his work, and this seems to me rarely to be the case. Facts about the life of an author, while sometimes a legitimate digression for the critic and often a pleasant diversion for the reader, too often become ends in themselves and an escape from the more serious responsibility of grappling with the work itself. In *Jean Santeuil* Proust himself has something to say on this subject, and though he seems to confine his remarks to the painting of Gustave Moreau, the sense of these remarks covers a much wider area in the problems of criticism:

If you wished to try to fathom the meaning of those mysterious nude forms, with hair woven like the lotus and heavy eyes filled with dreams, which can be seen in all the canvasses of Gustave Moreau, or if you wanted a deeper understanding of those cliffs where a statuette rises in one of the anfractuosities of the landscape in his pictures, it would be entirely useless to you to know in detail the life of Gustave Moreau, to speak with him on the subject of art, of life and of death, or to dine with him every evening. You would be no closer to the solution of the mystery of their origin and of their significance, since he himself, to tell the truth, no longer knows them; they were all borne to him with exact precision, like strange sea-nymphs, on the tides of inspiration which assailed him. What he should be able to tell you would carry no resemblance except to the outward circumstances of their invention, that is to say the earthly part of their construction (such and such a landscape which he had actually seen, such a cultivated plot of land which he had once admired) but would contain no hint of the analogy which united them, the essence of which, though it must have been present once in his mind, since he alone had isolated it and bodied it forth, is nevertheless unknown to him.[3]

The main idea of this passage seems to be that found originally in the Platonic dialogue *Ion*. There, Socrates reaches the conclusion that the poets themselves are often the most ignorant of the meaning of their own works and the very last who ought to be appealed to for an interpretation of them. For the poet, according to Plato, works not according to science but by inspiration. He is the instrument used by powers higher than he realizes. The criticism which brings us nearer to an awareness of the ultimate source of the poet's inspiration and the meaning of the reflections of the ideal which are seen in his work is alone worthwhile according to this criterion. True criticism of art, far from being helped by the humble and sometimes actually sordid details of an author's personal history, is more likely to be hindered and distracted by them. The contrast between what artists produce and what they themselves are is often so great that the attempt to connect them is like trying to bring heaven and

[3] *Ibid.*, II, 12.

earth together. See what a confused clod the man proves himself in life, and yet see the magnificence of what he has done. No, better say, see what has been done through him and almost in spite of him! Only by surrendering himself wholly to that power which inspires him can the writer totally surpass himself, and only by surpassing that poor miserable self of his can he hope to become of permanent value and interest to other people.

There is, of course, a connection between the life of an artist and his art, but this connection is sometimes negative and indirect rather than positive and direct, and it has at all times to be approached with a great deal of skepticism. The quality of the connection is of gossamerlike delicacy and subtlety. We must be prepared to approach the matter from the side of the light which his art throws upon his life rather than the other way around, which is the usual approach. In the case of the real artist, it is art which is the more important part of the equation. The man lives in order to create, and without the creation his life would seem to be void and meaningless.

A generation of living with the work of Proust has left me with the thought that three things within it, at least, are vitally connected to the known facts of his biography. But before mentioning what these are, I should note that his poor life has become the subject of much scandalous surmise, which is perhaps as significant of the psychology of the critics themselves as it is of that of the man they are criticizing. To one group he has become a kind of aesthetic martyr, to another group he appears to be a moral leper, and to both something more or less than what he intended to be. These interpretations are achieved by magnifying still further certain aspects of Proust's own creative magnifications, and the result is not clarity but obfuscation. The drawing of Proust as either saint or devil is possible only by the method of distortion, and the resulting picture has most meaning in relation to the image-making needs of the critics themselves. I grant that every person's image in this world must be seen by another person through the refraction of an alien vision (we cannot see him "face to face" in the Scriptural sense even when we are face to face with him—perhaps in such physical proximity least of all), but the success of each effort is measured by the ability to see the vision *more* or *less* darkly. And if one thinks that he sees it less darkly, he must plot the outlines of the main features more simply and clearly than has hitherto been done—the result to be measured by the conviction which it carries and the satisfaction which it gives.

The first fact of basic significance in the relation of Proust's work to his life seems to me to be that the narrator of *A la recherche du temps perdu,* who is identified in the course of the narrative as "Marcel," is normally constituted in being heterosexual, unlike Proust himself who was a homosexual. The second significant fact is that the narrator's mother in the story is not a Jewess, unlike Proust's own mother, who was born Mlle Weil and came of a prominent Alsatian Jewish family of financiers and merchants. The third fact to be remembered is that the narrator of the story is an only child, unlike the author himself, whose brother Robert played so great a part in the early days of the formation of the Proust cult.

These are not the only changes, but they are the important ones, in the sense that all the others seem to stem from them. The change of both sex and occupation which Proust's chauffeur Agostonelli underwent in being transformed into the model for Albertine in the novel is the result of the initial assumption of the hero's own normality. Similarly, the hero's rise in high society is easier and more unhindered than Proust's own would appear to have been because, unlike Proust, his fictitious alter ego does not have the handicap of his Jewish ancestry to contend with. And finally, the hero's being spoiled and treated with the excessive indulgence of an only child (his mother's allowing him, for example, to bring an unmarried girl to live in their house—a license of invention with which Mauriac and other critics find fault as being insufficiently motivated) is rendered less incredible by the assumption that there are no other children in the house to share his mother's love. It is evident that the changes in these basic facts imply necessarily countless other transpositions to be consistent with them.

But what is my interpretation of the meaning of these changes? I think that the work of art has something in common with both the dream and the confession, though dream and confession are superficially antithetical to each other. Dreams, as good observers must have known before Freud made it explicit, are created by the wish fulfillments of the dreamer which are pleasurable. Confessions, on the other hand, if they are genuine and not merely sham, are invariably self-destructive and full of torment. There are, however, as we all know by experience, tormenting dreams also, which seem to deal with pleasures which our wakeful minds find it difficult to confess, and which are very difficult to remember with any clarity of detail. The dreams easiest to recall are those which make us feel good about ourselves, for such dreams create and reinforce the personal image which we would impress upon the world, while confessions mercilessly criticize and tear that same image down.

The pleasurable dream element in the work of Proust is the elimination in his fictional representation of all those aspects of himself or of his family situation which gave him pain. The most persistent fantasy of Proust hinged on three possibilities which had been contradicted by reality—*if* only he could display his tastes in love with the freedom of other men, *if* only he were not the offspring of a mixed marriage but had Christian parents on both sides, and *if* only there had been no other child in the family to share his mother's love. The qualities of the good brother, the dutiful son, and the aberrant lover which he was in recalcitrant reality were transposed in his fantasy into those of a character whose sex life is normal, whose mother's origin causes no conflict within him, and who has her alone to himself. Such ruthless transformations are permissible only in dreams and in art, which has been called a type of play or pleasurable make believe.

What would life have been like could these three wishes have been realized instead of being vetoed by a malignant fate? Perhaps Proust originally undertook his vast work partly as an experiment to find the answer to this tantalizing question. Through the medium of his narrator, Proust was able imaginatively to live another life, a life like his own in most ways and yet in some crucial respects utterly unlike his own. The pleasure which he found in this so slight break with reality may account in part for the enthusiasm which carried him through so many volumes with so little encouragement at the beginning from the world.

In one sense, then, his work was for Proust a method of escape from the most painful psychological realities of his life. To the imagination, as Aristotle noticed, there is no difference between the merely possible and the actually real.

Proust retreated from reality first of all, and his readers have followed him afterwards. But the figure for the artist's effort seems to be that of the boomerang or the "bad" dream, which causes us to cry out with more pain than we feel when awake. Proust is not simply the clever escapist. He does not rid himself magically of his concern with homosexuality or the Jewish nation or his mother's love by taking the conflicts involving these away from his narrator hero. In fact, the very points eliminated from his direct confession, which made it so pleasurable to begin with, are precisely the loci around which his concerns obsessively revolve. Outside the narrator, the story teems with characters who are either homosexuals or Jews (and sometimes, as in the case of Nissim Bernard, a combination of the two), and it is saturated in mother love.

Proust turned the image of the world as he experienced it inside out. The positive picture which he printed was developed from the negative of himself, and this was the necessary condition for its development with any art or equanimity. Perhaps this was what Wilde meant when he said to Gide: "From now on, don't write *I* any more. In art, don't you see, there is no first person." [4] That is to say: Don't attempt direct confession; find some oblique angle or mask for yourself before you attempt to communicate the truth which is closest to you. What Proust represents himself as only watching or witnessing (the scene involving Mlle Vinteuil and her friend at Montjouvain,[5] the scene involving

[4] André Gide, *Oscar Wilde* (New York, 1949), p. 28.

[5] It is perhaps interesting to reflect, considering the vice of Mlle Vinteuil, on the similarity of the second syllable of her name and that of Santeuil, whose sex life is normal. In the newly discovered work, there is more than one flirtation with unconventional subject matter (for example, the story of the wayward nun in volume III, and the passage in the same volume dealing with the blackmail and suicide of a homosexual), but this is no more than

Charlus and Jupien in the courtyard of the Guermantes and later in the room where the narrator spies on them by standing up on a chair and peeping through the transom above the door, and the scene in the house of sado-masochistic delights during the World War) he had once acted out in reality himself; and, on the other hand, what he shows himself as acting out in the story (the psychology of one untroubled by conflicts caused by an abnormal sex life and an unmixed national origin) he had really only seen in the lives of others. The moving accents with which Proust describes the plight of homosexuals and Jews would not have been present to the same degree had he not known what it was to be stigmatized himself.

"Tell all the truth but tell it slant," said Emily Dickinson and, in giving the advice, spoke on behalf of all artists for whom the literal truth is too shameful to confess, yet who cannot rest in the concealment of their secret. I think that this attitude is also at the bottom of Hawthorne's summation of the moral of the Reverend Mr. Dimnesdale's harrowing experience: "Be true! Be true! Be true! Show freely to the world, if not your worst, yet some trait whereby the worst may be inferred!" For the artist, the inference to his innermost truth is to be drawn from his work of art. Everything essential is really there, but it is stated from an angle. Even such a seemingly naive and "direct" poet as Whitman was forever stressing *indirection* as the inescapable characteristic of art, and the proof that he himself achieved this indirection in his own work is that the hidden facts of his life have been raked over as mercilessly and suspiciously as

a hint of the concentrated attention which such material receives in the later work. *Jean Santeuil,* composed while Proust's parents were still alive, is still relatively repressed and "decent," though it several times skirts upon the dangerous and forbidden territory which he was to make peculiarly his own.

those of Proust's. The secret of art is an open secret. But it must be added, from the noise always made about the lives of artists, that it is apparently far from being obvious. Essential revelations in the most prominently publicized places have been missed by the critics with a consistency which suggests an analogy between the technique of artistic concealment and that practised by the sly fox in Poe's *Purloined Letter*. The critics, it seems, outsmart themselves, ransacking the subtlest crevices of a work in search of hiding places, when all the while the sought for revelation declares itself plainly in the largest features. It literally "leaps to the eyes," and is therefore rejected as too obvious and innocent of meaning.

The fundamental importance of the changes which Proust introduced into the transposition of his own character to his pages is that they enabled him to tell the truth about himself. The slight break which he made in the straightness of his confession is what accounts for the success of its *seeming* straight when seen through the eyes of the reader, because of the inevitable subjective refraction which such vision necessarily implies. Had Proust attempted to be more direct, he probably would have failed and begun to posture and to sound completely false. The device which enabled him to appear before the world in a mask, however light and transparent, permitted him to speak without excessive self-consciousness and therefore to tell the truth which hurt without taking personal responsibility for it—as Gide, for example, had to do. The problem, of course, is finding the proper angle to compensate for the reader's refraction. Infinitesimally out of the way one way or another, and the artist is at once lost in the poseur. The difference may be so small that it is invisible to the critical intellect, but it will be absolutely and immediately clear to the intuitive feelings. The penalty of artlessness is to be mistaken for imposture. This is shown in an odd way by the history of language, in which it is the fate of words originally denoting simplicity eventually to degenerate to mean foolishness.

It is interesting to note that the vital changes of identity which constitute the Proustian mask did not await the composition of *A la recherche du temps perdu* but had already all been present in the earlier *Jean Santeuil,* where, as a matter of fact, one of them appears to have been much more heavily emphasized and unmistakably underlined. There is a marked insistence on the fact that Jean Santeuil's mother is not Jewish, though she is represented as being magnanimously tolerant of her Jewish friends.[6] The author goes to the length of depicting his mother as a *blonde,*[7] the very inverse, in other words, of Proust's actual mother, who, to judge from her extant portraits, belonged to the characteristically dark-haired, Alsatian Jewish type. In *A la recherche du temps perdu,* it is tacitly assumed that the narrator's mother is not Jewish, though no such obvious indications as those in *Jean Santeuil* are given. In this respect, then, the later treatment is subtler than the earlier one.

There are other respects, too, in which the author's transformation of his wish fulfillments about his family life into the material of his art is in a much rawer, less advanced, and more obvious state in *Jean Santeuil* than it was to become in *A la recherche du temps perdu.* There are a number of scenes, for example, in the earlier book which parallel the primal scene of the great novel, involving the narrator's feelings as a child about his mother's goodnight kiss. The opening of *Jean Santeuil* provides the most obvious and

[6] *Jean Santeuil,* II, 72.

[7] *Ibid.,* p. 69.

direct equivalent to the introduction of the novel, but I think that the deepest and most significant similarity of feeling in the two books occurs towards the end of *Jean Santeuil,* where Proust describes Jean's reaction to a day when his father departs from home and he has his mother all to himself, just as he did on the memorable night of parental "abdication" later in Combray. The day of Jean's father's absence is compared, in a poignant figure of speech, to a day of *convalescence* for the son. The frankness of the acknowledgment of hostility which this figure of speech implies is to be softened during his maturity, and the final scene of the earlier composition, which contains a premonition of Jean's father's death, is entirely eliminated from the later one.

There are scenes of family life in *Jean Santeuil* which are so ugly and brutal in their unadorned naturalism that they come as a positive shock to the reader of Proust's later work. Scenes in which the son is driven in desperation to call his parents "imbeciles" to their face, and they are hardly more gentle in their retorts to him, form no part of his recaptured memories, which seem, by comparison, to be misted over and softened in a golden haze of Watteaulike romance and nostalgia.

The reasons for Jean's clashes with his family are clearly rooted in his emotional isolation among them and their hostility towards everything he represents. In his later book the narrator's difficulty in finding his way to art is explained as being entirely inward, but in the earlier book it is parental opposition which is largely responsible for his failure of self-realization as an artist. Jean Santeuil's grandfather is contemptuous of poets and poetry, and his father evidently shares the aversion.[8] Jean's mother, though much more sensitive and sympathetic to her son, has an attitude not really much more helpful to him, summed up in these words: "Frivolous as a study, but noble as a pleasure, poetry appeared to her to be the delicate flower of wasted time." [9] To such an attitude of mind, a serious poet could have appeared to be little better than a wastrel. Jean's mother always has good intentions towards her son to begin with, but she is too self-deprecating in the face of an obtuse and uncomprehending world, which is represented by the rest of her family, resolutely to assert these initial impulses of sympathy. This is evident in the ironic characterization of Jean's parents: "Much more intelligent than her husband, endowed with an artistic sense, general intelligence, tact and sensibility, which were almost entirely lacking in him, Madame Santeuil was nevertheless convinced that all these gifts mattered little, since a man so superior as her husband was lacking in them." [10]

But such critical and even contemptuous feelings towards his parents are compensated by other feelings. There is in Jean Santeuil a very strong identification with his father (against whom he has sinned mentally so often through his hostility), so that he finally goes to the length of preferring his father's candidates to political office in place of his own.[11]

With such a background, it is small wonder that Jean feels that our own past always constitutes an inimitable work of art,[12] and that as early as his twenty-second year he is already tormented by the thought of "temps perdu." [13]

[8] *Ibid.*, I, 77.
[9] *Ibid.*, pp. 84–86.
[10] *Ibid.*, p. 76.
[11] *Ibid.*, III, 288.
[12] *Ibid.*, I, 185.
[13] *Ibid.*, III, 284.

This literal feeling of waste and loss preceded both the conception and title of his principal work.

### THE QUESTION OF PROUST'S STYLE

Since this book is to be so largely devoted to ideas and abstractions, which are nearly the same for all languages, I think that something ought to be said too about Proust's quality in French. It is to be noted as an interesting fact that his style, which seems to me the least debatable part of his equipment as an artist, has, from the very first, been more heatedly discussed, argued, and even denied altogether than any other element of his work. I have seen the view expressed that C. K. Scott-Moncrieff's translation into English is so much better and more lucid than the original, that it should be translated back into French. Even if it is obvious that such an eccentric opinion merely expresses its author's taste for outrageous paradox, it still remains the statement of a view which, in a more moderate form, is apparently shared by other readers.

Proust has been described as having a style which, in its extremely intricate involvements and convolutions, is reminiscent of the obscurity attending certain German philosophers rather than of that classic purity which is the hallmark of the genius of French prose. But much as I admire Mr. Moncrieff's excellent translation, it does not seem to me to compare in quality with the original. In any writer who is a master of the music of his own tongue, the echo of that music in any other language must remain just that—an echo. Cervantes long ago accurately remarked of the relation of a literary masterpiece to its translation that it resembled that existing between the two sides of a Flemish carpet. The design on the whole is the same on both sides, but on the wrong one it is a little faded and in places gets to be stringy and disheveled.

No work of secular literature has had the advantage of the devotion bestowed upon the King James Version of the Bible by its translators. The secular work has one or two translators at most, instead of the fifty-four who worked on the Bible. But in the matter of translation precisely, the rule is different from what it is in creative work where the individual imagination reigns unchallenged. In translation, as anyone may find by experience, two heads are always better than one, three than two, and so on. And no amount of collaboration can entirely reproduce in a foreign language the complete charm of an original master. Not the greatest and most famous translations in world literature have succeeded in doing this, not the Bible in English or Shakespeare in German. I am not saying this with the object of denying to the English translator of Proust the value of his magnificent accomplishment, which was not completed because of his death, but of restoring the credit to whom it principally belongs—to Proust himself.

It must be noted that Proust apparently disagreed with many of his critics and took infinite pains with his style, saying that it was his final intention to write his book so that it could be read aloud like a poem. This intention has either been ignored or scoffed at by those critics for whom he plainly failed to fulfill it, though some of these critics are attracted by other psychological and philosophical powers which are displayed in the work.

It would be tempting to believe that for anyone who still remained to be convinced of the euphony of Proust's style the discovery of *Jean Santeuil* should definitely settle the question. But this temptation must be resisted if only because of the reflection that a man who has not been pleased by the harmonies of Proust's prose before this time is hardly likely to hear what the lovers of his style hear not only in *Jean Santeuil* but throughout his work.

It is not inconceivable, indeed, that a writer may be great because of the predominant power of other more important elements of literary composition and be notoriously deficient in his feeling for words and their arrangement, as is said to be the case with the journalistic sloppiness of Dostoyevsky's Russian and as is manifestly the case with the boorish awkwardness of Dreiser's English. One of the chief beauties of Proust to me, however, is his style in French, and whoever does not read him in the original must, I feel, be necessarily deprived of an important element, the absence of which helps to highlight some other aspect—Proust's thought, his characters, his story. In French, the latter elements are combined with a vivacity of language which at times almost puts them in shadow and always manages to keep them in their place. If Proust had no substance but only style, he would seem to me a kind of John Lyly of the French language, and this is no mean compliment when we consider that Shakespeare himself had something to learn from the author of *Euphues.* As a matter of fact, the extant imitations of Proust's style have all leveled against him the implicit accusation of being the French equivalent of what we mean by Euphuism in English—that is to say, the commander of an impressively weighty machinery of artistic expression, with nothing correspondingly important in the subject matter to express.

But though Proust is much more than a stylist (I shall not say "mere" stylist, for the attribute of style, even in the absence of any other quality, is more important than the adjective "mere" implies), still he seems to me to be nothing if not a stylist. It is difficult to communicate with other readers on this score. Style is something apparently more delicate and elusive, more fragile to the questioning touch however sensitive, than ideas or characters or plot. Style is of the very essence of the subjective experience of art, as distinguished from the other elements which are more nearly objective and the same for all readers, and it is this subjectivity of the impressions of artistic style which accounts for amazingly different evaluations of the same style and renders so futile when it does not make completely ridiculous the attempt to translate these impressions into something more tangible.

The critic seeking to communicate to his readers his thoughts and feelings about a writer's style must often content himself with the quotation of felicitous passages. But he can't avoid the responsibility of giving at least some general indications of the grounds of his judgment. To me the overall merit of Proust's style is defined by the phenomenally close adherence of the flowing robe of his language to the body of feeling which I sense underneath. The twisted shapes often found in his expression must seem willful to those who do not see in these shapes the outward and accurate renditions of something below the language itself. But to those who sympathetically follow the hidden movements, the fidelity of the imitations in the draperies above will seem wondrous. Proust's language is like some very soft, very clinging, very bright and precious material, which betrays by its glancing lights and spreading shadows the faintest stirring of the sensitivities. It is like sea water troubled by a nervous shimmer of light, whether because it is blown by the wind or heaved up by some pressure it is difficult to say. We only know that it seems continually filled with brilliant flashes of excitement and is never for a moment still.

"The sound must seem an echo of the sense," says Pope in the *Essay on Criticism.* So it always does in Proust. Ben Jonson expresses the same idea as Pope does about the relation of the drapery of words to the informing thought, when he praises Shakespeare by saying that "Nature herself . . . joyed to wear the dressing of his lines." If I had to choose one word to convey my impression of Proust's style, it would be the word *scrupulous,* which is a term equally applicable to technique and ethics; for ultimately, as Proust himself said, style is a matter of vision and even more of life-evaluation. Such formulations, I am afraid, must begin to sound mystical, but for some people there is no way of avoiding them and remaining true to their perceptions.

The feelings of the reader glide over the periods of Proust's prose without awareness of any difference between sound and sense. Proper words in proper places was the phrase with which Jonathan Swift, himself a magnificent stylist, tried to catch the essence of what must ultimately remain a private experience because it is enclosed within each reader's own sensibility. This sort of thing defies logical definition and lends itself, if at all, only to sensible appeals based upon similar experiences.

The intimate clasp between ideas and words, the closeness of their touch and adherence to each other, has always been the measure of good style. And the gift of Proust as a stylist, if I attempt for a moment to fix its sensuous quality as it comes through to me, is that his words have the genius of following the shifting contours of his feelings with the immediacy with which the edge of darkness closes in upon the twitching and tremblings, the slidings and leapings of a flame.

This is the reaction of a reader to so large a mass of the work that it cannot be satisfactorily illustrated through isolated quotations, though it is the most important recommendation of his style. In a sense, this *is* the style of a writer's *whole* work. Fortunately there are other elements of style which do not resist supplying concrete examples. One of these elements is the felicitous comparison which shoots up in the text a brilliant firework of simile or metaphor, supplied by that eye for resemblances which from the most ancient times has been recognized as the prime sign of poetic genius. By the quality of their metaphors, the quality of poets is made known as by an abbreviated symbol. From this point of view, *Jean Santeuil* supplies the most impressive confirmations of the poetic powers of Proust. When he speaks of "those moments of profound illumination in which the mind descends into the depths of things and lights them up like the sun going down into the sea," [14] he not only supplies us with a beautiful example of simile but states its function very clearly and exactly. For it is the perception of true analogies underneath superficial differences and true differences underneath superficial analogies that enables the poet, by means of his figures of speech, to penetrate into the deeps of reality.

Proust realized the rarity of the inspiration which resulted in really memorable metaphors and when he discovered them he hoarded them very carefully for use later on. The most telltale sign in *Jean Santeuil* is the presence of certain striking figures of speech immediately recognizable to the reader of Proust's masterpiece.

[14] *Ibid.*, I, 45.

Occasionally a simile is drawn out by Proust to almost epic length, concealing a shock of surprise in its very tail which none but he seems capable of inventing:

His love escaped his feverish grasp. He searched for its mysterious essence and found only a host of petty actions by which he had sought to bring her pleasure and, more than anything else, to see her; he found only little feelings which he had noticed in her and which she had awakened in himself, all of them very generous feelings and common actions which were not at all like his love for her, that is to say something unanalyzable and unique; it was as if his love had been an obscure, fallen deity, obliged to speak the language of men and to assume, like the ancient gods, a human shape. And yet at times, he had felt near his love, like the voyagers to Emmaus, a Presence which was more than human.[15]

Here the author seems to hover over his quarry in lazy circles and then, with a sudden pounce, to dive to the heart of the matter. We see that he has known what he was up to from the beginning. Wit is always accompanied by rapidity of association, which, whether it has come after long preparation or without any warning, completes its arc more quickly than we have been quite able to follow. He's there before we know it. It is the speed of the sally not the seriousness of its subject which makes us smile when Proust tells us that a man with cancer is like one who unexpectedly possesses "an inner life."

The art simile, of which I shall have more to say later on, also finds a striking illustration in *Jean Santeuil:* "It is said that age brings with it a weakening of our sensations. Perhaps this is so, but these are accompanied by the echo of much older sensations like great singers past their prime whose failing voices are reinforced by an invisible choir." [16]

And as a final example of his metaphorical genius as it

[15] *Ibid.*, III, 254.

[16] *Ibid.*, II, 10.

was expressed in his earlier work, it is worthwhile considering how the feelings and limitless fancies of elementary school days are recaptured in single figure depicting a classroom to which the teacher suddenly returns after being away for a little while: "The pupils—who were still parading fearlessly on top of the rows of desks like sailors on a boat, clambering the beams or balancing precariously between two planks, amidst noises as numerous and deafening as the sounds of the winds, the rigging and the sea—rushed back to their seats in a split second." [17]

There is another element of Proust's style that seems adequately demonstrable and this is the quality and conciseness of his early aphorisms. Here, too, quickness of association is essential, and yet it is something more than mere cleverness which results: "We trust ourselves to love as we do to life without taking account of the nothingness of either one." [18] And it is Proust at his best who remarks of love in *Jean Santeuil:* "What we call our power over things is perhaps nothing more than our lack of demands upon them. One must be in love in order to know that one is not loved in return. When one is no longer in love, one is always certain of being sufficiently loved." [19]

The short, sharp observation from his newly discovered work, "Life is never pretty except at a distance," [20] is good enough to justify the observation of Mauriac about the work of Proust: "What a collection of admirable maxims could one not extract from this book for the profit of busy people." [21]

The mention of Mauriac reminds me that his witness to the magical qualities of Proust's style is the most im-

[17] *Ibid.*, I, 240.
[18] *Ibid.*, III, 244.
[19] *Ibid.*, pp. 250–51.
[20] *Ibid.*, p. 284.
[21] François Mauriac, *Proust's Way* (New York, 1950), p. 55.

pressive I know outside of Gide's belated tribute. Mauriac's passage is worth quoting in full:

> [Proust's] existence and genius were revealed to me through the translation of *Sesame and Lilies* by Ruskin, for which [he] had written the preface. From the first lines of that Preface, I felt myself on the frontiers of an unknown country. . . . That simple Preface threw me into a sort of stupor. From that moment I never stopped asking people about Proust, and I was told about his strange secluded life into which I did not expect ever to penetrate. If I own a copy of the first printing of *Swann's Way*, it is because I had scarcely deciphered the name of Proust in the bookstore windows when I hastened to obtain the book.[22]

It is style which communicates first the news to our nerve ends that a writer whom we have never read before is sending out his message on the wave length of our own sensibility. The other qualities of literature, being strained through the meshes of our intellect, take more time to make themselves felt by us. It is the immediate, overpowering fragrance of personality present in the style which overpowers the sensitive reader, throws him "into a sort of stupor," makes him vibrate in sympathy with the writer, and convinces him that he is on "the frontiers of an unknown country." But style, just to the degree that it is calculated to cause the strongest initial impression on the delicately attuned aesthetic response, escapes the notice of less gifted readers and those with grosser sensibilities, who are invariably more interested in penetrating first *what* a writer has to say rather than being aware of *how* he is saying it. These readers are not aware that the two considerations, though in some sense separate, are also intimately joined together and that one may be a clue to the other. Missing the significance of one may mean missing the significance of both. That seems to have been for a long time what happened to Proust. People

[22] *Ibid.*, pp. 8–9.

who were insensitive to the distinction of his style were also unaware of the importance of what he had to say through his style about art and life. When the more sensitive had shown the way to Proust's value as a writer, many who had not perceived this to begin with came to respond to his work through the power of suggestion and imitation, and these latecomers, not feeling the inner reason which had given rise to the fashion in the first place and responding only to the grosser features of the work visible to those who read as they run, the sensational subject matter, the portrayal of society, and so on, are probably responsible, either through indifference or through active sponsorship, for the pernicious myth that Proust is a writer primarily of content and that he is negligible as a stylist.

### THEMES OF *Jean Santeuil* DEVELOPED IN THE LATER WORK

In addition to the scenes and characters in *Jean Santeuil* which have already been cited as being similar to those in *A la recherche du temps perdu*, it is interesting to see in the newly discovered earlier work those central themes which were destined for much fuller exposition and development later. For example, the idea expressed in this passage: "That sense of exaltation which compels us to offer up beautiful words to achieve some interested object is precisely the contrary of the literary spirit which is forced to express exactly what the writer feels. From which difference undoubtedly springs the antagonism between art and life." [23] Art here is conceived of as the refuge, the sanctuary from an affected and insincere world. Art offers the sole possibility of an escape from tormenting reality.

To the eye grown accustomed to the finer shadings of

[23] *Jean Santeuil,* III, 143–44.

Proust's meaning and to a mind knowing something about Proust's intellectual influences, the source of this antagonism between art and life is contained for us in the single word "interested" in the preceding passage. The trouble with the actions of life is that they are necessarily *interested* actions, which find their motivations and consequences in the present, the immediate past, or the immediate future. Art, on the other hand, takes for itself the subject and the object of eternity. It can draw its material from the remote past and address itself to the most distant future. Art is, whenever it is genuine and truly deserving of its name, *disinterested.* And this distinction, furthermore, is the same as that drawn by the philosopher whom I shall show as influencing Proust so greatly—namely, Schopenhauer. Life for Proust, too, is the restless expression of the unceasingly striving will, and only in art do we manage briefly for a moment to transcend this will, whose principal characteristic is its changeableness, and manage to reach a more secure and permanent ground of judgment. Proust's language leaves us in no doubt about the extent of his debt to Schopenhauer:

> Each time an artist, instead of locating his happiness in his art, puts it in his life, he experiences a feeling of deception and almost of remorse which warns him infallibly that he has deceived himself. So that to write a novel or to live one is not at all the same thing, no matter what is said. And yet our lives are not absolutely separate from our works. I have lived through every scene which I have depicted. How is it possible, then, that they were less valuable as scenes in my life than they are as scenes in my book? *That is so because at the moment I was actually experiencing them, it was my Will which apprehended them within a purpose connected with pleasure or fear, vanity or transgression. And so it happened that their innermost essence escaped me.*[24]

[24] *Ibid.*, II, 253. Italics mine.

Life is the subject of art, but to grasp its meaning we must first stand aside from it and rid ourselves of the distortion which our will introduces between our experience and our understanding. The tonality of disillusion is as strong in the earlier Proust as it is in the later one. He saw through the deceptions of desire, and the terms in which he tells us how he saw through them suggests that his formulation was helped substantially by the German philosopher:

> Why indeed torment ourselves because we do not have what we have desired. For in the course of their perpetual revolutions these things will inevitably end by coming to us. Circumstances change, and what we have once desired we always end by having. Yet circumstances change less quickly than do our own hearts, and if we always end by having what we desire, it is only when we desire it no longer.[25]

With such an attitude to both life and art, it is not surprising that we find in *Jean Santeuil,* as we are to find several times in *A la recherche du temps perdu,* an artist who puts the value of art so far above that of life that the latter appears to him much less precious than do those thoughts which he is able to transpose into his work. The theme of the self-sacrificing artist is foreshadowed as soon as the value of the will is negated. The novelist Bergotte, created by the later Proust, who, in a vision as he is dying, sees life and art in two opposite scales before him and regrets that he has too often sacrificed the permanent joys of one for the ephemera of the other, is clearly germinating in the character of Santeuil, whom Proust describes as follows:

> The various thoughts which he loved to set down seemed to him much more important than himself, to the extent that he was always dreaming, found himself good for nothing if for several days they

[25] *Ibid.,* III, 16.

did not appear in his brain, and when he had them nearly all written down he no longer saw any serious inconvenience in the idea of dying and was entirely resigned to it.[26]

Also in *Jean Santeuil* is the most important point in Proust's psychology of love—namely, that love is essentially a subjective phenomenon and that the overwhelming attraction which the object of our desire exercises upon us is created by our desire itself rather than by its object. This theme, stated in bare abstraction in the earlier book, is destined to be the basis of innumerable ingenious variations later on.

The advice of Proust (quoted at the head of my chapter on his social theme) that if we would understand society and its motions we must first of all descend into the depths of the individual psyche has its counterpart in *Jean Santeuil* in the observation that history is composed of exactly the same stuff as our petty lives.

And, finally, the central motif of Proust's most mature reflections on morality is beautifully expressed in his appeal for kindness and universal toleration found in his recently uncovered work: "We cannot draw near to the most abandoned creatures without recognizing in them the images of men. And the sympathy we feel for their humanity compels our tolerance of their perversity." [27]

The imaginative development of these themes is, of course, only barely suggested in the earlier work, and certainly the lack is felt of that coherence, order, and "architecture" which is Proust's glory in his maturity, but his basic thoughts remain largely unchanged. *Jean Santeuil* holds many novel delights but few real surprises for those who have mastered the materials of which *A la recherche du temps perdu* is composed.

[26] *Ibid.*, pp. 299–300.

[27] *Ibid.*, p. 319.

# The Aesthetics of Proust

*Art is the most real of all things, the sternest school in life and truly the Last Judgment.*
MARCEL PROUST [1]

THE ARTISTS in Proust's work are the only characters who are built up in the reader's esteem instead of being broken down. He is disillusioned with the values of worldly creatures like the Duchesse de Guermantes, but he does not at first realize fully the worth of those who have devoted their lives to art. The highest place in Proust's spiritual hierarchy belongs to the creative artist; below him come the interpreter of art and the aesthetes (or, as Proust calls them, "the celibates of art") who are limited to the appreciation of the works of others. All of these are distinguished from society in general which does not know the transcendent reality embodied in works of art and spends its time on different forms of vanity and "striving after wind."

[1] *The Past Recaptured*, p. 206.

All translated portions from the volumes of *Remembrance of Things Past—Swann's Way, Within a Budding Grove, Guermantes Way, Cities of the Plain, The Captive, The Sweet Cheat Gone*, and *The Past Recaptured*—are from the translation, the best known perhaps in contemporary literature, made by C. K. Scott-Moncrieff and Frederick Blossom and published in New York by Random House in 1934 with an Introduction by Joseph Wood Krutch.

When the writer Bergotte, the painter Elstir, and the composer Vinteuil first appear in *Remembrance of Things Past,* they seem to the reader to be the most ordinary and insignificant creatures of Proust's imagination. Only gradually does the reader become aware that whatever their appearance may indicate, they are all a portion of what Proust calls "the eternal mind." Not only is their intellectual importance revealed, but even their personal lives seem to improve under our observation. They seem to be frivolous or snobbish or ostentatious at the beginning, but this is only a protective coloration which they have assumed from the unredeemed society of which they are a part. We come to see that their devotion to something that is greater than themselves separates them from the world and saves them. Elstir first comes before us in the guise of M. Biche, the silly painter who loved practical jokes; he is affected in his speech and forms part of the Verdurin drawing room during the courtship of Swann and Odette. Vinteuil appears to be a harmless old music master, the obscure neighbor of the narrator's family at Combray, the father of a notorious daughter, and the somewhat vain composer of what are taken to be the feeble trifles of a provincial teacher. As for Bergotte, though he is introduced to us as a famous and important writer, our keyed-up expectations, like those of the narrator himself, are let down by the actual first impression which he makes: "The name Bergotte made me jump like the sound of a revolver. . . . I bowed . . . my salute was returned by a young common little thickset person, with a red nose curled like a snail shell and a black tuft on his chin. I was cruelly disappointed." [2]

But while other characters begin with an impressive ap-

[2] *Within a Budding Grove,* Part 1, p. 169.

pearance and then go on to reveal their spiritual nullity, the development of the artists is a process of creative growth. We become aware later on of the wealth of spiritual feeling that is hidden under the commonplace surface of Vinteuil. Bergotte is less pure, for there struggle in him two distinct personalities—that of the artist and that of the social climber. In the end, the artist in Bergotte wins out, and the scene describing his death shows him in torments of regret not for any worldly ambitions but for his failure to sacrifice himself after the manner of his idolized painter Vermeer in order to change his life into a lasting monument of art. As for Elstir, who made possibly the most trivial impression of any character at the start of the story, he ends in the book as a recluse who has broken entirely with the foolishness of fashion, after the Verdurin episode of his life, in order to live only for his art. When we see him at Balbec in his later years, he seems worthy of the comparisons with saints and heroes which the author lavishes upon him: "Elstir loved to give, to give himself. Everything that he possessed, ideas, work, and the rest which he counted for far less, he would have given gladly to anyone who could understand him. But failing society that was endurable, he lived in an isolation, with a savagery which fashionable people called pose and ill-breeding, public authorities a recalcitrant spirit, his neighbors madness, his family selfishness and pride." [3] That last sentence could apply equally well to Proust's own later years, and his voluntary withdrawal to his cork-lined chamber, where he wrote his books.

The artists in the book have to go through a period of trial and temptation by smart society, the survival of which confirms them in their call. An artist's material, like the

[3] *Ibid.*, Part 2, pp. 176–77.

saint's sanctity, originates in the mistakes of his youth.[4] The final confirmation of reality in the artist is his self-sacrifice to some vision. He must stop "living" in the ordinary sense so as to make of his life a reflection of experience. "Genius," says Proust, "consists in the reflective power of a writer and not in the intrinsic quality of the scene reflected." [5] And in another place, he writes: "It is not the cleverest nor the most learned man nor the one with the best social connections who becomes a Bergotte, but the one who knows how to become a mirror and thus is able to reflect his life, however mediocre." [6] For renunciation of self is the universal rule in art, and if, on the contrary, artists are so often filled with egotism and self-assertion, that may be why there is so much bad art in the world.

The interpreters of artistic works rank far below the creative artists in the realm of art. The actresses Berma and Rachel, the violinist Morel, and the pianist at the Verdurins are the interpreters whom Proust describes. They, too, in order to excel have to have the ability to forget themselves and to think only of the feelings in the work which they are doing. If the ideal for the creator is to make himself a mirror, the ideal for the interpreter, according to Proust,[7] should be to become a transparent medium revealing the work of art. In both cases, the artist himself must remain as unobtrusive as possible. When the narrator went to the theater to see the famous actress Berma for the first time, he was aware of the talents of everybody in the cast except herself—not because she didn't possess any talent but because she had identified herself so completely with the part of Phèdre which she was playing that to an untrained eye

[4] *Ibid.*, Part 1, p. 186.

[5] *Ibid.*, pp. 180–81.

[6] *The Past Recaptured*, p. 29.

[7] *The Guermantes Way*, Part 1, p. 55.

she could no longer be distinguished from it. But most interpreters in Proust are very shallow-minded (Morel is an excellent example of this), and so they do not recognize this great truth—which is the reason why actors, singers, and performers in general have always enjoyed so bad a reputation for vanity that Voltaire uses the expression: "bête comme un musicien." [8] So it often happens that the best interpreter of a given work, in spite of his lack of technical virtuosity, is the composer himself: "His playing is become so transparent that himself one no longer sees and he is nothing now but a window opening upon a great work of art. . . . It appears that this was the case with Vinteuil when he played the piano." [9]

Morel and Rachel, in spite of their being among Proust's most egocentric and morally obtuse characters, are partially redeemed for us by the fact that they are serious about their art if about nothing else. They are concerned about their reputations as artists more than they are about either money or worldly position. They are covetous of the latter, it is true, but only when such covetousness does not seem to conflict with their careers. Since they are interpreters of other men's work only, it could justly be said that their vices cast as little aspersion on the elevating nature of art in general, as might the corruptions of some few petty, minor officials upon a great government which they are supposed to serve. The interpreters are servants to something that is far greater and purer than themselves, and in spite of all their pettiness and meanness they know this and are deeply proud of it. Rachel's reputation as an actress is more important to her than all the wealth and social rank offered by her aristo-

[8] Louis Abatangel, *Marcel Proust et la musique* (Paris, n.d.).
[9] *The Guermantes Way,* Part 1, p. 55.

cratic lover, Saint-Loup. When she is convinced that her profitable connection with him can affect her art badly, she doesn't hesitate to drop him. It is this standard of values which, in spite of all her viciousness, cruelty, and prostitution, raises her in Proust's pages far above the fine but vapid society women who fancy themselves her superiors. It is Rachel who reveals the genius of Maeterlinck from the stage, not they. The same quality of pride in his possession of first prize in the violin from the Conservatory leads Morel to break with his powerful protector, Charlus. It is in vain that Charlus offers his protégé titles of nobility; Morel's accomplishments have made him prouder of the name Morel than he could be of any titles. When the Verdurins wish to part him from the unhappy Baron, they play (as villains like Iago always seem to do instinctively) upon his best qualities. They convince him, therefore, that Charlus is dangerous to the development of his art and its recognition. From then on, no material gain can keep him from breaking as suddenly with his patron as Rachel had broken with hers.

Next to the respect and tenderness which Proust shows for his artists is that which he has for his "celibates of art," the aesthetes who, though they have been unable to create, are best qualified to appreciate the accomplishment of the artist. The difference between a character like Swann and Charlus, on the one hand, and a Mme Verdurin or Mme de Guermantes, on the other hand, is that the former really appreciate art and seem almost to live for it, while the latter only simulate their appreciations. Art enables the aesthete to see the world through new eyes. "The world," says Proust, "was not created once and for all, but is created afresh as often as an original artist is born." [10] It is not easy to grasp the

[10] *Ibid.*, Part 2, pp. 21–22.

essential originality of an artist's vision, just as it was not easy for him to put it down. That is why masterpieces have often failed of immediate recognition—including Proust's own, the first volume of which was rejected by numerous publishers and had to be brought out finally at his own expense. It is a gift to be able to submit ourselves to an artist's vision, and so people are legitimately proud of their good taste, when it is genuine and not simply imitative.

Swann carries his tendency to see the world through the eyes of his favorite painter to the point where he initially loves Odette, whom at first sight he had found somewhat displeasing, as soon as he begins to perceive a resemblance between her and a certain figure in a work by Botticelli.[11] He adores Odette on the assumption that "the divine Alessandro" would have found her beautiful, without reflecting that what was natural to the Italian artist is extremely artificial in himself. He is not the only aesthete in the pages of Proust who falls into such error. Charlus, too, is a connoisseur who compares his beloved Morel to various works of art. And the narrator does the same thing with his friend Albertine:

> Then, just as those works of art which seem to address themselves to the eye or ear alone require that, if we are to enjoy them, our awakened intelligence shall collaborate with these organs, I would unconsciously evoke from myself the dreams that had been stifled by the routine of everyday life. I cast them into the composer's phrase or the painter's image as into a crucible, or used them to enrich the book that I was reading. And no doubt the book appeared all the more vivid in consequence. But Albertine herself profited just as much by being thus transported out of one of the two worlds to which we have access, and in which we can place alternately the same object, by escaping thus from the crushing

[11] *Swann's Way*, p. 289.

weight of matter to play freely in the fluid space of mind. I found myself suddenly and for the instant capable of feeling an ardent desire for this irritating girl. She had at that moment the appearance of a work by Elstir or Bergotte, I felt a momentary enthusiasm for her, seeing her in the perspective of imagination and art.[12]

### WAGNER'S INFLUENCE

The most important influence upon Proust, from the point of view of both his aesthetic theory and practice, is that of Richard Wagner. If Proust's outlook upon life as a whole, as I shall show in the next chapter, is that of Schopenhauer, his view of art originates with Wagner. The coupling of the names of the two great Germans (philosopher and composer) is not accidental, for it was Wagner who said that "Schopenhauer was the first to perceive and point out with philosophic clearness the proper position of music with reference to the other fine arts." [13]

Every reader of Proust must soon note his exaltation of music above the other arts. Before the appearance in print of the first volume of his great work, Proust gave an interview about it which was printed in the newspaper *Le Temps* in which he said:

> If I presume thus to reason about my book, it is because the book is in no way a work of reason; it is because its most trifling details have been supplied to me through feeling; because I first of all noticed them deep within myself, without understanding them, having as much trouble to change them into something intelligible as if they were foreign to the realms of the intellect just as is—how shall I put it?—a theme of music.[14]

It is not often that an artist puts another art in a position above that which he himself practices, but Proust unmis-

[12] *The Captive,* p. 67.
[13] Richard Wagner, *Beethoven* (London, 1880), p. 8.
[14] Marie Scheikévitch, *Time Past* (New York, 1935), p. 206.

takably does so, on the rather strange ground, considering his own gifts of analysis,[15] that music is the art which is least analytic in its effect:

Every human and external word left me indifferent, compared with the heavenly phrase of music with which I had been engaged. . . . I asked myself if music were not the unique example of what might have been—if there had not come the invention of language, the formation of words, the analysis of ideas—the means of communication between one spirit and another. It is like a possibility which has ended in nothing; humanity has developed along other lines, those of spoken and written language. But this return to the unanalyzed was so inebriating, that on emerging from that Paradise, contact with other people who were more or less intelligent seemed to me of an extraordinary insignificance.[16]

Another passage, some hundreds of pages later, makes still clearer, I think, the place of music at the apex of Proust's hierarchy of the various arts, and in at least one of its phrases—that in which it is said that "sounds assume the inflexion of the thing itself"—reminds one forcibly of Schopenhauer's theories about music,[17] in which the phi-

[15] Joseph Conrad has said: "I don't think there has been such an example of the power of analysis, and I feel pretty safe in saying that there never will be another." *Marcel Proust—Reviews and Estimates,* comp. by Gladys Dudley Warner (Stanford University Press, 1942), p. 235.

[16] *The Captive,* p. 349. It is interesting to read in this connection Régis Michaud's *Modern Thought and Literature in France* (New York, 1934), p. 34: "We obtain another clue to the Symbolist esthetics through Paul Valéry's statement that Symbolism meant, most of all, for the poets a way of appropriating to themselves what belonged to the musicians. Music was to the symbolists what eloquence had been to the Romanticists and painting and sculpture to the Parnassians."

[17] There are other passages in Proust reminiscent of Schopenhauer's writing about music—for example, the following from Louise Varèse's translation of *Les Plaisirs et les jours,* published under the title *Pleasures and Regrets* (New York, 1948), p. 169: "[The sea] refreshes our imagination because it does not remind us of the life of men, but it rejoices the soul because like the soul it is infinite and ineffectual aspiration, striving, forever broken by a fall, eternal and sweet lamentation. It enchants us like music, which, unlike language, bears no trace of material things, which never speaks to us of men, but imitates the movements of the soul."

losopher attributed the effect of music to its tracing more intimately than was possible in any other art the pattern of the human will:

This music seemed to me to be something truer than all the books I knew. Sometimes I thought that this was due to the fact that what we feel in life, not being felt in the form of ideas, its literary (that is to say, an intellectual) translation in giving an account of it, explains it, analyzes it, but does not recompose it as does music, in which the sounds seem to assume the inflexion of the thing itself, to reproduce that interior and extreme point of our sensation which is the part that gives us that peculiar exhilaration which we recapture from time to time.[18]

It is Proust's great regard for music which makes him value what might fairly be called the musical qualities of literature, the aura surrounding the qualities of language and almost independent of the literal statements. He thinks that the secret of things, which every writer seeks to deliver, may perhaps be found in the form of a charmingly turned phrase rather than in any intricate intellectual concept.[19] There is for him, in other words, a correspondence between a higher reality which is to be found behind the world of appearance and the way in which words are put together. It is this feeling for the unexplainable musical effects of literature that makes Proust so skeptical of the claims of so-called realists who are to him merely superficial and vulgar materialists, who do not recognize that the spiritual trans-

[18] *The Captive*, p. 510. A parallel passage from Schopenhauer is the following from *The World as Will and Idea* (London, 1909), III, 232: "That music acts directly upon the will, i.e. the feelings, passions, and emotions of the hearer, so that it quickly raises them or changes them, may be explained from the fact that unlike all the other arts, it does not express the Ideas, or grades of the objectification of the will, but directly the will itself. . . . Music, far from being a mere accessory to poetry, is an independent art, nay, the most powerful of all the arts."

[19] *Swann's Way*, p. 233.

position of this world which is achieved in music is likewise the aim of literature and indeed of all art.

When we examine his book itself, we find that, as Proust prepares us to expect from his opening pages (which resemble the prelude to a music drama by introducing the principal characters and themes of the whole four-thousand-page work), instead of narrative in the older style of the novel (which in relation to Proust became what the previous opera was to Wagner—that is, a method of composition not discarded but rather incorporated to a higher purpose), we have no single story-line progressing more or less simply, but rather the continual interweaving of a number of leitmotivs [20] such as habit, dreams, time, art, love, society, and friendship—none of which is permitted to reach the stasis of a complete resolution before being interrupted by one of the other themes. Just as in Wagner, there are few completely enclosed arias but instead, as his earliest critics bitterly complained, broken bits of melody fantastically intertwined (like endless strings of macaroni, according to one critic quoted by Ernest Newman), so in Proust there are no complete stories—with one exception which I shall presently note—but rather incidents, scenes (some of them hundreds of pages long, it is true), which are not permitted to round off to any real conclusion.

The exception to this, of course, is the second half of the volume *Swann's Way*, which is entitled "Swann in Love"

[20] Proust himself employed the word leitmotiv earlier than any of his critics in a letter to Lucien Daudet in 1913. See also Douglas W. Alden, *Marcel Proust and His French Critics* (Los Angeles, 1940), pp. 125–26: "Writing an essay *Sur la composition wagnerienne de l'oeuvre de Proust*—a title suggesting the musical comparison so frequent with modernist interpretation—Pierhal declared that this method of Wagnerian 'leitmotifs' employed by Proust, this interweaving of recurring themes, is a 'démarche consciente de l'activité créatrice.' "

and which is almost a novelette in the older sense, a story with a beginning, a middle, and an end, a single unifying theme, jealousy—all of which makes it roughly analogous, save in greater fineness of texture perhaps and in depth of psychological sensitivity to such a book as Somerset Maugham's *Of Human Bondage.* It is said that Wagner composed *Die Meistersinger* as an answer to those who held that he wrote according to his new principle because he could not master the old one. And Wagner showed his critics in his Prize Song of that music drama that he could compose a single, unified, classically distinguished melody which should be treated more or less like the traditional operatic aria, that is, exhibited by itself, neatly framed, and separated from its surroundings. Perhaps Proust told the story of Charles Swann's love affair with Odette de Crécy for a similar reason. He proved (to himself no less than to his readers) that, if he wrote his work according to an untried plan (untried in literature, that is, but not in music, where it had been tried by Wagner), it was not because he could not create a novel in the more familiar form. He put this love duet near enough to the opening of his work and filled it with amazingly fresh perceptions in order to reassure us that he has not escaped from the yoke of old-fashioned controls but has satisfactorily mastered and gone beyond them.[21]

[21] Concerning the yoke of traditional controls on the artist and Proust's ability to create in familiar patterns, I am reminded of an ironic observation made by Paul Valéry in a letter—that in our disordered times, an artist who formerly might have been dismissed as obviously devoid of talent, can always be promoted and sold to the public as "a genius."

I wonder if among the legitimate uses of the musical analogy in criticism of Proust may not be put the three-part structure of his work as a whole—its ABA form. By his ABA form, I mean, of course, that Proust begins with a scene in Combray, the sound of Swann's ringing of the doorbell, and after innumerable excursions in the middle sections, he returns at the end to the

There is another analogy which brings the names of Proust and Wagner together in my mind and that is the enormous structure of their chief works. *Remembrance of Things Past* is in the literature of the world what *The Ring* is in the world of music—that is to say, a masterpiece of such imposing scope that size alone would be sufficient to guarantee it a permanent regard as one of the wonders of the human mind.[22] Who but the German master could have inspired Proust to undertake such an enormous task? Bayreuth had become a place of worship towards the end of the nineteenth century (in the book, we hear of several of Proust's characters who make pilgrimages there); it was a shrine for spiritually homeless aesthetes who had lost every religion but that of art. It may be remarked parenthetically here that if music, beginning with Handel, had transformed the church into a theater, in the next century music repaid her debt by making the theater into a church. It is not accidental that Proust, inspired by the accomplishment of Wagner, should aim to fill a similar need in literature: "I knew not whether it would be a church in which the true believers would be able little by little to learn some new truths and discover some harmonies. . . . But I had decided to devote to it all my strength." [23]

That art for Proust is a kind of half-way house if not to

---

same point. The simplicity of this large pattern so familiar in music is emphasized by a letter of Proust to the critic Paul Souday: ". . . the last chapter of the last volume was written immediately after the first chapter of the first volume. All the 'in-between' part was written subsequently." *Letters of Proust*, ed. by Mina Curtiss (New York, 1949), p. 338.

[22] Douglas Alden in *Marcel Proust and His French Critics* expresses a sentiment very similar to this.

[23] *The Past Recaptured*, p. 393. This figure of speech, comparing his work to a church, is of course not unique to Proust. In my Introduction to Céline's *Death on the Installment Plan*, New Directions reprint in 1947, I quoted Céline as saying that he wanted to create his work "like a Gothic Cathedral."

religion then at least to a Platonic awareness of a region beyond the reach of sense is shown in that place in his last volume where he speaks of the necessary awareness by the artist of "those mysteries whose explanation is probably to be found only in other worlds and the presentiment of which is the quality in life and art which moves us most deeply." [24] In saying such things, Proust was surely following in the steps of Wagner, who has written that music "is a spiritual revelation throughout, that rouses unspeakable emotion, as it brings us nearer than aught else to the essential nature of religion." [25] It was Wagner, too, who wrote that "as Christianity arose from under the universal civilization of Rome, so from the chaos of modern civilization Music bursts forth." [26] Making the connection still more plain, he writes of the symphonies of Beethoven that "these wonderful works preach repentance and atonement in the deepest sense of a divine revelation." [27]

Wagner tried to combine many arts in his own so that there would be no temptation for his faithful to stray in search of other satisfactions. Proust, too, tried to include more than one type of literature in his book—which is clear from his saying that it was intended to be at the same time a novel, an autobiography, and the history of a certain period in the form of memoirs.[28] Such enveloping ambitions are proper to artists in a time when they can no longer regard art as the legitimate handmaiden of some other social activity, and consequently try to absorb their audience into a complete, many-faceted world of their own constructive imagination. It seems as if the efforts of some of the greatest,

[24] *The Past Recaptured,* p. 384.
[25] Wagner, *Beethoven,* p. 33.
[26] *Ibid.,* p. 102.
[27] *Ibid.,* pp. 55 ff.
[28] Michaud, *Modern Thought and Literature in France,* p. 60.

the most serious, and the most ambitious modern artists are devoted to gathering their audience into a lifelong dream.

It is fitting that in connection with a passage in Proust which concerns itself with the question of the superiority of art to life,[29] the name of Wagner should enter and that there should then follow several pages of eulogy and analysis of his work, which have no parallel in *Remembrance of Things Past,* except for the passages about the fictitious Vinteuil, whose music, as Proust describes it, seems to contain certain Wagnerian characteristics combined with those of other composers, César Franck for example. "I began to perceive how much reality there is in the work of Wagner," says Proust. Even without this explicit acknowledgment, the debt of the writer to the composer would still be clear to anyone sufficiently acquainted with the work of both. In an article on Baudelaire written only a year before Proust's death, he speaks of his continuing admiration of Wagner dating back to his childhood. He writes of "the genius" of Wagner and deplores an iconoclastic trend which he detects in the latest school of modern composers to deny it.[30]

### THE ART SIMILE

Wagner helps us to understand the over-all form of Proust's work, its method of composition, and the meaning which art had for him; but Proust's novel is, after all, a work of literature and not of music, and therefore it contains many things which require literary analogies. What I wish to emphasize in this section is a characteristic literary device of Proust which, if it has been noticed, has not

[29] *The Captive,* p. 209.

[30] Marcel Proust, *Chroniques* (a collection of his occasional pieces selected by his brother, Dr. Robert Proust, and posthumously published in Paris, 1927), p. 218.

sufficiently been dwelt on, I think. That is how characteristic and original is Proust's use of a certain figure of speech, which I shall call the art simile. This kind of simile, which I shall presently define and illustrate, is as much a part of the texture of his work as the epic simile is of Homer's. By the art simile I mean that Proust consistently makes his most effective comparisons between what we call the real world and the various arts. It is this quality which has made him pre-eminently an artist for artists. The composer, the painter, the choreographer, and the sculptor must at once recognize in Proust a writer who, when he chooses to draw for his similitudes upon the various arts (as he does more frequently than any other modern writer), knows what he is talking about with an intimacy and accuracy rare in literature. Proust naturally appeals to art when he wishes to make his observations and feelings about the real world clearer to us. Art for him reflects the essence of all things, and it is far removed from the accidents we encounter in experience.

That is why the steeple of the Church of Combray, seen in outline from a distance, appears to the narrator "so sharpened and so pink that it seemed to be no more than sketched on the sky by the finger-nail of a painter anxious to give to such a landscape, to so pure a piece of 'nature,' this little sign of art." [31] A still more vivid musical analogy follows:

> The topmost pinnacles [of the Church] at the point where they entered that zone of sunlight and were softened and sweetened by it, seemed to have mounted suddenly far higher, to have become truly remote, like a song whose singer breaks into falsetto an octave above the accompanying air.[32]

[31] *Swann's Way*, p. 78.

[32] *Ibid.*, p. 79.

A prematurely rising moon evokes a curious theatrical comparison:

Sometimes in the afternoon sky, a white moon would creep up like a little cloud, furtive, without display, suggesting an actress who does not have to "come on" for a while, and so goes "in front" in her ordinary clothes to watch the rest of the company for a moment, but keeps in the background, not wishing to attract attention to herself.[33]

Sometimes, moreover, a single observation of nature (a sudden ray of sunshine in the following instance) is conveyed by a whole cluster of comparisons, bound together in a bouquet, stemming from many different arts:

The sun, bursting out again from behind a threatening cloud and darting the full force of its rays on to the Square and into the sacristy, shed a geranium glow over the red carpet laid down for the wedding, along which Mme. de Guermantes smilingly advanced, and covered its woolen texture with a nap of rosy velvet, a bloom of light, giving it that sort of tenderness, of solemn sweetness in the pomp of a joyful occasion which characterize certain pages of *Lohengrin,* certain paintings by Carpaccio, and make us understand how Baudelaire was able to apply to the sound of the trumpet the epithet "delicious." [34]

It is passages like this one, characterized by what is almost too much of a muchness, a kind of overripe aestheticism, a little ornate in its loveliness, that made certain early readers of Proust's work ridicule what seemed to them a transplantation of euphuistic exaggeration into the sober garden of French prose.

The central aesthetic moral of Proust's work, to which his whole last volume is given over, that art is "the most real of all things" seems to me to be implicit in his similes.

[33] *Ibid.,* p. 187. [34] *Ibid.,* p. 229.

When Proust has occasion to liken his impressions of nature with his memories of art experiences, it is in a tone almost of apology for nature. To Proust, as to Yeats in "Sailing to Byzantium," art is something precious and permanent rescued from the destructive changes of the natural world. Proust prefers the golden bird to the feathered one. He asks forgiveness from the reader at one point of his story for *daring* to compare the "humble landscape" of Combray with certain "glorious works" of art—"those old engravings of the 'Cenacolo,' or that painting by Gentile Bellini, in which one sees, in a state in which they no longer exist, the masterpiece of Leonardo and the portico of Saint Mark's." [35]

There seems to me no aspect of Proust which makes him more "modern" than this elevation of art to a position superior to nature. One must have traveled very far indeed away from the romantic poets in terms of aesthetic theory if one is to think of a pastoral landscape as *humble* when compared with certain paintings. Is it possible to conceive of Wordsworth or Shelley valuing a work of art above nature? For these poets, the highest aspiration of the artist was to produce something which merited comparison with nature, while for Proust it seems to be the highest praise of natural beauty that it suggests a work of art. See what becomes, for example, of Keats's "murmurous haunt of flies on summer eves" when Proust is the listener: "the flies . . . performed for my benefit, in their small concert, the chamber music of summer." [36]

[35] *Ibid.*, p. 213.

[36] *Ibid.*, p. 103. If among the poets of the last century, Baudelaire, like Proust and Yeats, shows his preference for the imitation of nature rather than for nature itself, it is just this quality which brings him so close to the literature which is characteristically modern, so much closer than any of the Romantics, including Poe.

Proust is able to put the art simile to a variety of uses. Sometimes, as in most of the examples I have given, he uses it, as the simile is used generally, simply to make the feeling which surrounds a given term clearer by a felicitous comparison. But sometimes he uses it as a conscious comic device, making the analogy tremble on the edge of the ridiculous without quite allowing it to topple over. This use of the figure of speech then becomes so intimate and personal a thing that I can describe its effect best as Proustian irony—that is, an irony which is kindly rather than cruel, an irony which, like that of the grandmother's smile as Proust describes it, is directed at himself rather than at a victim. A good example of this is his description of the trouble his poor cook takes in honor of an important diplomat who is to be their dinner guest: "She had gone herself to the Halles to procure the best cuts of rump-steak, shin of beef, calves' feet, as Michelangelo passed eight months in the mountains of Carrara choosing the most perfect blocks of marble for the tomb of Julius II." [37] Or again when he compares the cries of street peddlers outside his window to passages from Mussorgsky and Debussy.[38] These conceits make us smile, but it is an affectionate humor, for it would be too gross and out of character for Proust to have intended such extravagant comparisons to dwarf still further the modest stature of a servant or of a peddler. Rather (if I may be excused for analyzing with so heavy a hand what is so feathery a touch of fancy) he seems to me to imply here that all those who serve their purposes well, whatever these purposes might be, resemble each other. Françoise, the cook, as he points out on other occasions, is, in her own way, an artist; the narrator admires not only her cooking but her

[37] *Within a Budding Grove,* Part 1, p. 22. [38] *The Captive,* p. 152.

poetic speech—he admires what the Existentialists would call her *authenticity*. And the great artists who are thus compared to the most humble tradesmen and workers would probably have been the least distressed or amused by the contrast. Certainly the narrator of Proust's book, as I indicate in the chapter on his sociology, declares his preference for workers above all the other classes of society. It is idlers who make Proust angry. Françoise is no Michelangelo, but she is far closer to him than either Mme Verdurin or the Duchesse de Guermantes.

But it is in an altogether different emotional tonality that the most tragic occasions of the book are graced by the imagery of art. The passage of the work which some very good readers have thought its high point, that describing the death of the narrator's grandmother, is climaxed by a wonderful art simile: "On that funeral couch, death, like a sculptor of the middle ages, had laid her in the form of a young maiden." [39]

Art had a reality for Proust which compared so well with what ordinarily passes for reality to the rest of the world that he must have been continually tempted to enclose himself in the experience of art to the exclusion of the most pressing social and moral obligations. How easily he might have become like those eccentric old aunts of the narrator who, when their sister is dying, refuse to answer the summons to her bedside, because down in their town of Combray "they had discovered a musician . . . who gave them excellent chamber music concerts, in listening to which they thought that they could find, better than by the invalid's bedside, food for thought, a melancholy form of exaltation the form of which was, to say the least of it, unusual." [40]

[39] *The Guermantes Way*, Part 2, p. 48.

[40] *Ibid.*, p. 18.

The tendency to see life and its issues in artistic terms is as marked in Proust's letters as it is in his books. Writing to his friend Mme Straus in 1898, he indicates that the Dreyfus Case, in which he was so vitally concerned (a concern which will be dealt with in the chapter on his ethics), seems to him like something out of the best French fiction or the greatest English drama: "I haven't seen you since the so Balzacian Affair (Bertulus the police magistrate in *Splendeur et misère des courtisanes,* Paty du Clam the Rastignac who makes appointments with Vautrin in distant suburbs) has become Shakespearean with its accumulation of sudden dénouements." [41]

Proust himself must have realized how distinctive such similitudes were of his vision, for, having to choose samples of his work which might give to the readers of the newspaper *Figaro* a foretaste of it, he picked passages containing such images in the greatest profusion. In a passage from an essay, which, but for a change of place names, completely parallels his well-known impression of the steeples of Martinville in the novel, which figures there as the first original and characteristic composition of the narrator's youth, there is an even greater abundance of art similes than are to be found in the version appearing in *Remembrance of Things Past.* A very beautiful simile which Proust for some reason sacrificed from the pages of his book is that in which he says that "the city . . . took sudden form and began to develop in a mounting figure, a complex, clear-cut fugue of roofs." [42]

These images, drawing with such fine discrimination upon Proust's immense erudition in the various arts, are signs

[41] *Letters of Marcel Proust,* ed. by Curtiss, p. 47.

[42] Marcel Proust, *Selections from His Miscellaneous Writings* (London, n.d.), pp. 156 ff.

that his own art is itself a distillation of his appreciations. That is not to say that what is at this time the most famous literary accomplishment of the first half of the twentieth century is not an independent and original creation. But the book is also undoubtedly a confession of his taste, and in that sense it resembles a number of other important art works of our time—Joyce's *Ulysses,* Eliot's *Wasteland,* and Pound's *Cantos.* In all of these works, we sense the artist, not only in a fresh relation to the world, but also as the heir of a great tradition of culture. An artist must be the honest and sensitive recorder of the most vivid perceptions available to him. In our time, coming as it does at the end of several millennia of cultural development, the experience of tradition is more important than it has ever been before to the artist. To this truth Joyce testifies by his mastery of so many languages and literary styles, and so do Eliot and Pound. As for the art simile in Proust, it is the development in modern French literature which seems to me the best parallel to the one in English literature which produced the galactic footnotes to *The Wasteland.*

There is a scene in the novel in which the narrator talks to Albertine about the moon, and this talk becomes almost a lecture on the changing epithets that have been applied to the moon by different French poets in the course of time. Every generation has had to discover the moon for itself. It apparently is the characteristic of our time, however, that even an impassioned lover can hardly look at the moon without remembering the lines in which it has been described by his poetic predecessors. And it is this very excess of his awareness of the tradition that is precisely the most up-to-date quality of Proust.

He is conscious of the element which sets his style apart

and which I have attempted to isolate for observation here. He introduces a parody of himself from the lips of Albertine, who has lived with him long enough presumably to mimic him successfully. Her pastiche necessarily is overdone, but the features which she caricatures are present in the original:

> What I like about these foodstuffs that are cried is that a thing which we hear like a rhapsody changes its nature when it comes to our table and addresses itself to my palate. As for ices (for I hope that you won't order me one that isn't cast in one of those old-fashioned moulds which have every architectural shape imaginable), whenever I take one, temples, churches, obelisks, rocks, it is like an illustrated geography book which I look at first of all and then convert its raspberry or vanilla monuments into coolness in my throat. . . . I set my lips to work to destroy, pillar after pillar, those Venetian churches of a porphyry that is made with strawberries, and send what I spare of them crashing down upon the worshippers. Yes, all those monuments will pass from their stony state into my inside which throbs already with their melting coolness.[43]

Even to the most uncritical reader, this passage seems to give the show away. To the one whose consciousness is already attuned to Proust's artistic device, it increases his awareness. It is a kind of play within the play, which underlines the essential pattern of the original. Proust has slipped the key to his own method under the door mat.

It is a great achievement, I think, that Proust's use of the art simile was recognized as so distinctively original a stylistic element of his work that he was able eventually to parody himself. We know from his correspondence with the novelist Louis Martin-Chauffier, who had written a pastiche of Proust, how much he appreciated such things when they

[43] *The Captive,* pp. 168 ff.

were cleverly done. His pleasant reaction to Chauffier is reminiscent of a similar reaction by A. E. Housman to the brilliant parody of his verse done by Hugh Kingsmill. It is, after all, the best sign that an author has found his own manner of projecting his vision, when this manner can by a slight distortion be changed into mannerism.

### IMAGERY, THE TOUCHSTONE OF PROUST'S GENIUS

Proust's use of the art simile naturally leads us into the wider subject of the image-making ability in general. Like Aristotle, Proust thought of metaphor as the touchstone of poetic genius. He approached the difficult aesthetic question of what made good literary art through the back door by inquiring as to the qualities which made literature bad. And in this approach to the question, he was using the same caution as Samuel Johnson when he said to Boswell on one occasion that, though he could not perhaps tell what poetry was, he could tell what poetry was not. According to Proust, I gather that all bad literature can be said to have one common denominator—namely, stale impressions of the world, or, strictly speaking, no real and lively impressions at all, but merely simulacra of such impressions, trite and defaced counterfeits of them. He gives an example of what he means when he writes of the First World War as it became the subject matter of poor art:

> heros of mediocre and commonplace intelligence, writing poems during their convalescence, tried to put their description, not on a level of the incidents which are nothing in themselves, but on a plane of banal aesthetics, following the old, familiar rules and writing as they would have done ten years before of "the bloody dawn," "the quivering flight of victory," etc.[44]

[44] *The Past Recaptured,* p. 60.

Proust's complaint seems to be that in order to compose such banalities, it was not necessary for the writers to go through their harrowing experiences at all. Bad poets either do not have any fresh feelings, because their consciousness has been entirely flooded with familiar images and they do not experience anything in life but what has already been reduced before them to literary equivalents (of which they make an unself-conscious use instead of a conscious one, as artists like Proust and Joyce and Eliot and Pound do), or else, a more probable hypothesis, bad poets do have some new feelings but they either dismiss them as unseemly or else have not the intellectual energy, patience, and courage (of a different kind from the one needed on the battlefield) to translate and define those feelings, which might constitute their own irreducible contribution to art.

As the opposite of such bad art, I shall risk an example of good art from Proust's own work, which seems to me to abound with such examples. From the volume *The Captive* which describes the narrator's affair with Albertine, I choose this remarkable touch of a sensitive, poetic imagination:

We left our motor car and walked a long way together, indeed for some moments I gave her my arm, and it seemed to me that the ring which her arm formed round it united our two persons in a single self and linked our separate destinies together. . . . At our feet, our parallel shadows, where they approached and joined, traced an exquisite pattern. No doubt it already seemed to me a marvellous thing at home that Albertine should be living with me, that it should be she that came and lay down on my bed. But it was, so to speak, the transportation of that marvel out of doors, into the heart of nature, that by the shore of that lake in the Bois, of which I was so fond, beneath the trees, it should be her and none but her shadow, the pure and simplified shadow of her leg, of her bust, that the sun had to depict in monochrome by the side of mine upon the gravel of the path. And I found a charm that was more immaterial doubtless but no less intimate, than in the drawing together, the fusion of our bodies, in that of our shadows.[45]

The exact notation of the feelings conveyed by those shadows is the concrete perception of a "trifle," a mere bagatelle, but it communicates with our own feelings at once, for we recognize in it a symbol of a vast and inexpressible emotion (inexpressible that is by direct means but not inexpressible as Proust proves by oblique ones). If imitative art is counterfeit, original art is a mint which issues coins passing at their full value, because the materials of which they have been made are real, and their colors remain fresh and unfaded. Proust's images are not promissory notes drawn against a bank with no deposit of lively impressions. His observation of the effect of the shadows of himself and his loved one on his feelings is a "trifle" of a kind which we recognize as making up our own significant sum (not a very large one) of moments when life has become a memorable thing and something else than a dark liquid through which we seem to glide like blind fish. Proust has succeeded, in other words, in *rendering* his experience of love for us; he has restored all of its poignancy of the time. He has delivered himself of his subjective awareness of a universal experience, and that is why he lives for us as the mediocre poets to whom he refers do not. War, like love, has to be recreated for each of us in subjective terms in order to become convincing. Bad poets are incapable of going beyond worn generalities; consequently they can't communicate *their* war or *their* love.

Examples of such beautiful observations may be multi-

[45] *The Captive,* p. 232.

plied. In *Swann's Way*, Proust has occasion to dwell on the difference between the effect of a name as it first strikes us and the effect of the actual thing or being in the world which corresponds to that name. It is a subtle distinction, and Proust seeks a comparison which will succeed in making it more clear. To illuminate the effect of the imagination as distinguished from material reality, he says that it is "something as delicious as might be for a human race whose whole existence had passed in a series of late winter afternoons, that inconceivable marvel, a morning in spring." [46] We admire, among other things, the simplicity of means which underlies his superior image-making ability. He secures the novelty of his effect through the use of the most familiar realities. By a slight turn and the sudden juxtaposition of hitherto separate memories, he gives an almost startling vividness to what was before an abstraction.

How sharp is his vision of timeworn things! Whose memory of an old man's hands is not renewed by Proust's phrase—"gentle hands, white and crumpled, which looked as though they had been left lying too long in water"? [47] While the powerless writer goes through the most unheard-of and nerve-racking experiences only to bring us a commonplace account of them, the powerful artist takes up materials which have been handled a thousand times before and by some mysterious lighting effect of his own sensibility reveals aspects of them which we had never seen. This is the reason why Proust was so fond of the painters of Dutch interiors and of still life like Vermeer. To change hackneyed materials into striking pictures with the help of light and shade and patient execution is his forte as well as theirs. In large parts of his book, as will be evident in my later chapters,

[46] *Swann's Way*, p. 504. [47] *Within a Budding Grove*, Part 1, p. 69.

Proust deals with bizarre materials, but he is no less a master with the subjects which originate in everyday life. He says at one point that the artistic creation which transforms the most ordinary experiences into something rich and strange enjoys the largest domain in the field of art, and he is capable by his own practice of giving substance to this generalization.

In his novel, it is to the painter Elstir that Proust attributes the appreciation of domestic scenes which he had actually learned from the Dutch artists and from certain contemporary French painters whom he liked, like Cézanne. The following passage is as illustrative of Proust's own power of alchemically transforming and meticulously drawing the poetic essences of the most familiar objects as it is a tribute to what he has learned from the art of painting:

> Since I had seen such things depicted in water colors by Elstir, I sought to find again in reality, I cherished, as though for their poetic beauty, the broken gestures of the knives still lying across one another, the swollen convexity of a discarded napkin upon which the sun would patch a scrap of yellow velvet, the half-empty glass which then showed to greater advantage the noble sweep of its curved sides, and, in the heart of its translucent crystal, clear as frozen daylight, a dreg of wine, dusky but sparkling with reflected lights, the displacement of solid objects, the transmutation of liquids by the effect of light and shade, the shifting color of the plums which passed from green to blue and from blue to golden yellow in the half-plundered dish, the chairs, like a group of old ladies, that came twice daily to take their places around the white cloth spread on the table as on an altar at which were celebrated the rites of the palate, where in the hollows of oyster-shells a few drops of lustral wine had gathered as in tiny holy water stoups of stone; I tried to find beauty there where I had never imagined before it could exist, in the most ordinary things, in the profundities of still life.[48]

[48] *The Guermantes Way*, Part 2, p. 235.

The effect upon me of such a passage is comparable to that produced by some of the sensuous images of food and drink in "The Eve of Saint Agnes," except that the aestheticism of Keats, already so marked as compared with his Elizabethan models, is raised to a still higher power by Proust, which is not the same thing as saying that the art of Proust is the more powerful.

Proust can record the finest shades in perceptions which to grosser sensibilities must seem of one uniform tone. Sometimes he does this with an art simile, which in the following instance helps him to render those various planes of consciousness which we traverse in the subtle transition of the mind from the state of sleep to that of waking:

> Similarly, in later years, at Venice, long after the sun had set, when it seemed to be quite dark, I have seen, thanks to the echo, itself imperceptible, of a last note of light, held indefinitely on the surface of the canals, as though some optical pedal were being pressed, the reflexion of the palaces unfurled, as though for all time, in a darker velvet, on the crepuscular greyness of the water.[49]

### ART AND SOCIAL VALUES

It is an interesting aspect of Proust's aesthetics that he continually insists on the international quality of all artistic culture. He lived and wrote before the full eruption of those chauvinisms which followed in the wake of the First World War, but signs of the disease that was coming were not lacking for the attentive observer. During the war which Proust survived by only four years, German composers and writers long dead and even the German language itself had been made the scapegoats in France and elsewhere in the Allied world for the actions of the Kaiser and his generals. Writing to the German critic Ernst Curtius, Proust underlines the

[49] *Ibid.*, Part 1, pp. 194 ff.

fact that neither he nor his brother are French "nationalists" (the quotation marks are Proust's own).[50] What his reaction to the later postwar world would have been is sufficiently indicated, it seems to me, by these words from one of his articles: "Fortunately for the sympathy and understanding which are among the great happinesses of life, our different individualities are worked on a woof that is made of all mankind."[51]

Proust was especially troubled by the cultural intolerance which sprang out of political conflicts, and he makes it the special merit of his heroic character Saint-Loup that he has risen above such prejudices. Describing Saint-Loup's letters to him from the front during the war, the narrator of the novel says that the soldier

> did not hesitate to refer to a page by Romain Rolland[52] or even Nietzsche, with the independence of men at the front, who were not afraid, as were the people at home, to utter a German name. . . . If Saint-Loup mentioned in his letters an air of Schumann's, he always gave the title in German, and he did not beat about the bush to tell me how, at dawn at the edge of a forest, he had been thrilled as if he had been listening to the bird in "the sublime *Siegfried*" which, indeed, he hoped to hear again after the war.[53]

In his articles, too, Proust satirizes the postwar tendency to put national feeling before feeling for quality in art and philosophy. He tells us of a contemporary history of philosophy which leaves unmentioned the names of Leibniz, Kant, and Hegel![54]

Proust thinks that art can serve no cause but its own. He

[50] *Proust's Letters*, ed. by Curtiss, p. 404.
[51] Marcel Proust, *Selections from His Miscellaneous Writings*, p. 19.
[52] Rolland took a pacifist position during the First World War and was consequently as unpopular with the Allied authorities as if he had been a German spy.
[53] *The Past Recaptured*, p. 61. [54] Marcel Proust, *Chroniques*, pp. 218 ff.

rejects the notions, widespread in his time and even more widespread since then, of Popular Art, Patriotic Art, and Revolutionary Art.[55] He finds it anomalous for art, which seems to him far more important than any of them, to subordinate itself to a revolution, or to a particular nation, or even to "the people." If art could serve society, this service must always be an incidental by-product of its main purpose, which is concerned with the revelation of the essential nature of things. Art can serve people as individuals, if they are willing to submit themselves to its rigid demands, but not as members of groups. Proust seeks no self-justification as an artist by any social criterion other than this—that he retires from the world, like the hermit, to work for the salvation of the world in a way which, just because it is the world, it can never understand: "If I was going to live apart from people who would complain of not seeing me, was it not precisely so that I might devote myself to them—more thoroughly than I could have done in their company—seek to reveal them to themselves, to arrive at their true natures?" [56] In another place, he defines the function of the artist as the demonstration by the artist to the individual of the infinite richness and variety contained in his soul "which we have been content to regard as valueless and waste and void." [57]

That was Proust's answer in advance to all the criticisms of his work which have not changed their tune in a quarter of a century and will probably remain the same as long as he is read. These criticisms, whether they come from socialist critics or from socially conscious ones, are that the interest of the work suffers from the useless and parasitic people

[55] *The Past Recaptured,* pp. 216 ff. [56] *Ibid.,* p. 331.
[57] *Swann's Way,* p. 452.

whom he has chosen for his subjects.[58] They find an echo even in such a place as Albert Thibaudet's notice of Proust in the fourteenth edition of the *Encyclopaedia Britannica.* From a vantage point where presumably eccentricity of views and merely personal predilections are least allowable, Thibaudet says that "the very thing that is likely to tell against his lasting reputation" is "the fact that his characters . . . are exceptional, an erotic and mysterious group having little in common with the generality of mankind." He speaks of "the idle life and ultimate nothingness of the people of his world . . . and the indifference that the ordinary reader must always feel as to their fate." [59]

Proust was certainly aware of what has become a standard criticism of him, and in his work he speaks of

> the literary theories that had disturbed me for a time, more especially those the critics had developed at the time of the Dreyfus Case and revived during the war, which sought to "make the artist come out of his ivory tower," scorn frivolous and sentimental subjects, depict great working-class movements, and, if not huge crowds, at any rate no more insignificant idlers.[60]

I shall have much more to say on these matters in the chapter on Proust's sociology. Here I wish to confine myself to Proust's answer to his critics—which is that a consideration of art will show that the least important thing in determining its value is the nature of its subject matter. Not "what it is about" is the thing that ultimately matters, but what is done by the artist with whatever his work is about. Whitman says somewhere in his "Song of Myself" that "there is no trade

[58] Alden, *Marcel Proust and His French Critics*, p. 148: "In 1930, at the Soirée franco-russe recorded by the *Cahiers de la Quinzaine*, Boris Vycheslazeff said of Proust: 'La grande arène où se jouent les destins des nations et de l'humanité n'existe pas pour lui.' "

[59] Volume XVIII, p. 636, of the 14th edition published in 1929.

[60] *The Past Recaptured*, p. 208.

or employment but the young man following it may become a hero," and Proust seems to think that there is no subject in art so trivial, no character so worthless, but that in the hands of a great artist they may be made to yield up the most important truths. If subject matter had any great importance in itself apart from the artist's treatment of it, there would be little use in his intervention at all. Perhaps there may even be some bravado on Proust's part in showing us his powers of sorcery on the unlikeliest materials, the ones from which it seems almost impossible to extract anything precious. Proust says:

> When it comes to studying the laws of character one can do this quite as well on a frivolous as on a serious subject, just as a prosector can study the laws of anatomy precisely as well on the body of an imbecile as on that of a man of talent, for the great moral laws, like those governing the circulation of the blood or renal elimination, vary but little with the intellectual worth of the individual.[61]

After reading Proust, most other novelists begin to seem like phrenologists of the soul. They seek to discover by the merest external and accidental bumps of the personality what goes on in its depths. It was Proust's objection to the school of literary naturalism that it was satisfied with the surface impressions of objects instead of with the really deep and significant ones. He concluded that the literature which had the approval of the social-minded critics was one "which is satisfied to 'describe objects,' to give merely a miserable listing of lines and surfaces." [62] This literature, he says, is "the very one which, while styling itself 'realist' is the farthest removed from reality, the one that impoverishes and saddens us the most." [63]

Reality, for Proust, is much too complex a thing to be

[61] *Ibid.*, p 209. [62] *Ibid.*, p. 213. [63] *Ibid.*

caught by such a simple net. "An hour," for him, "is a vase filled with perfumes, with sounds, with moments, with changing moods and climates." [64] There can therefore be no limited number of aspects of reality which art must imitate. Art must choose its own level of imitation, and the criteria which were meant to apply to another level could not then legitimately apply to it. He has a very optimistic view (in contrast to his prevailing pessimism on so many other matters) concerning the future possibilities of modern art. In one place, he suggests that the potentialities of the musical scale, for example, far from having been exhausted, as some people think, have barely been touched. In another place, he illustrates what he means by the different levels of reality with an example from painting:

> If a portrait brings out certain truths with regard to mass, light or motion, does that make it necessarily inferior to another portrait of the same person which does not resemble it at all and in which a thousand details omitted from the first one are minutely recorded, so that one might conclude from the second portrait that the model was a raving beauty, but from the first that she was ugly—a point which may have a documentary and even a historic importance, but which is not necessarily a verity in the realm of art.[65]

The possibility of meaningful artistic creation begins for Proust when the artist recognizes the many-layered nature of reality, and when he reconciles himself to the essential subjectivity of his vision. Most artists, like people in general, seem to him never to quit the shallows of the objective world we all know in common because they are afraid of plunging more deeply into themselves and perhaps never coming to the surface again. His point is that whatever force Schopenhauer's sentence "The world is my idea" may have

[64] *Ibid.*, p. 212.

[65] *Ibid.*, p. 25.

for everybody else, it has an inescapable truth for the artist. The artist is the one who must have the courage to say "This is my world" as he presents his picture, even at the risk of being taken for mad because so little of his impression corresponds with that of anybody else. But "the proof of a poet is that his country absorbs him as affectionately as he has absorbed it," as Whitman said; and no matter how strange an artist's work may have seemed at the beginning, eventually, if it is a genuine work of art, it will begin to impress with its possession of a nameless internal consistency. If it is a possible vision of reality and if it is looked at with some patience, then at a certain point it will begin to set up echoes and reverberations even in the minds of those who have mocked it. Convention, which is another name for habit, is inimical to a new work of art, because each new work of art reaffirms the fact that

> every impression has two parts, one of them incorporated in the object and the other prolonged within ourselves and therefore knowable only to us—we are quick to neglect the latter, that is to say, the one part to which we ought to devote our attention, and consider only the other half, which, being outside ourselves, cannot be studied deeply and consequently never will cause us any fatiguing exertion.

The human eye is not a camera, or, if it is a camera, it is one with a lens so special and a background of mind film on which each picture is to be developed so individual, that no two snapshots of the same object will ever completely resemble each other, and the problem of determining if there is any single thing in the field of vision to be captured will not be a slight one. The artist is the one with courage to believe in the truth of the color and angle of his own vision, and the ability to project that vision into the consciousness of others. Only then can there be any reward for his honesty and for the success of his struggle with himself to bring before the world his weirdly lighted personal pictures as true representations of reality. One by one, other sincere and groping minds will recognize the intentions and even the outlines of his work, and will come forward hesitatingly and shamefacedly with the admission that he may have caught something elusive and important after all. This is, after all, the history in brief of Proust's own recognition which turned the book that had been rejected by all publishers in 1913 into a world-famous achievement less than ten years later. The world of *Remembrance of Things Past* which Proust had presented modestly enough to the public at his own expense was subsequently recognized as a profound vision by some critics who had been resentful skeptics when they first beheld it.[66]

### SUFFERING AND ARTISTIC CREATION

"Habit," says Proust, "is a second nature [which] prevents us from knowing our original nature."[67] By "our original nature" I think Proust means something that is very primitive, very individual, something that we perceive with our nerves before the intervention of education, society, and their conventional languages. Habit is the cotton-wool wrapping of stinging, untutored sensation. As such, it is absolutely necessary to life at the same time as it takes all the distinctive savor out of it. Habit is "anaesthetic";[68] and therefore it is the foe of the aesthetic life, which is the life of the feelings. It drugs us through life, the pain of which might otherwise become unbearable. The narrator notices

[66] Clive Bell, in his *Proust* (New York, 1929), confesses that he was one of these.

[67] *Cities of the Plain,* Part 1, p. 215.

[68] *Swann's Way,* p. 10.

even as a child how any defiance or breaking of the rules of habit caused him to think "very melancholy things." [69] Habit was an anodyne which inhibited his perception of his surroundings: "the door handle of my room was different to me from all the other doorhandles of the world, inasmuch as it seemed to open of its own accord and without my having to turn it, so unconscious had its manipulation become." [70] On the other hand, when the child is forced to go away from home and to lie in a strange room in a hotel where his sensations are undrugged by familiarity, he feels convinced

> of the hostility of the violet curtains and of the insolent indifference of a clock that chattered on at the top of its voice as though I were not here; while a strange and pitiless mirror with square feet, which stood across one corner of the room, cleared for itself a site I had not looked to find tenanted in the quiet surroundings of my normal field of vision.[71]

If all of our nights had to be spent in such alarmingly strange surroundings, we should get little rest, and we should probably end with nervous exhaustion if not in entirely losing our wits. But fortunately a natural process of conservation enters (like that healthful sleep in *Macbeth* which knits up the ravel'd sleeve of care)—habit which

> changed the color of the curtains, made the clock keep quiet, brought an expression of pity to the cruel, slanting face of the glass. . . . Custom! That skillful but unhurrying manager who begins by torturing the mind for weeks on end with her provisional arrangements, whom the mind, for all that, is fortunate in discovering, for without the help of custom it would never contrive, by its own efforts, to make any room seem habitable.[72]

Or, we might add, any social situation either. The unsettling effect of habit is always a poignant thing for Proust,

[69] *Ibid.* [70] *Ibid.* [71] *Ibid.*, pp. 7 ff. [72] *Ibid.*

though the cruelty is mixed with enchantment as well. Even long familiar lodgings and people may be made very mysterious and strange by the simplest change of lighting. Thus the presence of a magic lantern in the child's room at Combray makes him feel as uneasy as if he had moved to a hotel:

> My sorrows were only increased, because this change of lighting destroyed, as nothing else could have done, the customary impression I had formed of my room, thanks to which the room itself . . . had become quite endurable. For now I no longer recognized it, and I became uneasy, as though I were in a room in some hotel or furnished lodging, in a place where I had just arrived, for the first time.[73]

Habit, being a second nature, softens the original impression, slowly effaces it altogether and substitutes another impression, more in line with our desires and tastes and expectations, more banal in one word. To put Proust's thought in the simplest possible way—*we can get used to anything*. Swann, who at first sight thought Odette's complexion too sallow, her eyes too large, and her whole appearance not in his style at all, gradually, under the combined influence of their physical intimacy, the pain which she causes him, and his artistic tastes, convinces himself that she is really beautiful, and it is under this false, anaesthetic impression (his second nature rather than his original one) that he lives out the agony of his love affair, only to have his first impression cruelly and rudely restored to him at the end, after untold suffering, through the agency of a dream. We may note in passing that the importance which Proust assigns the dream in the artistic process is due to such power of restoration of long-buried, "forgotten" impressions of reality. Our dreams are very disrespectful of our waking

[73] *Ibid.*, p. 9.

habits, of our whole moral life. They play the most preposterous games with time,[74] and by the close juxtaposition of long separated periods and consequent contrast of impressions, they provide the artist not only with materials but with a usable technique for operating in his own turn upon the imaginations of his readers.[75]

Habit, then, though as we shall see in the chapter on his ethics it is for Proust the effective basis of moral institutions and the friend of life, is the enemy of art. For art, as we have already seen, depends for its very inception upon the existence of fresh rather than stale impressions of reality, while it is the function of habit to reduce this freshness, because to the nervous system of man a fresh sensation inevitably involves a shock, or at least a kind of tang and sharpness which he cannot take in large doses any more than he can subsist on a diet of spices. The role of habit with regard to art is generally malignant. It could not be otherwise when "habit weakens every impression," [76] for it is upon the strength of impressions that art lives. Proust speaks of "the deadening effect of habit, which cuts away from things we have seen many times the taproot of deep impression and thought which gives them their real significance." [77] It is the triumph of good art which is "unusual and yet true to nature," [78] that it suspends the action of habit, and in so doing "it startles us, makes us emerge from our habits and at the same time brings us back to ourselves by recalling to us an earlier impression." [79] Later on, Proust applies this theme to literature directly and says that "certain novels are like great but temporary bereavements, they abolish our habits, bring us in contact once more with the reality of

[74] *The Past Recaptured*, p. 243. [75] *Swann's Way*, p. 106.
[76] *Within a Budding Grove*, Part 1, p. 308. [77] *The Past Recaptured*, p. 64.
[78] *Within a Budding Grove*, Part 2, p. 191. [79] *Ibid.*

life." [80] But if it is true that art can help to free us from habit, the converse is also true—namely, that freedom from habit is the source of art: "It needs only a modification in our habits to make . . . poetic . . . our perceptions of the external world." [81]

Such freedom has its price, which is suffering. For suffering, as Proust analyzes it, is simply the way in which a living creature learns to absorb a new condition of life, when the anaesthetic effect of habit can no longer protect it from feeling.[82] Hence the connection, emphasized throughout Proust, between art and suffering. Pain is the exaction of the creative process. Proust's pessimism prepared him for this view. No writer that I know of is more eloquent than Proust on the subject of the effort necessary to make a great work of art. He puts the matter in such a way that the magnitude of other forms of heroism shrinks by comparison. His words may inspire the elect, but they are calculated to frighten off from the attempt all but the strongest, the most courageous, the most rash, or the most possessed of spirits. Speaking of the artist's effort of creation, he says that he must "endure it like an exhausting task, accept it like a rule of conduct, build it like a church, follow it like a regimen, overcome it like an obstacle, win it like a friendship, feed it intensively like a child, create it like a world." [83]

Once we see clearly everything that creation implies, only an overwhelming urge will keep us from shying away from "the full extent of suffering." [84] But perhaps the most terrifying thing of all is that we have to undergo artistic creation, like birth and death and all of our most significant experiences, *alone*—"no one can stand in our stead, or even

[80] *The Sweet Cheat Gone*, p. 196.

[81] *The Guermantes Way*, Part 1, p. 108.

[82] *Ibid.*, Part 2, p. 15.

[83] *The Past Recaptured*, p. 384.

[84] *Cities of the Plain*, Part 2, p. 363.

collaborate with us." [85] And so, those who feel only half-heartedly drawn to art find all manner of excuses for slackness and evasion, and they invent the most plausible rationalizations for what is actually a nervous failure—"each happening, the Dreyfus case, the war, supplied fresh excuses to the writers for not deciphering that book. They wished to assure the triumph of right, rebuild the moral unity of the nation, and they had not time to think of literature." [86]

But the man who is really a writer (as distinguished from the man who merely wishes to be one) knows that he has only one essential duty to fulfill, and that is to write—everything that does not help to that end is indifferent to the purpose of his life, and he must have the courage to be misunderstood and considered unkind or even ruthless in his pursuit of that purpose. In the end, it will be clear that he has been the most selfless after all—"I would not even let people come to call on me at my home during my working hours, for the obligation to accomplish my literary task took precedence over the duty to be courteous or even kind." [87]

Suffering is inseparable from the conception and the final fruition of the work of art—the passages in Proust on this theme are innumerable:

> It is only while we are suffering that our thought, as though stirred up by perpetual, changing movements, bring up within our range of vision, as in a storm, all that boundless world, governed by laws, but of which we had no view from our ill-placed window, for the calm of happiness leaves it all too smooth and below our range of vision.[88]

> Happiness is beneficial for the body but it is grief that develops the power of the mind.[89]

[85] *The Past Recaptured,* p. 206.
[86] *Ibid.,* p. 206.
[87] *Ibid.,* p. 330.
[88] *Ibid.,* p. 226.
[89] *Ibid.,* p. 237.

It is our moments of suffering that outline our books and the intervals of respite that write them.[90]

Even when suffering does not supply, by disclosing it to us, the subject matter of our work, it is useful by impelling us to undertake it. Imagination and reflexion in themselves may be admirable machines, but they stand idle unless suffering furnishes the motive power.[91]

Happy years are wasted years; we wait for suffering before setting to work. The idea of suffering as an ineluctable prerequisite has become associated in our minds with the idea of work; we dread each new undertaking because of the suffering we must go through to formulate it in our imagination.[92]

Proust goes to such lengths in his praises of suffering, he exercises such fantastic ingenuity in weaving together variations around this single theme, that occasionally he begins to sound almost too precious in his exaggerations. I am thinking of a passage like the following one, which, if it has any charm for us (as I think it does), must owe that charm to its felicitous phrasing rather than to its force of truth. At his worst, Proust was still a very fine writer!

As for happiness, it has hardly more than one useful quality, namely to make unhappiness possible. In our happiness, we should form very sweet bonds, full of confidence and attachment, in order that the sundering of them might cause us that priceless rending of the heart which is called unhappiness. If one had not been happy, though only in anticipation, the misfortunes would have had no cruelty and therefore no good result.[93]

But this very forcing and straining of the theme to all kinds of incredible lengths emphasizes the importance which it has for Proust. The connection of fruitful artistic labor and suffering makes him finally doubt the desirability of life itself:

[90] *Ibid.*, p. 239. [91] *Ibid.*, p. 240. [92] *Ibid.*, p. 241. [93] *Ibid.*, p. 238.

When a living being—and perhaps in nature that creature is man—is so poorly constituted that he must suffer in order to learn new truths, the existence of such a creature becomes very wearying in the long run. . . . And when we understand that suffering is the best thing we can encounter in life, we contemplate death without dismay as a sort of emancipation.[94]

The artist for Proust is necessarily a sufferer, though suffering is not enough to make him an artist. "The training of poets, as of children, is accomplished by cuffs and blows." [95] Furthermore, the final product of the artist will be marked for the sensitive by the suffering which its maker has had to undergo. Art, when it is properly and sympathetically understood, seems to contain a message, a whole philosophy of life. Thus it is that the aesthete Swann, after listening to the little phrase of Vinteuil's sonata, "thought that he could now discern in it some disenchantment. It seemed to be aware how vain, how hollow was the happiness to which it showed the way. In its airy grace, there was indeed something definitely achieved and complete in itself, like the mood of philosophic detachment which follows an outburst of vain regret." [96] Yet Swann notes the paradox that even the suffering which is depicted in art becomes transformed somehow into a source of delight for the beholder: "He began to reckon up how much secret and unappeased sorrow underlay the sweetness of the phrase; and yet to him, it brought no suffering." [97]

[94] *Ibid.*, pp. 240 ff. [95] *Ibid.*, p. 150. [96] *Swann's Way*, pp. 81–82.

[97] *Ibid.*, p. 208. Schopenhauer notes the same phenomenon in his chapter "On the Metaphysics of Music," *The World as Will and Idea* (London, 1909), III, 237: "Music never causes us actual sorrow, but even in its most melancholy strains is still pleasing, and we gladly hear in its language the secret history of our will, and all its emotions and strivings, with its manifold protractions, hindrances, and griefs, even in the saddest melodies. When, on the other hand, in reality and its terrors, it is our *will itself* that is roused and tormented, we have not then to do with tones and their numerical relations, but are rather now ourselves the trembling string that is stretched and twanged."

It took great fortitude of spirit, in other words, for Proust to desire to become an artist, and this desire is a theme running from the beginning of the book to the end. His great fear was that he might not after all be able to become an artist; he was never afraid of the price of suffering that he would have to pay. He was like the hero who fears, not the sacrifice which heroism calls for, but only that during his unfortunate lifetime there might be lacking the occasion on which he could display his heroism. If art for Proust is inevitably accompanied by pain, it does not in that respect differ very much from the other activities of life; but it is superior to them, for the man who has chosen the difficult journey of art experiences, after all the pain, one moment of exultation which quite surpasses the satisfactions of love, friendship, business, or the other activities of society. He has fulfilled the purpose for which he was given life, and the awareness of that discharge is ecstatic. Proust experienced that exultation once in his youth when he composed his first successful page of writing, which he found worthy of inclusion in his masterwork;

> At the moment when . . . I had finished writing it, I found such a state of happiness, felt that it had so entirely relieved my mind of obsession . . . that, as though I myself were a hen and had just laid an egg, I began to sing at the top of my voice.[98]

Once he has created his work, the artist can afford to catch sight of himself in that unflattering mirror which

---

The first part of Schopenhauer's passage might be applied to describe Swann during his happy time with Odette when Vinteuil's *little phrase* was the anthem of his love. The latter part of the passage might be applied to the later Swann, himself now become the trembling string twanged by his helpless jealousy of Odette. Vinteuil's phrase, reminding him of happier days, now comes to taunt him by its association with his most excruciating pain, not because the nature of the music had changed in any way but because Swann himself had changed.

[98] *Swann's Way*, p. 234.

conscience sets up for us in the darkest night without any fear or doubt. He will see in his own features no ugliness or guilt, which are the portion of those who have lived for themselves alone without realizing anything objectively worthwhile in their lives.

# The Philosophy of Proust

*L'oeuvre de Proust . . . laisse . . . un amer bouquet de désenchantement.*

RAMON FERNANDEZ [1]

*For in much wisdom is much grief and he that increaseth knowledge increaseth sorrow.*

ECCLESIASTES

A MAN'S GENERAL OUTLOOK upon life, his *Weltanschauung*, is one of the first things that is formed complete in him. That is because philosophy, far from being useless as some people think, is really indispensable. If a man is an artist, it may be a long time before he achieves mastery and it may even take him long to realize fully his artistic vocation, but his *Weltanschauung* will be fashioned long before then, simply because he must live and, if he enjoys the capacity of thought at all, he must think about life.

These are some of the considerations suggesting themselves about Proust's earliest writings. The philosophy of *Les Plaisirs et les jours,* his first book, is much more mature than his art; the similarity of tone between some of his first polished maxims and his later ones is most striking. Gide

[1] Ramon Fernandez, *Messages, première série* (Paris, 1926), p. 147.

is certainly right in tracing some of the most characteristic themes of Proust back to his first volume, but a distinction ought to be made between the perfection of his aphorisms and his fumbling with problems of plot and character. In Proust's early sketches, there are, both in style and content, innumerable echoes of his literary admirations. Anatole France, in his preface to Proust's book, invoked the names of Bernardin de Saint-Pierre and Petronius. Much closer to the surface, I hear the voice of Poe in the story, "A Young Girl's Confession," and that of Tolstoy in "The End of Jealousy" and in some of the prose poems. The difficulty with the use of these models is that Proust in his twenties lacked the creative strength to embody his tastes in his own unmistakable pattern. His incompletely digested artistic enthusiasms leave disfigurements in his work. Gide's astute critical parallels between the importance to the child of the mother's good-night kiss or the guilt of children in the death of their parents, as these themes are treated in Proust's earlier and later work, nevertheless leave out of account the decisive part played in art not by the bare statement of a theme, which is after all not very important, but by its handling, its development, its variations and complications. The poorest and best of artists may both make use of the same theme to entirely different effects. The notation of similarity of theme, while of some intrinsic interest then, is of negligible importance in deciding the value of art.

But when it comes to the philosophy of *Les Plaisirs et les jours* and its expression in brief, thought-packed sentences, then indeed the work, on a few occasions at least, challenges comparison with the best that Proust has done, not only because of the maturity of his early thoughts but also because of the sharp and memorable form in which the words have been arranged. In a fairly long story, for example, in which the characters are pasteboard and the plot unsteady, there is at least one passage which leaps out of the faded context with terrific force. It is a reflection which is only incidentally connected with the immediate story and can certainly stand up by itself. Proust's narrator in the story, a growing boy watching an older relative slowly dying, is struck by what he calls "the universal scandal of human lives that walked toward death backward with eyes turned toward life." [2] It is evident where the young writer has made an idea his own, where the voice is his own voice, where the manner and the image in which he has incorporated his thought are original.

It is in such rare philosophical metaphors that Proust's latent powers first showed themselves; the book did not gain too much notice because they were hidden from the eyes of most readers by their scarcity among masses of more obvious matter. The brilliant metaphors all have one thing in common—they describe feelings about death or else they deal with the sufferings of life, the futility of desire, the necessity of renunciation. In one figure, he summons up the tragic image of "a young man, who has all his life been mistaken about the country of his birth [and] felt homesick for death which at first had seemed to him a land of eternal exile." [3] He traces the fact of the universal dissatisfaction and misery of mankind to the existence of "two worlds, the world of reality and the world of desire [which] are parallel [to each other, so] that it is impossible for them ever to meet, as a shadow the body that projected it." [4] The themes

[2] Proust, *Pleasures and Regrets*, trans. by Varèse, p. 11.
[3] *Ibid.*, p. 20. [4] *Ibid.*, p. 190.

of his stories, however incomplete his powers to treat them, are often philosophical themes. In one story, a girl who is remorseful for her vicious sex life goes into society to be distracted from her morbid desires but finds herself there freed of her vices and bereft of her virtues (solitary thought, deep feelings, dreams, and art). In desperation at this unlooked-for misfortune, she turns back to sex in order that it might reawaken her affective, intellectual, and aesthetic life. Proust is keenly aware of the plight of the poor human being caught in a dilemma between spiritual pain and the stagnation of boredom, and ceaselessly tossed between them. The girl says, "I would go into society to calm myself after sinning, and, no sooner calm, would sin again." [5]

Proust is aware that there is only one exit from such a dilemma aside from death and that is renunciation. The girl says: "I put off from day to day the final decision, the choice, the truly free act, the option of solitude." [6] The expression "truly free act" reminds us forcibly of Schopenhauer who says that the self-suppression of the human will is the greatest possible assertion of human freedom. Young Proust is also distinguished by a very delicate moral sensitivity (which should claim our attention later in a chapter on his ethics). The troubled girl tells us that "the accomplices of my sins made themselves apologists to my conscience." [7]

Perhaps it may be said that Proust's reading in La Rochefoucauld, La Bruyère, Chamfort, and Schopenhauer help to account for his pessimistic maxims, as his reading of Poe helps us understand his style in one story and his admiration of Tolstoy the sentiments of a character in another story.

[5] *Ibid.*, p. 40. [6] *Ibid.* [7] *Ibid.*, p. 39.

The difference is that the philosophy sounds personal, convincing, and distinguished in expression, while much of the art seems simply imitative.[8]

SCHOPENHAUER'S INFLUENCE

Schopenhauer is, I think, the most literary of our modern philosophers. Even those who admit the intellectual preeminence of other philosophers could hardly claim that they compare with him in verbal brilliance and lucidity. I do not mean to be needlessly iconoclastic in suggesting the following comparison or to revive the sterile seventeenth-century quarrel (slain by Swift) over the relative merits of ancient and modern learning, but I think that Schopenhauer is as outstanding on grounds of literary art and style among the philosophers since the Middle Ages as Plato was among those of Greece. And just as literary men often find their bridge into philosophy through a reading of Plato because his beautiful words and phrases find so pleasing an entrance into our ears which remain recalcitrant to other deep but unmusical thinkers, so Schopenhauer has owed his initial

[8] The critic Paul Rosenfeld in his book *Men Seen*, part of which is reprinted in Lindner, *Marcel Proust—Reviews and Estimates*, p. 83, writes: "It has been said that one could gather a new La Rochefoucauld from the novel." Justin O'Brien actually tried to give concrete evidence to this observation by compiling a volume of *The Maxims of Marcel Proust* for the Columbia University Press in 1948. F. L. Lucas (quoted in Lindner, *Marcel Proust—Review and Estimates*, p. 192) makes a distinction which I have not thought fruitful enough to use myself in this chapter: "In Proust, indeed, France has added one more to her numerous *penseurs*, not to her few philosophers. He has the quick perception of a woman, not the organizing logic of the builders of systems." It seems to me to restrict the meaning of philosophy too greatly to find room in it only for "systems." Behind every great aphorist, there has certainly been implicit some kind of system. It is the purpose of this chapter to show that Proust has such a system without giving to it a connected formal utterance, and that his system has important points of resemblance to that of Schopenhauer.

and continuing fashion not so much to professional philosophers as to artists, musicians, writers, and what Johnson would have called "common readers." The first great name in the difficult history of his recognition is that of Wagner. Proust mentions Schopenhauer's name several times in the course of his work.[9] Proust sums up (as we shall see) not only the main ideas of the German philosopher but some of his subordinate ones as well (such as are found, for example, in an essay like "The Metaphysics of Love between the Sexes"). That Schopenhauer's name has not occurred in Proustian criticism as much as that of other philosophers—like Bergson, for example—is, I believe, because Schopenhauer's influence on Proust is easily taken for granted, without a serious, conscious effort to define it precisely and it is just as easy to miss that influence entirely because of the very obvious magnitude of its importance. Then, too, critics proud of the fineness of their perceptions often turn their attention to secondary details before settling the questions about the main outlines and in this way often ignore important causes in favor of recondite ones.

Some critics—Edmund Wilson, for example—have de-

[9] One of the few scholars who accords to Schopenhauer some of the importance (though not enough, it seems to me) he deserves in a study of Proust is Harold March, *The Two Worlds of Marcel Proust* (Philadelphia, 1948), pp. 16–17. Maurois makes two brief, tantalizing references to Schopenhauer in his biography of Proust. One of these references reveals that Schopenhauer had a vogue among the young men with whom Proust was associated in editing *Le Banquet* in his twenties, but Maurois does not explore the implications which this invites the reader to discover. Instead Maurois chooses to stay on the well-trodden ground of tracing the well-known and undoubted analogies between Proust's work and Bergson's. For an explicit appreciation of Schopenhauer in the pages of Proust outside his novel, see Marcel Proust, *Selections from His Miscellaneous Writings*, pp. 134–36, where, speaking of Schopenhauer's *Aphorisms on the Wisdom of Life*, Proust says that this essay "more than any other work I know presupposes in its author not only a vast amount of learning but great originality as well."

tected in writings such as Proust's or Leopardi's the characteristic mark of an invalid. Proust himself made no effort to suppress the fact of his invalidism in his work—he refers to it glancingly, by means of a figure of speech, in the very opening pages, and mentions it in passing often after that. But the invalidism which he and his critics refer to, the disability in his lungs, his suffering from asthma, is not really to the point when we consider Proust's thought. If Proust's ideas about retirement from the world of action, of the resignation of the will, stem from his physical illness, how is it that some invalids—like W. E. Henley, for example—have, on the contrary and perhaps in compensation for their physical handicaps, developed the most strenuous attitudes towards life? No, to trace Proust's pessimism to such a cause is much too simple. Perhaps there was in Proust, much more important than his physical ailments, a kind of mental invalidism, caused by the split in his sex and in his nationality (both of which, as we have seen, he did suppress from the pages of his novel, at least so far as the person of his narrator is concerned). It seems best not to risk falling into the genetic fallacy, and to treat Proust's ideas in themselves. We ought not to assume too easily that we can know their source or that we may dismiss them because of their origin. Pessimism has certainly a very long history in human thought, and not all of those who have been pessimists have been invalids in any obvious way. Even if we did agree to call them sick, it is not clear that such sickness is as far removed from the ordinary human condition as is usually assumed. The hypothesis that illness may be normal is supported by the fact that the issue of all human life is ultimately the same, no matter what optimistic ideas are entertained about it.

It was Plutarch, that great critic of the human soul, who pointed out a principle which is important to the reader of life—that an "accidental" expression or jest by a man is more important to our intimate understanding of him than an account of the greatest actions in which he participated. I think that something similar may be said about literature—that the key to a writer's philosophy may be contained in a parenthetical expression or in an adjective more often than in the obvious places of character and action where we would think of looking for them. In fact, just as a great man, more so than others, is perhaps one whose life is only an expansion of the pattern found in his everyday words and deeds, so a great writer may be one whose vision is so unified that it is contained not only in the form of his whole work but in the smallest phrase of its composition. I find, for example, the seed of Proust's large philosophic structure in a passing parenthesis from the volume next to his last: "Three events out of four are unfortunate." [10] From such a tiny phrase, as from the one by Housman which resembles it, "Luck's a chance, but trouble's sure," I think that a classical scholar of the future could, working with the same process of reconstruction which enables naturalists, sometimes with the shape of only a single bone to guide them, to tell with reasonable certainly what a long-vanished creature looked like, deduce fairly accurately the fundamentals of an author's view of life.

A man who believes that three quarters of the things that happen to us are bad is not likely to be a great believer in human virtue. Since evil is multiplied by *the* evil, life would be a great deal easier to take if the ratio of good people were increased. But for Proust, goodness, in all but a very few

[10] *The Sweet Cheat Gone,* p. 38.

men, is a superficial camouflage which soon wears thin and shows the baser motives underneath. Only those who have minds as tough as their stomachs are capable of taking this bitterness straight, and Proust admits his own squeamishness at believing people to be as mean and cruel as they really are, "the idea of deliberate wickedness being too painful for me to bear." [11] But Proust did not permanently turn aside from the unpalatable truth, which grew more strongly upon him all the time, about the overwhelming evidence of the inherent brutality and depravity of mankind. He schooled himself to terrible disillusion with the most painstaking assiduity, until at last he came to a great generalization: "Other people as we get to know them are like a metal dipped in an acid bath, and we see them gradually lose their good qualities." [12] It is true that he adds immediately, "and their bad qualities too, at times." That is because he is conscientiously and completely accurate, but the clear implication of that phrase "at times" is that while on some rare occasions our acquaintances improve with the length of our knowledge of them, in most cases the opposite is true. All we need is a gaze strong enough to take off the top layer of gilt which adorns them.

Life is irremediably painful [13]—that is what Proust tells us over and over again, what he illustrates with his stories in endless variations. Everywhere he turns his eyes, he sees misery:

What troubled me now was the discovery that almost every house sheltered some unhappy person. In one, the wife was always in

[11] *The Guermantes Way*, Part 1, p. 234.

[12] *Cities of the Plain*, Part 1, p. 269.

[13] Francis Birrell (quoted in Lindner, *Marcel Proust—Reviews and Estimates*, p. 15) says: "Man . . . is doomed by the nature of his being to unsatisfied desire and restless misery, till Proust becomes, as I have called him above, the prophet of despair."

tears because her husband was unfaithful to her. In the next it was the other way about. In another, a hardworking mother, beaten black and blue by a drunkard son, was endeavoring to conceal her suffering from the eyes of the neighbors. Quite half of the human race was in tears.[14]

There is nothing but eternal dissatisfaction, frustration like that of Tantalus, so terrible as to suggest some supernal malevolence. Happiness, like the horizon, is a goal towards which we are always striving but which we can never reach. As we are about to reach it, it is always being "snatched from us." [15] "If we succeed in overcoming the force of circumstances, nature at once shifts the battleground, placing it within ourselves and effects a gradual change in our heart until it desires something other than what it is going to obtain." [16] This is one of the tricks used by "nature" which "with diabolical cleverness" is bent upon frustrating us. It is nature which creates in us "the mental incapacity for happiness." Even when happiness does appear, it is followed "at once" by "the bitterest of reactions." [17] Proust's pessimism reaches a nadir when he says that "we are all of us . . . all living persons, really only dead men who have not begun to exercise their functions as such." [18]

Every love affair described by Proust is a study of the alternation of pain and boredom in life. As soon as one condition is absent, the other takes its place. There is hardly time to catch one's breath in between, and that hastily drawn breath is all that we ever know of happiness, which is simply the momentary absence of pain before boredom has had a chance to develop, "anguish the actual cessation of which

[14] *The Guermantes Way,* Part 2, pp. 86–87.
[15] *Within a Budding Grove,* Part 1, p. 282.
[16] *Ibid.* [17] *Ibid.*
[18] Marcel Proust, *Selections from His Miscellaneous Writings,* p. 136.

was so agreeable that it might even be called a state of happiness." [19] Not only are the large rhythms of life divisible into pain and boredom (that is to say the dominant feeling of one long period is deprivation of the objects of desire, while that of another period is surfeit), but every one of the smaller segments of which these are composed can also be divided into incipient sufferings and ennuis: "I felt that my life with Albertine was, on the one hand, when I was not jealous, mere boredom, and, on the other hand, when I was jealous, constant suffering." [20] Pain and ennui, as in the German philosopher's formulation, are the poles between which we are endlessly thrown, so that Proust is able to take certain days out of the life of his narrator and to report the almost hourly changes in the tone of his emotional life, showing him run the entire gamut from euphoric exaltation to almost melancholic despair.

Although pain is the more dramatic half of the seesaw of human misery, the torture of boredom is wonderfully illustrated by Proust with scenes from the uneventful life of the old invalid Aunt Léonie—boredom becomes as terrible to her as to a prisoner in solitary confinement, so that she longs for some positive pain as a relief from it!

> Although Saturday, by beginning an hour earlier and by depriving her of the services of Françoise, passed more slowly than other days for my aunt, yet the moment it was past, and a new week begun, she would look forward with impatience to its return, as something that embodied all the novelty and distraction which her frail and disordered body was still able to endure. This was not to say, however, that she did not long, at times, for some even greater variation, that she did not pass through those abnormal hours in which one thirsts for something different from what one has, when those people who, through lack of energy or imagination, are un-

[19] *Swann's Way*, p. 305. [20] *The Captive*, p. 537.

able to generate any motive power in themselves, cry out, as the clock strikes or the postman knocks, in their eagerness for news (even if it be bad news), for some emotion (even that of grief); when the heartstrings, which prosperity has silenced, like a harp laid by, yearn to be plucked and sounded again by some hand, even a brutal hand, even if it shall break them; when the will, which has with such difficulty brought itself to subdue its impulse, to renounce its right to abandon itself to its own uncontrolled desires, and consequent sufferings, would fain cast its guiding reins into the hands of circumstances, coercive, and, it may be, cruel.[21]

But the invalid (even the imaginary invalid) is not the one who is most threatened by boredom. Those who are rich enough financially to be idle and not rich enough spiritually to find creative occupation for themselves are in even worse case. Mme Verdurin literally dreads the prospect of being left alone to herself during a single day of the year by her chosen little circle. She makes plans far in advance of Christmas and Easter to keep her faithful from wandering off to their own families during the holidays.[22]

Pope says "man never is but always to be blest." Proust agrees about the absence of blessedness from the present but locates it in the past rather than in the future: "The only true Paradise is always the Paradise we have lost." [23] Happiness for him is an imaginary state. What we are conscious of in actuality is perpetual disillusion,[24] for either the objects of our desires remain unattained, or else our desires themselves change. As a final turn of the screw, our desires change more quickly when they are fulfilled than when they are frustrated. In either case, however, there is no such thing as permanence, only change, and change is always fatal to something in ourselves. Or, as Proust puts it at one

[21] *Swann's Way*, p. 146.
[22] *Ibid.*, p. 244.
[23] *The Past Recaptured*, p. 195.
[24] *The Guermantes Way*, Part 1, p. 52.

point: "I observe that each alteration of the brain is a partial death." [25] The object of our striving comes to us too late to satisfy:

> In love the barriers, do what one may, cannot be broken down from without by him whom they maddeningly exclude; it is when he is no longer concerned with them that suddenly as the result of an effort directed from elsewhere, accomplished within the heart of her who did not love him, those barriers which he has charged without success will fall to no advantage.[26]

As in any pessimistic philosophy, there is much emphasis in Proust upon the themes of transitoriness and mutability. Proust demonstrates, after an exhaustive catalogue of the various instabilities inseparable from life, that even grief itself which, considering his dark picture of the world would seem to have the best and most lasting claim upon us, is impermanent.[27] The duration of everything in the world—things, people, ideas, feelings—is relative and ephemeral. Flowers, which would seem to be the very embodiment and symbol of the concept of change, themselves seem relatively stable when compared with the clouds of sunset.[28] Society, which seems so fixed in its hierarchies to the short-sighted, presents a spectacle to Proust as sad as the statue of Ozymandias in the desert seemed to Shelley. "How perishable," says Proust, after describing how the almost blind Charlus bowed to a certain lady whom he had spent a lifetime in snubbing, "how perishable is the love of earthly grandeur and even human pride itself." [29]

But Proust would not be a great novelist if, in addition to stating his thoughts like any other writer of expository prose,

[25] *Cities of the Plain,* Part 2, p. 180.
[26] *Within a Budding Grove,* Part 1, pp. 264–65.
[27] *Ibid.,* p. 291. [28] *The Guermantes Way,* Part 1, p. 240.
[29] *The Past Recaptured,* p. 184.

he did not also find ways of illustrating them in terms of characters and stories. Thus, no amount of theorizing on the foolish tricks which desire plays upon poor human beings could equal the effect of the hilarious incident in which the narrator, catching sight of an intriguing woman walking quickly down a dark street, rudely leaves the friend with whom he has been driving in order "not to forfeit for a purely conventional scruple, my share of happiness in what may very well be the only life there is." [30] So, breathlessly running after that elusive phantom imaging all of our unknown desires, he catches up with her at last under a street lamp only to find—old Mme Verdurin, whom he had spent years in "carefully avoiding." No lament concerning the vanity of human wishes can quite equal the picture of Legrandin, who, after infinite plotting and conniving and snobbish strain, has attained his lifelong ambition to be invited out regularly to the best society, and then decides not to go, for two compelling reasons: first, that the actual fulfillment of his desire has robbed its object of the aura of the unattainable; and second, that, having nurtured, along with his snobbery, the vice of homosexuality, the strength of the latter supplants the satisfactions of the former, and he who had dreamed all his life of dining with dukes is now more contented with the company of hooligans.[31] The same thing, in slightly altered form, happens to the character Bloch, too, who had begun as a snob and then found that time, as it altered his social status, correspondingly altered his desires as well:

I observed that whereas he formerly used to pretend to believe that he had to take a two-hour railway journey in order to call on

[30] *Within a Budding Grove*, Part 2, pp. 14–15.
[31] *The Sweet Cheat Gone*, pp. 345–46.

someone who had given him but a perfunctory invitation, now that he was receiving many invitations, not only to luncheon and dinner but to spend a fortnight here and a fortnight there, he refused many of them without announcing the fact or boasting that he had received and declined them.[32]

The startling proximity with which the certainty of attaining something is related to the complete extinction of all desire for it is shown in a scene involving the narrator, his friend Elstir, and the "little band" of girls at Balbec. In the space of a few moments the state of the narrator's feelings, alternately based on the belief that an introduction to the girls is impossible and then later that it is inevitable and still later that it is difficult once again, undergoes the most amazingly swift, we may almost call them schizophrenic changes from feverish expectancy to bored indifference and then back again to the initial excitement.[33]

One of the greater resemblances between Proust and Schopenhauer lies in their similar attitudes to women. Proust does not go the whole length of the fierce contempt of the German philosopher, who called women the narrow-shouldered, broad-hipped, short-legged, unaesthetic sex, but he does indicate his conviction that there is nothing objectively to correspond to the needs of our instinctive enthusiasm for the female of the species. Such an attitude towards the other sex seems characteristic, furthermore, of nearly all

[32] *The Past Recaptured,* p. 312. In his recent book *The Mind of Proust* (Cambridge, 1949), Professor F. C. Green holds that while other characters in the novel undergo changes, Bloch remains the same from beginning to end. I don't see very well how this criticism can stand up in the light of such a passage as the one I have quoted. Bloch certainly does change no less than the other characters do. Proust underscores that by adding, beyond the text I have cited: "Discretion, in both word and deed, had come to him, along with social standing and age, with a sort of social age, if one may use the term."

[33] *Within a Budding Grove,* Part 2, pp. 215 ff.

pessimists. We find it in Ecclesiastes who says that once in a great while he has found a man who justified his hopes, but woman uniformly is "a snare and a deception." We find it in Juvenal who, in his sixth satire, wonders why men marry while there is still enough rope in the world with which to hang themselves. We find it in Swift, who concentrates an unhurried, relishing gaze upon all the more noisome physical attributes of a woman's bodily existence. For Proust there is certainly nothing individual essentially about women—at one point he suggests that all members of that sex are different means to an identical pleasure.[34] Cynicism, it would seem, could go no further. Proust thinks that that which makes a particular woman seem unique and irreplaceable is merely a painful illusion. We would love a great deal more lightheartedly did we not believe in the inevitability of that love and of its consequent sufferings. Even in the throes of his affair with Albertine, this truth is present somewhere in the back of his mind: "Over and above any personal considerations . . . I was performing the duties of an ardent and painful devotion dedicated as an oblation to the youth and beauty of Woman." [35]

It will occur to some readers perhaps, in contradiction to what is said here, that the two best characters in Proust's book, the purest and the most idealized are both women, the narrator's mother and his grandmother. But these two are far outweighed by a really phenomenal number of perfidious females: Mme Verdurin, the Duchesse de Guermantes, Mme de Cambremer, Odette, Gilberte, Albertine, Rachel—to name only a few. It seems to me one of the psychological difficulties of Proust's story that the mother and grandmother should be made to stand so alone in the midst of their sex.

[34] *Swann's Way*, p. 202. [35] *The Captive*, p. 94.

Even were there not other, more conclusive, evidence, this would indicate the probability of his tampering with the sexual identity of some of his characters. Since there seems now to be no reasonable doubt left of Proust's own inversion, and the original suspicion that the character of Albertine was based primarily upon a male model has been conclusively confirmed,[36] some of the looser ends of this question are tied up. Proust, like other pessimists I have mentioned, was undoubtedly a misogynist, and, like them too, his misogyny was only one corner of a more general feeling of misanthropy. The mother and grandmother in the book are such rare spots of light in the shadowy picture of mankind that they can only serve to set off the darkness of the rest. They have very few others to emulate them, either men or women. The statistically exceptional quality of goodness in this world and, conversely, the statistical predominance of evil are among the most potent reasons for Proust's despair of mankind's possibility of amelioration.

In the following passage, the reference evidently is to Schopenhauer's "Metaphysics of Love between the Sexes": "We are told that it is the preservation of the species which guides our individual preferences in love, and, so that the child may be constituted in the most normal fashion, sends

[36] Proust's inversion, which was an idle rumor in his lifetime and for years after his death, has been pinned down with decisive evidence which no reputable scholar would now care to controvert, I think. This has been done by the publication of Gide's Journals, where an entry tells us of the explicit confession made by Proust to Gide concerning his sex life. No one would suggest that Gide fabricated this, or suppose that Proust was trying to shock Gide by a false disclosure. Vigneron has, of course, done the best work of identifying Albertine with Proust's chauffeur-secretary, Agostonelli. One of the virtues of Maurois' biography is that he takes this scholarship into account and leaves no doubt of his own conviction of Proust's homosexuality. That it took so long for the world, in spite of its great interest in the fact, to make certain of it is a confirmation of Proust's emphasis upon the immense difficulties of making certain of the simplest, most obvious, and most necessary truths.

fat men in pursuit of lean women and vice versa."[37] Proust's view of love, like Schopenhauer's, was basically antiromantic. It is at the opposite extreme from such a worship of woman as we find in Rousseau or in Keats. Perhaps because he understood internally only too well the temptations of such an attitude and also its self-destructiveness, Proust was determined not to die for love. He was evidently much impressed with the story which he tells in *Swann's Way* about Mohammed II, who, having fallen in love with one of the wives in his harem, at once stabbed her because, as his biographer relates, he did not wish to live in spiritual bondage to another.

Proust emphasizes the accidental quality of love, its dependence upon circumstance and, above all, on our own subjective state. There is no such thing as "exclusive love," for him, except as our conditioning, the product of our environment combined with our laziness and willful self-deception, makes it so. We can love any one of a large class of beings interchangeably. The most that Proust is willing to grant to the romantics is that, were our present love to be taken from us, we could not fall in love again with "any other woman."[38] But even of this much degraded illusion, he does not seem very sure.

As in Schopenhauer, the blind, striving will is the sole permanent aspect of our varying personalities.[39] The will seems to be subservient to our higher intellectual centers, but so uncertain is the brain's mastery, so wavering and contradictory and self-indulgent are its commands, that this is another case where the nominal servant actually rules. It is the necessity of keeping the unruly will in check that

[37] *Within a Budding Grove,* Part 2, p. 33.
[38] *The Sweet Cheat Gone,* p. 118.
[39] *Within a Budding Grove,* Part 2, pp. 236–37.

makes Proust base the ethical life upon the secure foundation of habit rather than upon the spontaneity of the impulsive heart.

Whatever rest (it is too much to call it happiness) we can obtain in this life depends upon showing our will its proper place, which is to remain securely kenneled at home.[40] Proust, like Schopenhauer and those eastern mystics with whom the philosopher said he had so much in common, believes that renunciation and resignation of the will is the only course for a man who would achieve the relief of even comparative calm. Desire, as we have seen, leads nowhere; at best, desires that are attained soon begin to appear fantastic and are quickly forgotten.[41] "I found a certain wisdom in those philosophers who recommend us to set a limit to our desires." [42]

There are whole passages in Proust which, if they were taken out of their context and presented to us in another guise, might very well pass as Schopenhauer's. And I think that this mistaken judgment would not be at all due to our stylistic obtuseness or insensitivity—as in the case of those society "music lovers" in Proust who madly applaud what they think a piece by Debussy only to be frozen into embarrassed silence when they are told it is Meyerbeer's.[43] On the contrary, the better acquainted we are with the ideas and tones of the German master, the more likely it seems to

[40] Van Meter Ames in his book on Proust and Santayana, parts of which are included in Lindner, *Marcel Proust—Reviews and Estimates*, p. 236, correctly says: "His [Proust's] joy in the aesthetic attitude, induced chiefly by art, lay in the release that Schopenhauer called relief from the Will." Harold March, whom I have credited earlier with recognizing the resemblances between Proust and Schopenhauer to some extent, says (*The Two Worlds of Marcel Proust*, p. 246): "Like Schopenhauer, whom he read and admired, Proust believed that in the world of ordinary experience illusion was inescapable, desire insatiable and always frustrated, and happiness impossible."

[41] *Within a Budding Grove*, Part 1, pp. 155–56.

[42] *Ibid.*, Part 2, p. 16.

[43] *Cities of the Plain*, Part 2, p. 138.

me would we be to accept the following as a passage from the fourth book of *The World as Will and Idea* or from one of his numerous essays: "If happiness or at least freedom from suffering can be found, it is not the satisfaction, but the gradual reduction, the eventual extinction of our desire that we must seek." [44]

It is a lack of realization of how central the pessimistic philosophy is in Proust's work that makes certain critics regard as useless digressions some passages which, when they are more deeply considered from this point of view, are revealed as adding much weight to the gloomy atmosphere of the whole thing. Thus, a generally sympathetic critic like Derrick Leon can say that "it is difficult to find any adequate justification for the lengthy exposition of military tactics, or Brichot's endless dissertations upon the meaning of place-names about Balbec. The sum of many such digressions when it does little to advance the portrayal of character or the development of action, merely serves to weaken the cumulative effect of a work which was composed with the most detailed and passionate care." [45] In a general treatment, I can only suggest the lines of refutation of this criticism. Saint-Loup's military theories, which serve as background for the passages on the First World War in the last volume, generally aim at the point that, as in all fields, there is a well-defined tradition in war, and not only have there been a limited number of battle types in history, but even the same fields have been used over and over again throughout many centuries by different nations. What better evidence could there be for the Preacher's saying that there is nothing new under the sun? Even the ways of killing and

[44] *The Sweet Cheat Gone*, p. 46.

[45] See Derrick Leon's contribution in Lindner, *Marcel Proust—Reviews and Estimates.*

destruction are stereotyped in the annals of mankind. Pessimists in general love to dwell on the subject of war, because it is so hard to derive any comfort from its spectacle. The business of killing men and brutalizing them has gone on since Cain, and the methods of doing so, except perhaps for progress in efficiency, have not really changed. I cannot agree that the disquisitions on military science are useless from the philosophical point of view in Proust.

Nor can I agree that Brichot's lectures on place names are without point either. In fact, these talks, far from serving no purpose at all, really serve two at the same time. We must recall the context in which they take place. A curé of the church of Combray has written a little book purporting to give the origins of the place names around the seaside resort of Balbec. Brichot, the Sorbonne pedant, sets to work with great delight before an appreciative company to destroy the last shred of these theories; instead, he supplies his own derivations of these place names. Now this is not only a satire on battles of the books in general, but a commentary on the hopeless ignorance of humanity about its origins. Everything changes with time, and the memory of whole communities is as fallible as that of any individual. No other interpretation can be put upon our inability to account definitely and accurately for the origin of names of places, where many generations have lived and died—generations which knew the secret but imparted no memorials of it to anybody. Knowledge, it is said, is the light of the world, and yet what a feeble light it is. Perhaps that is why Ecclesiastes says that the increase of knowledge also increases sorrow. Those who are totally ignorant may be happy, and those who have a little knowledge may be hopeful, but those who have the deepest knowledge must learn what a flickering illumination it gives over the vast abysses of what we can never know. It takes an indefatigable, self-assertive, and confident scholar like Brichot to point more sharply this melancholy truth for Proust.

Perhaps the most effectually terrifying picture which Proust uses to illustrate the fate of humanity is to be found in his last volume. No part of the whole work seems more powerful in evoking feelings of disgust and horror than this one, in which he describes his sudden realization of the meaning of old age, which, while he wasn't looking, so to speak, has overtaken himself and all the friends of his youth. It is Proust's *Lear*. He puts into this panel the best of his talent. It is a grisly tale of how Time, which is ordinarily so modest as to be scarcely noticeable, suddenly turns a pleasant party into a macabre masquerade. The scene reminds us of a possible crossing between a story by Poe and Hamlet's address to Yorick's skull: "Get you to my lady's chamber, and tell her, let her paint an inch thick, to this favour she must come. Make her laugh at that! . . ."

As to that young Lezensac, I cannot imagine what he had put on his face but, while the others had whitened, some one-half of their beard, others merely their mustaches, he had not bothered with dyes, but had managed to put wrinkles all over his face and add bristling hairs to his eyebrows. The general effect was not at all becoming; his face seemed hardened, bronzed, solemn-looking, and he appeared so old that no one would have taken him to be a young man. I was greatly surprised at the same time when I heard someone address as the Duc de Chatellerault a little old man with the silvery moustache of an ambassador, who had retained just a glance of the eye which enabled me to recognize in him the young man I had once met calling on Mme. de Villeparisis. With the first person whom I thus succeeded in identifying by trying to disregard his masquerade and supplement by an effort of memory such features as had remained unchanged, my first idea should have been, and probably was for a fraction of a second, to congratulate him on being so wonderfully made up that one was not able at first to recognize him, just as when a great actor appears in a role very different from his natural self, the first moment he comes on the stage, the audience, although fully informed through the program, sits for an instant open-mouthed with astonishment before breaking into applause. From this point of view the most remarkable of all was my personal enemy, M. d'Argencourt, the real "hit" of the entire affair. Not only had he disguised himself with an extraordinary beard of an impossible whiteness in place of his own, scarcely touched with gray, but also with the aid of many slight physical changes calculated to make a person look smaller and stouter and, what is more, change his outward character, his personality, this man, whose dignified mien and starchy stiffness I still remembered, had turned himself into an old beggar who no longer inspired the least respect, and he put so much realism into his character of a driveling old man that his limbs shook and the flaccid features of his usually haughty face smirked continually with a stupidly beatific expression. Carried to this point, a disguise beomes something more than that, a transformation. And in truth, although certain small details testified that it was indeed M. d'Argencourt who was offering this picturesque but indescribable spectacle, how many successive facial stages I had to reconstruct in order to get back to the M. d'Argencourt I had known, who had changed himself so completely with merely his own physique to work with. He evidently carried the travesty to the extreme limit possible without bursting; what had formerly been the haughtiest countenance and the most erect carriage was now merely a limp rag tossed hither and yon.[46]

If objection is made that the predominating note in this last volume is joy at having found his artistic vocation, my answer is that Proust has had to transcend this world in order to reach his mystical sublimity and that Schopenhauer's Nirvana is a genuine and not entirely joyless hope

[46] *The Past Recaptured*, pp. 254–55.

which he holds out to us without his passing properly for anything but a pessimistic philosopher. Pessimism refers to a feeling of hopelessness about the possibilities of this world, and in this sense no one could be more pessimistic than Proust. I think that, though he overstates the case a little, Paul Elmer More is essentially right: "Humanity as portrayed in Proust's imagination is without aim, without joy, without peace, without outlook of any sort; his people have no occupation save to think about themselves, and in *le néant* beyond the phantasmagoria of unsatisfied and forever insatiable desires the only reality for them is the grinning face of Fear." [47]

For Proust, the individual exists irremediably alone; no real tie is possible between him and any of his fellows. Consequently, if there is to be any solution for his problems at all (which is exceedingly doubtful) it must always be an individual rather than a collective solution. Proust's, like Schopenhauer's, is basically an individualistic philosophy:

> The bonds that unite another person to ourself exist only in our mind. Memory as it grows fainter relaxes them, and notwithstanding the illusion by which we would fain be cheated and with which, out of love, friendship, politeness, deference, duty, we cheat other people, we exist alone. Man is the creature that cannot emerge from himself, that knows his fellows only in himself; when he asserts the contrary, he is lying.[48]

It is what has been called "the great human pretension to happiness" which leads to most of the positive ills of the world, whereas idleness results in the negative ones. Idleness results in boredom which in turn is the cause of mischief. Like Ecclesiastes, Proust thinks that work is good

[47] Lindner, *Marcel Proust—Reviews and Estimates,* p. 166.
[48] *The Sweet Cheat Gone,* p. 47.

because it distracts our attention from the vain bubble of happiness.[49]

But better than anything else is resignation of the will. While desire and the expenditure which it entails steadily weakens us, resignation "allows certain elements of our strength to be indefinitely increased." [50] The things we wish for in life, if attainable at all, can be achieved only at the end of a "heartrending" course of pain and renunciation.[51] Those who have accomplished great things in the spiritual realm—the artist, the priest, the hero—have all learned the lesson of renunciation, says Proust.[52] They have even found that, though it is very hard to discipline the rebellious will at the beginning, eventually, like other great and good things, the curb pleases us and it also makes us better. About the artist Elstir, who had been a silly and trifling worldling in the Verdurin salon before submitting himself to the self-imposed yoke of his work, he says: "The practice of solitude had given him a love for it." [53]

That last phrase reminds us that in the case of the narrator of the novel, too, while he was trying to find his way to the vocation of writing, the most potent rival which his sweethearts had to fear was his love, not for others, but for solitude itself, and the lonely condition of creation eventually wins out.

For Proust, as for the most stoic philosophers, the practice of resignation of the will is incomplete until it prepares us to part with equanimity from life itself. Life to him seems only the most ingrained of our habits, the hardest to break; but there comes a point for the thoughtful and long-suffering man when, having broken his most persistent and seemingly

[49] *Cities of the Plain*, Part 2, p. 3.
[50] *Within a Budding Grove*, Part 1, p. 278.
[51] *Ibid.*, p. 312.
[52] *Ibid.*, Part 2, p. 177.
[53] *Ibid.*

ineradicable habits and himself with them, he is ready for the last and hardest step—not suicide, for suicide, as Schopenhauer says, is only the sign of impotent rebellion of the will rather than its complete suppression, but what may be called nonresistance in the face of death or any illusions about its personal finality. Proust shows himself reaching this conclusion through a line of reasoning growing out of his abandonment by Albertine:

I reflected: I used to value Albertine more than myself; I no longer value her now because for a certain time past I have ceased to see her. But my desire not to be parted from myself by death, to rise again after my death, this desire was not like the desire never to be parted from Albertine, it still persisted. Was this due to the fact that I valued myself more highly than her, that when I was in love with her I loved myself even more? No, it was because having ceased to see her, I ceased to love her, whereas I had not ceased to love myself because my everyday attachments to myself had not been severed like my attachments to Albertine. But if the attachments to my body, to myself were severed also . . . ? Obviously it would be the same. Our love of life is only an old connection of which we do not know how to rid ourself. Its strength lies in its permanence. But death which severs it will cure us of the desire for immortality.[54]

Proust's own manner of facing death was apparently worthy of these words, for he did not flinch, did not even stop working at his book, as the doctors, one of whom was his own brother Robert, ordered him to do, but continued at his post to the last, dictating, it has been said, his famous passage on the death of the novelist Bergotte, just before he met his own death. It is evident that Proust, like Schopenhauer, does not put much faith in consolations about the possibility of personal survival after death. In spite of the unbelief, however, which most critics find in Proust, there

[54] *The Sweet Cheat Gone,* pp. 314–15.

seems to have been a great struggle on the part of Proust to reach a belief in immortality. He approached the problem from all possible angles, from the point of view of science as well as from that of religion.[55] At one point in his book, so great is his need of consolation for the death of his beloved that he confesses having turned to table-rapping and spiritualism. But in the end it was the nineteenth century which triumphed in him.

The belief in immortality seems to Proust the last triumphant assertion of the human will, and for that reason alone it is suspect. The will, after all, had always led him in the pursuit of phantoms and illusions—why should this final manifestation of it be anything but false? The connection of faith and desire is emphasized strongly by Proust on the two most critical occasions of the book, the illness and death of his grandmother, and the flight and death of Albertine:

> Desire is very powerful; it engenders belief; I had believed that Albertine would not leave me because I desired that she might not. Because I desired it, I began to believe that she was not dead; I took to reading books upon table-turning, I began to believe in the possibility of the immortality of the soul.[56]

The very tone in which Proust tells us this signifies that he regards this desire of man for personal perpetuity as the most futile of all his desires, a desire which comes from his weakness and one which "death will cure." Proust turns the question of immortality round and round for examination. Even if we were to grant the possibility of life after death, Proust shows how many difficulties are inherent in the concept. For example, which of our successive and varying

[55] This will be documented later with a quotation from de Lauris.
[56] *The Sweet Cheat Gone*, p. 132.

personalities in life will be the one chosen to last forever. If, actually, the continuity of our personality is merely a convenience of nomenclature, and all of us die many times before our death, do we not run the risk, asks Proust, of being eternally condemned to the companionship of people whom we have outgrown, separated from, and discarded in our lives?

The general view of Proust is stated in the words: "the dead exist only in us." [57] That Proust regards belief in personal immortality as human weakness, as an evasion of the unbearably painful consciousness of the permanence of death, is shown by his words of praise for his own strength in rejecting such easy comfort when the memory of his greatly beloved grandmother returns to torture him:

> I . . . should have liked to feel driven yet deeper into me those nails which fastened the memory of her to my consciousness. I did not seek to mitigate my suffering, to set it off, to pretend that my grandmother was only somewhere else and momentarily invisible, by addressing to her photograph . . . words and prayers as to a person who is separated from us but, retaining his personality, knows us and remains bound to us by an indissoluble harmony.[58]

This skeptical attitude towards immortality naturally does not prevent the narrator, while his grandmother is still alive but when he is already troubled by the possibility of her death, from consoling her in the traditional way—I suppose with the same kindly justification which keeps us from telling an invalid that the illness which he assumes to be temporary is mortal after all, and that all of the roseate plans and hopes which he has are bound to come to nothing, because he is not going to come out of this room alive: "I began to talk to her about philosophy. . . . I remarked

[57] *Cities of the Plain,* Part 1, p. 222. [58] *Ibid.*

what a curious thing it was that, according to the latest scientific discoveries, the materialist position appeared to be crumbling, and the most likely thing to be, once again, the survival of the soul and reunion in a life everlasting." [59] Parallel to this passage from the novel may be one contained in a dedication of a copy of it to a friend of his mother's in which he tells her that he believes "at times" in a recent philosophy which holds that the soul survives death.[60]

But the more steadfast attitude leaves no room for such anodynes or palliatives. Proust not only doubts immortality, but, as I have said, emphasizes the impossible number of logical contradictions in which we would be involved by accepting it as a premise. Or, as he says:

> We passionately long that there may be another life in which we shall be similar to what we are here below. But we do not pause to reflect that, even without waiting for that other life, after a few years we are unfaithful to what we have been, to what we wished to remain eternally. . . . We dream much of Paradise, or rather of a number of successive Paradises, but each of them is, long before we die, a Paradise lost, in which we should feel ourself lost too.[61]

Among such intimations of mortality, Proust introduces some softer feelings. If his basic ideas are stoically pessimistic, his philosophy is not impervious to sentiment. In fact, throughout the book, we get the distinct impression that Proust has come to a renunciation of his dearest hopes by the hardest and most impassable of all roads, for, being a man in whom the affective side of his nature was extraordinarily developed, it took strength and heroism quite out

[59] *Within a Budding Grove,* Part 2, p. 35.
[60] Marcel Proust, *Lettres a Mme. C.* (Janin, 1946), p. 199.
[61] *Cities of the Plain,* Part 2, p. 8.

of the ordinary to renounce the dearest of his heart's desires. We are not surprised by the revelation of Proust's learning in religious literature and philosophy as it is made in the reminiscences of him by his friend Georges de Lauris:

I remember a conversation with Mme. Lucie Felix-Faure Goyau in which he revealed a subtle and varied erudition on most difficult subjects of religious philosophy and exegesis. Had he then read the whole of *The Golden Legend* and the work of the learned Hollandists—both chronicles of the Lives Of The Saints, the former by Jacobus de Voragine, thirteenth century bishop of Genoa, the latter the work of the Belgian Jesuits? [62]

The strength of Proust's expression of disbelief is in direct proportion to the strength of the impulses to belief which he had to overcome first. Few writers have written more eloquently of a premise which intellectually they have come to reject:

I asked nothing better of God, if a Paradise exists, than to be able, there, to knock upon that wall the three little raps which my grandmother would know among a thousand, and to which she would reply with those other taps which said: "Don't be alarmed, little mouse, I know you are impatient, but I am just coming," and that He would let me remain with her throughout eternity which would not be too long for us.[63]

In the same tenor are the words from a letter of Proust in 1904 to Georges de Lauris:

. . . what madness, what intoxication, if I could be sure of immortal life. How can you really, I won't say not believe, because the mere fact that a thing is desirable does not result in one's believing it—alas, on the contrary—but be satisfied with non-belief (not the intellectual satisfaction of preferring the sad truth to the

[62] Marcel Proust, *Letters to a Friend* (London, 1949), p. 12. The reminiscences about Proust by Georges de Lauris, given in a long introduction, seem natural and convincing, in other words somewhere in between hero worship and flat iconoclasm into which so much of biography falls.

[63] *Cities of the Plain,* Part 1, p. 227.

sweet lie). Would it not be sweet to find again, under a different sky, in the valleys vainly promised and futilely awaited, all those whom one has left or will leave? And to realize oneself at last.[64]

In 1906, he writes to the same correspondent: "I never asked you whether your mother was religious, had the consolation of prayer. Life is so horrible we might all come to this; alas, to wish for it is not enough." [65]

The key word in his most moving passages on this subject is always the word *if!*

The nearest that Proust approaches to a consolation of humanity for the necessity it is under to die comes in those passages which are devoted to art. Proust clearly had the will to believe, but lacked the capacity to do what he thought believers did—that is deceive himself. He was ready, as an artist, to do what Yeats said was now up to the poets to do—to assume the burden that had dropped from the shoulders of the priests. The whole existence of Proust testifies to his readiness to sacrifice himself for the truth, his voluntary immurement in his cork-lined chamber, his solitary devotion to an ideal of art long misunderstood by the public, and finally his sacrificial death. All of these things, like the legendary mutilated ear of Van Gogh, have become a part of that inspiring hagiography which, in the desert of the complete rejection of all spiritual values, has served to keep modern art alive. In the following passage which is about the piano sonata by Vinteuil, we feel how hard it is for Proust to admit the possibility of annihilation for art:

Perhaps it is not-being that is the true state, and all of our dream of life is without existence, but, if so, we feel that it must be that these phrases of music, these conceptions which exist in relation to our dream, are nothing either. We shall perish, but we have for our hostages these divine captives who shall follow and share our

[64] Marcel Proust, *Letters to a Friend,* p. 57. [65] *Ibid.*, p. 67.

fate. And death in their company is something less bitter, less inglorious, perhaps even less certain.[66]

It was never harder for Proust to cleave to his stoical acceptance of personal extinction than when the person to be extinguished was that of an artist, and on the occasion of Bergotte's death, though he steadfastly remains as equivocal on the subject of a life after death as Socrates is in "The Apology," Proust moves us most deeply when he relies upon the rhetoric of a religion that often flickered but feebly within him, a rhetoric, moreover, which, when it is used in this unusual connection with art, acquires new powers. It is part of the single passage in Proust which is most often quoted when there is room for only one quotation, so that many readers must have felt that it is most representative of him: "They buried him, but all through the night of mourning in the lighted windows, his books arranged three by three kept watch like angels with outspread wings and seemed for him who was no more, the symbol of his resurrection." [67] A parallel to this well-known passage from his fiction is to be found in a passage from a letter to his English friend Marie Nordlinger on the occasion of the death of Ruskin, whom they had both admired so much and had worked together in translating into French. Ruskin, incidentally, is the model for at least parts of the character of the writer Bergotte in the novel: "But when I learned of Ruskin's death, I wanted to express to you before anyone else, my sadness, a healthy sadness, however, and indeed full of consolations, for I know how little death matters when I see how powerfully this dead man lives on, how much I admire him, listen to him, try to understand him, to follow him more than I do many of the living." [68]

[66] *Swann's Way,* p. 453. [67] *The Captive,* p. 251.
[68] *Letters of Marcel Proust,* ed. by Curtiss, p. 64.

But such iridescent emotions are perhaps most striking for their extreme rarity in Proust, and even in them there is obvious the sign of the severe struggle which any faith in the supernatural has to make against the prevailing scientific and naturalistic current of Proust's time, so that he cries out once: "No one believes in heaven." [69] The parallel to this sentiment in his creative work is in a letter which he once wrote to Madame Straus, where he speaks of "heaven, in which neither of us believes, alas." [70] Proust's general feeling is the same as that in Shakespeare's most famous lines from *The Tempest;* Proust says once: "There is no great difference between the memory of a dream and the memory of a reality."

Proust is of that line of pessimistic thinkers which stretches from the mountain peaks of Ecclesiastes to Schopenhauer, though many more humble adherents of the same views have dwelt in the valleys in between. His friend Georges de Lauris is certainly right when he says about Proust: "His pessimism was fundamental." [71] Many of his most sensitive foreign critics have felt the same thing—the English Clive Bell,[72] for example, and the German Ernst Curtius.[73] Proust's experience of life seemed to have taught

[69] *The Sweet Cheat Gone,* p. 70.

[70] *Letters of Marcel Proust,* ed. by Curtiss, p. 182.

[71] Marcel Proust, *Letters to a Friend,* p. 20.

[72] Clive Bell (in Lindner, *Marcel Proust—Reviews and Estimates,* p. 127) says: "And is there a moral? To be sure there is; a philosophy of life at all events. It is not very new but it is true enough. Proust has explored depths hitherto unplumbed, he has stripped the dirt and varnish from reality till his fingers ache and our eyes, he has seen life from a new angle and described what he saw with a frankness and precision unmatched in prose; and the conclusion to which he has come is the conclusion to which came the Preacher—and Shakespeare:

All is vanity. . . .
. . . . it is a tale
Told by an idiot, full of sound and fury,
Signifying nothing."

[73] Ernst Curtius, *Proust* (Paris, 1928), p. 142.

him, as I said earlier, that the unhappy choice had three chances out of four of being the correct one. "The most gifted people I had known had died young," he says characteristically in one of his volumes.[74]

Proust does not deny the possibility that his philosophy may be due in part to his temperamental and constitutional defects. He speaks of "my disordered nerves . . . my morbid tendency to melancholy, to solitude." [75] He confesses to feeling that "health and sanity" were always in opposition somehow with "spiritual pleasures." [76] And though he says that he has always preferred health and sanity to illness and insanity, he makes us believe that it has been cowardly on his part to do so. Proust hesitated to give to any of his conclusions any absolute certainty, and so he carefully makes us aware of all of those subjective deficiencies and disqualifications which may serve to make the skeptical reader question the applicability of these pessimistic dicta and observations to himself, who is perhaps not an invalid, nor morbid, nor solitary, and who has never felt that sanity and spiritual pleasures were in any kind of mortal opposition to each other. Proust, in other words, is interested in making us aware, for the sake of completeness and impartiality, of the nature and coloring of the special lens through which he saw his vision of the world.

In spite of this, I cannot agree with those critics who see in this book the inevitable failings of an invalid. My own feeling is that, though few suffer from Proust's asthma, nevertheless all men as well as Proust himself, in one way or another, are invalids. Surely, Proust's is not the only world view possible, but it is a classic one with the most

[74] *The Guermantes Way*, Part I, p. 18.
[75] *Within a Budding Grove*, Part 2, p. 33. [76] *The Captive*, p. 163.

distinguished possible antecedents from ancient to modern times. Its proponents have been among the most fortunate of mankind (emperors and kings like Marcus Aurelius and Solomon) as well as the least fortunate (slaves like Epictetus). The dominant tendency of modern thought, perhaps, has tended to be optimistic, evolutionary, and progressive, but we have seen that for Proust, as for some other modern thinkers, it was science and the strict adherence to what he thought scientific method (that is, the rejection of any evidence that can't be made clear to the senses) which brought him to the most pessimistic conclusions. He was more ambitious than the utilitarians and progressives. Having been born into the most "privileged" strata of society, he could not be satisfied with a vision of reality which promised as the solution of all of our troubles and problems more electric lighting, more sewers, more washing machines, more television sets and gadgets for the future. Rather he wanted an answer to the most basic questions and hopes for humanity, and he found none at all for them in science. The progressive critics, then, may choose to reproach Proust for his pessimism as they reproach Schopenhauer and all other pessimists, if they like, but they ought not to permit themselves simply to attribute his philosophy to his illness.

### THE RELATIVISM OF PROUST

Any consideration of Proust's philosophy, however brief, would be incomplete without some remarks on what may be called his relative relativism. Even before his death, this aspect of his work had evoked the name of Einstein [77] from

[77] I think that it was Vettard who first made the comparison with Einstein. This line of criticism reaches its climax in Edmund Wilson who says in *Axel's Castle:* "He has recreated the world of the novel from the point of view of

some of his critics, and Proust himself seems to have been pleased by the comparison. It is true that Proust stresses the existence of both subject and object in relation to any perception, and makes the reader particularly aware of the importance of the position of the former to account for the impression that is made by the latter. Experience, rather than any intellectual theory, tells us how difficult it is for an eternally mobile, restless mind with imperfect senses at its command to form any accurate idea of things in the external world. Proust asks that we be true to our experience rather than to any prefabricated theories. In that sense he could not help being a relativist, and it was not necessary for him to wait for Einstein, because the philosophical essence of relativism is stated with perfect clarity by Schopenhauer, whose language he was better qualified to understand. Proust delights in showing how possible it is for anyone, even with the best will in the world, to be mistaken about things. That is the basis of his theory of metaphor and of his theory of love. Love, as we shall see in the chapter on his psychology, is to Proust mainly a subjective projection rather than a response elicited by an external object. And metaphor originates in the partial knowledge which we suffer from in our first impressions, and the consequent distortions which our eyes make in reality. In a passage describing a visit of the narrator to the room of his friend Saint-Loup in the barracks at Doncières, Proust in a comparatively short space summarizes his belief in the relativity of all our feelings and impressions, and the inseparable dependence of the objective world upon a percipient subject:

---

relativity: he has supplied for the first time in literature an equivalent on the full scale for the new theory of modern physics." Lindner, *Marcel Proust—Reviews and Estimates*, p. 146.

I was shewn Saint-Loup's room. I stood for a moment outside its closed door, for I could hear some one stirring; he moved something, let fall something else; I felt that the room was not empty, that there must be somebody there. But it was only a freshly lighted fire beginning to burn. It could not keep quiet, it kept shifting its faggots about, and very clumsily. I entered the room. . . . I heard the tick of Saint-Loup's watch, which could not be far away. This tick changed its place every moment, for I could not see the watch; it seemed to come from behind, from in front of me, from my right, from my left, sometimes to die away as though at a great distance. Suddenly I caught sight of the watch on the table. Then I heard the tick in a fixed place from which it did not move again. That is to say, I thought I heard it at this place; I did not hear it there; I saw it there. . . . We may ask ourselves whether, in the case of love, we ought not to act like those who, when a noise disturbs them, instead of praying that it may cease, stop their ears; and with them for our pattern, bring our attention, our defensive strength to bear on ourselves, give ourselves as an objective to capture not the other person with whom we are in love but our capacity for suffering at the other person's hands. . . . We have only to thicken the wads which close the aural passages, and they confine to a pianissimo the girl who has just been playing a boisterous tune overhead. . . . Take away for a moment from the sick man the cotton-wool that has been stopping his ears and in a flash the full daylight, the sun of sound dawns afresh, dazzles him, is born again in his universe. . . . When we increase or reduce the wads of cotton, it is as though we were pressing alternately one and the other of the two pedals with which we have extended the resonant compass of the outer world.[78]

A great many of the detailed actions of the rest of the book are simply variations of the themes of relativity sounded in this passage. A good illustration of Proustian relativity is contained in his analysis of the nature of drunkenness [79] as a state where alterations in subjective feelings are possible while the objective world remains what

[78] *The Guermantes Way,* Part 1, pp. 93 ff. [79] *Ibid.,* Part 2, p. 161.

it was and the confusion that results from this. Or take, for example, the theme of relativity as it is illustrated by a passage like the following:

> When M. de Guermantes, to explain how he was related to Mme. d'Arpajon, was obliged, going so far and so simply, to climb the chain formed by the joined hands of three or five ancestresses back to Marie-Louise or Colbert, it was still the same thing in each case; a great historical event appeared only in passing, masked, unnatural, reduced, in the name of a property, in the Christian names of a woman, so selected because she was the grand-daughter of Louis-Philippe and Marie-Amélie, considered no longer as the King and Queen of the French, but merely in the extent to which in their capacity as grand-parents they bequeathed a heritage. (We see for other reasons in a gazetteer of the works of Balzac, where the most illustrious personages figure only according to their connection with the *Comédie Humaine*, Napoleon occupy a space considerably less than that allotted to Rastignac, and occupy that space solely because he once spoke to the young ladies of Cinq-Cygne.) [80]

Every reader of Proust must notice that things, people, names, and places are forever changing their aspects in correspondence with the changing position of the individual point of view. But this undeniable quality is apt to mislead some readers, whose notions of the meaning of relativity are as wrong in the field of physical science as they are mistaken about Proust. For such readers, relativity may appear to be another name for complete Pyrrhonism, whereas nothing could be further removed from it. An extreme skepticism like Pilate's may imply the nonexistence of truth or the impossibility of finding it. Proust, on the other hand, believes that there are truthful explanations of things, but shows the immense labor and difficulty involved in finding them. Just as in physical science, the recognition of the im-

[80] *Ibid.*, p. 313.

portant role which relativity plays in our awareness is the first step to our escape from drowning in an eternal flux of things and to the achievement of a more secure standpoint of knowledge, so, for Proust, relativity is only a means to an end, which is the discovery of truth. Proust, in other words, is no Montaigne, as Gide once implied, and his endless qualifications and hesitations in the explanations he offers are only the sign of his seriousness about the possibility of going beyond the merely relative.

Some critics have seen in Proust's assertion of the relativity of our perceptions a denial of the whole concept of causality—which would certainly make a complete skeptic of him. Dandieu says: "Proust destroys the entire objective notion of causality. He takes a mischievous pleasure in showing how many plausible explanations can be offered for the same event." [81] This critic forgets one vital thing. Aside from the fact that there seems to me something more tortured than mischievous in Proust's eternal quest for truth and the description of his confused wanderings (a tortured quality which, for me at any rate, links his name more closely with Pascal, whose faith he never succeeded in achieving, than with Montaigne), Proust is not satisfied with finding merely *plausible* explanations—of which, it is true, he recognizes that an endless number might exist—but goes on to the discovery of the *one* explanation which is correct. This is exemplified most strikingly perhaps in some of the minor actions of the book. For example, the narrator's grandmother is ill. She thinks that it is a physical ailment and wants to rest. But a certain celebrated Dr. du Boulbon is called into the case unfortunately, and since he is a specialist in psy-

[81] Arnaud Dandieu, *Marcel Proust; sa révélation psychologique* (Paris, 1936), p. 22.

chiatry with such quaint notions as that neurotics are "the salt of the earth," he ascribes her symptoms to a disturbance of the mind and orders her to go out for exercise and fresh air. She follows his advice unhappily, goes out with her grandson to the Champs Elysées, and promptly suffers a stroke which soon carries her off to the veritable Elysian fields. Or let us take the case of the Russian Grand Duke who gets an eye infection and goes to the celebrated specialist Cottard, who, for a very substantial fee, puts down the inflammation as a toxic condition and prescribes a course of treatment which leaves the nobleman worse instead of better. Whereupon the sufferer goes to the obscure general practitioner at Balbec who simply removes a piece of dust from his eye, which makes the infection subside at once.[82] Proust is generally ironic on the subject of medicine, but the precise point of the irony here certainly goes beyond the field of medicine. For obviously, though there are many analysts of illness, as there are of events in general, only one among them is right, because only one can be in perfect accord with the facts. Proust, in other words, does not lose himself, in spite of his critics, in a wholly fuzzy subjectivism. The hope of man in general, not only of the doctors among them, is in finding the elusive explanation which will clear up the disturbing symptoms. It is true that in certain psychological states like love the difficulty of finding the truth is much greater than in purely physical illnesses, but Proust is not content to let the truth slip away from him in a variety of plausible conjectures. Thus, he pursues the facts about his dead sweetheart Albertine with almost fanatical and heartbreaking patience and at last pins down the decisive evidence of her depravity.

[82] *Cities of the Plain,* Part 1, p. 275.

An error in the interpretation of Proust's relativism similar to that made by Dandieu was made by the German critic of *Remembrance of Things Past*, the celebrated and gifted Ernst Curtius. For Curtius, Proust's relativism amounts to saying not, as Dandieu and others would have it, that *no* point of view is the true one but rather that *all points of view are true!* [83] Both these formulations, I think, are erroneous, and at bottom, furthermore, they seem to me to amount to the same thing.

Fortunately, we can call Proust himself to witness in the controversy of interpretation. He foresaw that his recognition of the importance of awareness of the relativity of our judgment might become distorted, as it actually has been, into a dreadful universal skepticism, which is not his and which he explicitly warns against. The warning occurs in the last volume of his novel, where he is discussing the First World War, and notes the intrusion of an emotional subjective bias into the various points of view of it, including his own. Those who were pro-German, for example, were led by their prejudice to stop listening as soon as their opponents mentioned facts which were embarrassing for them to own, such as the German atrocities against the civilians of Belgium. "And yet," says Proust, "they [the atrocities] were real. The subjective element I had noticed in hate, as in sight itself, did not prevent the object from having real qualities and defects and did not by any means cause the reality to vanish away into pure 'relativism.' " [84]

He evidently wished to separate himself from the vulgar, easy, and lazy interpretation of relativity, which had little in common with his own strenuous, tortured search for truth. If Proust ultimately turns aside from the world and its

[83] Ernst Curtius, *Proust*, p. 135. [84] *The Past Recaptured*, p. 245.

ready-made solutions, it is not with supercilious contempt for the world but because the world is not enough for him. There is nothing relative to the narrator about the guilt or innocence of Dreyfus any more than there is anything relative about the goodness of his grandmother. These truths are real and self-evident to him, and they have what might be called an axiomatic value for him. The strength of his conviction about a few facts in this world, though, as we have seen, it was not enough to lift him up to the acceptance of personal immortality, did nevertheless draw him out of the morass of complete skepticism. Like the physicist, the purpose of Proust's recognition of the existence of relativity was to accept its inevitable distortions and to reach a more secure ground of judgment.

It was the Ruskinian moralist in Proust, for example, who wrote the following words to Anatole France at the time of the Dreyfus Case:

> No one has shown higher courage than you who have so nobly hymned that virtue. . . . Indeed, you have stepped down into the arena of public life in a way not hitherto seen in this century, not as Chateaubriand, not as Barrès, for the purpose of winning yourself a name, but determined to make the great name that is already yours weigh in the scales of justice. Not that I needed any such excuse to admire you as a just, good, and honest man. I have loved you, and have, therefore, known your qualities.[85]

And it was no skeptic who wrote this sentence in another letter to France: "The greatest men are always the best men."[86]

It is true that though Proust is not a self-satisfied skeptic, neither does he have much respect for a type of dogmatism, which he finds in many scientists, who pride themselves upon

[85] André Maurois, *Proust: Portrait of a Genius* (New York, 1950), p. 86.
[86] *Ibid.*, p. 125.

lack of dogma, no less than in some of the philosophers whom they despise. I could cite his satiric vignette of the great medical "specialist x——" who believes that all human ailments, "whether headache or colic, heart disease or diabetes," are really disturbances of *the nose* which have been wrongly diagnosed. Just as du Boulbon, whom we have spoken of earlier, had traced all maladies to the psyche, so this other doctor lights on the human nose. Such scientists with their pet theories, their hobby horses which spring from a mixture of excessive pride and excessive specialization, cannot be swerved from the single track which they have chosen for themselves. In this sense, they resemble those politicians who have monomaniacal cures for the ills of the world, and these politicians in turn are like clocks that have stopped—at only one moment of the day and night do they show the correct time, and if by accident we happen to look at them at that moment we are under the illusion that they are really running, not standing still, but if we continue to observe them, we are soon corrected of our error. A clock that has stopped is right only once, and a man with a hobby horse may be right once, too, but neither is very useful. A timepiece that is five minutes slow or fast is never actually right any of the time, yet it always points to the truth.

Proust rejects a rigid dogmatism (like that of the "specialist x——") because he thinks that he sees in it the setting in of intellectual rigor mortis, just as he has already rejected a certain soggy form of popular relativism. Truth for him is precious and infinitely difficult to find, but once found and certified, it must be held on to almost desperately, and that is where he parts company with those for whom the truth is either nonexistent or else too easy of attainment. That is why I have spoken of the relative relativism of

Proust. I meant to indicate that his relativism has limits. When we have understood him to his deepest foundations, I would say, we realize that his vision included the relative as a way of discovering something beyond it. If it is argued that he did not, after all, discover very much beyond it, I still think that the seriousness of his search ought to be stressed.

# The Psychology of Proust

*Our critical estimation of Proust will depend largely on our estimation of the soundness or unsoundness of his psychology.*
PAUL ELMER MORE [1]

*In psychology no novelist has ever shown a more scientific interest than Proust.*
F. L. LUCAS [2]

*Proust is one of the great psychological instructors.*
PAUL ROSENFELD [3]

*Proust is beyond doubt the greatest literary psychologist we have yet encountered in fiction.*
F. C. GREEN [4]

PROUST is the discoverer of the hidden things in character, and the deepest influence which he can have upon his reader's understanding of other people is to convey an awareness of another dimension in them. Men in general are satisfied to deal with each other as if the apparitions of their surface lives were the real thing, because they are frightened of the psychological deeps. They suspected that monsters lurked there, I suppose, long before Freud ever confirmed

[1] Lindner, *Marcel Proust—Reviews and Estimates,* p. 163.
[2] *Ibid.,* p. 187. [3] *Ibid.,* p. 83. [4] *Ibid.,* p. 152.

their suspicions. But Proust is too honest a writer to anchor upon social superficiality, where, as the poet puts it, a smile "falls heavily among the bric-a-bric," and a man must grimace and gesture according to certain rules, "dance, dance like a dancing bear." Proust has a natural affinity for the profound in man's nature. He penetrates the guilty secrets of people with the device of a Roger Chillingworth but without his malice.

And we see with Proust into the hidden lives of all his characters. This curiosity is marked in the narrator even while he is still a child in Combray, where he describes himself reading in an enclosed shelter of the garden, from which he can see visitors while he is unseen by them. That scene is symbolic of his role throughout. Though he is always alert and responsive, most of his important discoveries come to him almost by accident, it seems, as, for example, when he stumbles suddenly (without her knowing that he is there) upon his old aunt Léonie, awakening from a dream of her dead husband and thanking God aloud that he is no longer around to interfere with the proper care of her health. His aunt would probably have gladly died under torture rather than admit under any ordinary circumstances the existence of such "unnatural" sentiments. But she is surprised at a moment when her social guard, still reacting to her dream, is somewhat down, and besides she thinks that she is alone. Her nephew sees truly and deeply into her in that unguarded moment, as he sees truly and deeply into the nature of the servant Françoise, when he walks into the kitchen unexpectedly one day and finds her (who had seemed so gentle to him before that) killing a chicken and brutally cursing the poor inoffensive creature for struggling and refusing to die quickly enough to suit her. So, too, he accidentally witnesses the degrading scene at Montjouvain between Mlle Vinteuil and her Lesbian friend—a scene that is so important in the structure of the whole book. The encounter between Charlus and Jupien, which the narrator accidentally comes upon in the courtyard of the Hotel de Guermantes at the beginning of the volume *Cities of the Plain,* is perhaps the most important of his discoveries and revelations. In one stroke, the homosexual hypothesis to explain the puzzling actions of the Baron—a hypothesis which the narrator had previously not even entertained—is conclusively confirmed. Similarly, the cruelty and viciousness of Morel, already long suspected, is demonstrated in his inhuman scolding of Jupien's niece, which the narrator overhears by chance in that same courtyard.

Proust delights in demonstrating to us how prepossessions concerning another person's character make it almost impossible for us to recognize the actual truth about him. Thus, the evidences of Legrandin's snobbery are exposed on so many occasions that it would seem impossible to miss them, and yet a conservative observer of human nature like the narrator's father distrusted the evidence of his senses the first few times and was driven only by prolonged repetition of the offense to admit that he may have been hasty in his good opinion of their pleasant neighbor. Proust has the following reflection on the conduct of Legrandin which seems to me so important in an accurate reading of all his characters.

> It was like every attitude or action which reveals a man's deep and hidden character; they bear no relation to what he has previously said, and we cannot confirm our suspicions by the culprit's evidence, for he will admit nothing; we are reduced to the evidence of our own senses, and we ask ourselves, in the face of this de-

tached and incoherent fragment of recollection, whether indeed our senses have not been the victims of a hallucination; with the result that such attitudes, and these alone are of importance in indicating character, are the most apt to leave us in perplexity.[5]

We must lie in wait for the truth, according to Proust, we must *surprise* it, and then we must have the strength to hold on to it, no matter how little it fits in with our previous knowledge and ordinary conceptions and no matter how much it contradicts our wishes. The world is full of dissimulators, a few of them willful, most of them unconscious, and nearly all of them desiring to live by pleasant illusions rather than to be undeceived by unpalatable truths.

Since people, according to Proust, often do not understand themselves very well, since they have an interest in concealing things about themselves even from those closest to them, since our knowledge of them is intermittent and fragmentary, since the very senses with which we perceive them are tired or fallible, since we subject the evidence we receive from the external world to more or less rigid molds of interpretation which, like the bed of Procrustes, do not completely fit and often do violence to those fleeting travelers which we call our impressions, it is natural that the amount of error in the world will always be very great and the little truth there inaccessible save to the most patient and persistent search. Proust believed that we can sometimes get at that elusive truth more effectively by what might be called peripheral means than we can directly. Not the advertisement of a personality, writ large for the world to see, is the important thing—we might call this the public relations of the private life—but the small, characteristic sign, by which a man did not even know that he was expressing himself,

[5] *Swann's Way*, p. 161.

which he paid little attention to, and which comes to us consequently in a pure state. This is what makes handwriting, facial expression, and quality of voice so significant psychologically for Proust.

Perhaps what first attracted my attention to this aspect of him was a daringly melodramatic use which he makes at a crucial point of his story of the handwriting of one of his characters. Proust has been called to account by critics for the melodrama of the scene, but none of them seems aware that there is something more than melodrama here. The episode occurs in the volume before the last, *The Sweet Cheat Gone*. The beloved Albertine had been killed in an accident—as the narrator was informed by her aunt, Mme Bontemps—and then the narrator, after describing his journey through the jealous hell of his posthumous search for the evidence of his sweetheart's treason, at last forgets her. He grows a new self which has never known Albertine, and her name now is that of a neutral stranger to him. It happens then, in Venice one day, that a telegram reaches him—from the dead, it seems, for it is signed with the name of Albertine, who seems to be alive after all and wishes to see her lover again. In a typical twist of Proustian irony, the narrator is so far alienated from the dead girl's memory that he decides to ignore her message. Some time later, when he is back in Paris, another former friend of his, Gilberte, meets him and says she wired him while he was in Venice but received no reply. In an instant, it is clear to him that the telegram he had read as coming from Albertine was really that of Gilberte. And then it occurs to him, too, how the mistake arose. He remembers how difficult he himself had always found it to decipher the affected handwriting of Gilberte, and since so many letters in the names of the two girls are the same, the telegraph operator must have mistaken the signature of Gilberte to read Albertine.

That, I shall grant, is a far-fetched story, but it is evident that it was no mere unhappy improvisation on the part of Proust. Many volumes before the description of that fantastic Venetian episode, Proust had carefully prepared the foundations for it. In telling of the first letter he had ever received from Gilberte, in his early youth when it meant so much to him, he had said: "So far as concerns this letter, at the foot of which Françoise declined to recognize Gilberte's name, because the elaborate capital 'G' leaning against the undotted 'i' looked more like an 'A,' while the final syllable was indefinitely prolonged by a waving flourish." The later magical metamorphosis of this signature to read Albertine could not have been more clearly foreshadowed.

Proust speaks of handwriting in other places in his book. There must have been a family resemblance between the handwriting of Gilberte and that of her mother Odette, for, in the course of the latter's long affair with Swann, the narrator describes a letter which Swann received from her. Swann "at once recognized that florid handwriting, in which an affectation of British stiffness imposed an apparent discipline upon its shapeless characters, significant perhaps to less intimate eyes than his of an untidiness of mind, a fragmentary education, a want of sincerity and decision." [6] The reader recognizes that this estimate of Odette's character is much more profound and accurate than anything Swann was able to arrive at for a very long time through his merely physical proximity to Odette. In fact, proximity, as Proust implies both in this passage and elsewhere, misleads us more often than it enlightens. A romance introduces so many sub-

[6] *Ibid.*, p. 287.

jective factors into our judgment, so many wish fulfillments, that our analysis under such conditions is much more significant of ourselves than it is of the object we are analyzing. It is really safer to trust to our untutored impressions of a person's face, voice, and handwriting as the clues to the inner nature of that person. For example, Odette's feeling for the strength which stylization gives to an original weakness is evident not only in her handwriting, but also in her freezing of her beauty later in a certain pattern, which helps, according to the narrator, to give her the appearance of youth even in extreme old age, after the faces of her youthful friends have all fallen apart.

I turn to another example of his handwriting analysis. The following is a passage concerning an invitation to dinner which the narrator receives one day from one of the minor characters of the story, old Mme de Cambremer:

> With that faint trace of ink, the handwriting revealed an individuality which in the future I should be able to recognize among a thousand, without any more need to have recourse to the hypothesis of special pens, than to suppose that rare and mysteriously blended colors are necessary to enable a painter to express his original vision. Indeed, a paralytic stricken with agraphia after a seizure, and compelled to look at the script as at a drawing without being able to read it, would have gathered that Mme. de Cambremer belonged to an old family in which the zealous cultivation of literature and the arts had supplied a margin to its aristocratic traditions. He would have guessed also the period in which the Marquise had learned simultaneously to write and to play Chopin's music.[7]

Perhaps Proust's interest in handwriting originally was aroused by the role which graphology played in the Dreyfus Case, which, we remember, hinged on the identification of

[7] *Cities of the Plain*, Part 2, p. 126.

the origin of the scripts of a number of key documents.[8] That such interest was pretty general in the intellectual circles in which Proust moved is evident from a letter of his to Mme Straus,[9] telling of a mutually abrasive encounter between Proust and his friend Montesquiou on the subject of character revelations in handwriting. In the same class with Proust's acute observations on material which less sensitive novelists (this includes very nearly all who have written, for sensitivity is Proust's great quality, as Léon Daudet recognized when he called his friend a man living without a skin) would pass over in complete silence are his remarks on less unfamiliar subjects of fiction, such as facial features. Eyes have often been treated in imaginative literature, either as indices of beauty or of character. But I am sure that there must be few observations to match the delicacy of the following sentence about Albertine: "Her eyes, even when fixed on an object, gave one the impression of motion, just as on days of high wind the air, although invisible, lets us perceive the speed with which it courses between us and the unchanging azure." [10] An intuitive figure of speech such as this one immediately lays bare the whole fugitive nature of Albertine, which many years of the narrator's life with her serve to confirm.

The quality of the writer Bergotte's voice draws the following comment: "There is nothing that so much alters the material qualities of the voice as the presence of thought behind what one is saying; the resonance of one's diphthongs, the energy of one's labials are profoundly affected —in fact, one's whole way of speaking." [11]

But emotional truths about a person as well as intellectual

[8] *Letters of Marcel Proust*, ed. by Curtiss, pp. 54–55. [9] *Ibid.*, p. 113.
[10] *Within a Budding Grove*, Part 2, p. 216. [11] *Ibid.*, Part 1, p. 173.

ones may be communicated through the voice, as is evident from the way in which the deeply outraged snobbish feelings of Legrandin suddenly manifest themselves, as surprisingly to himself as to his hearer, in

> a coarse and angry voice which I had never suspected him of possessing, a voice which bearing no traceable relation to what he ordinarily said did bear another more immediate and striking relation to something that he was feeling at the moment. What happens is that we are determined always to keep our feelings to ourselves, we have never given any thought to the manner in which we should express them. And suddenly there is within us a strange and obscene animal making its voice heard, the tones of which may inspire as much terror in the listener who receives the involuntary, elliptical, irresistible communication of our defect or vice as would the sudden avowal indirect and uncouthly profferred by a criminal who can no longer refrain from confessing a murder of which one had never imagined him to be guilty.[12]

The key phrase in this description is, of course, "involuntary, elliptical, irresistible communication." It is such messages that are the deepest and truest. We understand why it is that Proust says that he is interested not so much in the intellectual content of what people say as he is in the manner in which they say it. The matter of speech may be falsified, but the manner, properly interpreted, being largely unconscious and uncontrollable, must be true. So when he looks at handwriting, he is aware, as much of the way in which the letters are formed, as he is of the meaning of the words themselves. The writing lies before him on the page as if it were a picture, and from this picture he surmises the soul that has made it. It is possible for the voice of a person to tell a sensitive listener a very different story from the one in the words that are used. And the eyes may

[12] *The Guermantes Way,* Part 1, p. 277.

confess their secret long before the lips are unsealed. In at least one place, Proust joins these various psychological clues together, just as I have tried to do in my synthesis. That is when the narrator receives a letter from his friend Saint-Loup:

> I could tell at once when it was from him that a letter came, for it always had that second face which a person assumes when he is absent, in the features of which (the characters of his script) there is no reason why we should not suppose that we are tracing an individual soul just as much as in the line of a nose or the inflexions of a voice.[13]

If we may return for a moment to Gilberte, we remember another devastating analysis which he makes of her character on the basis of a slight change in her signature. One of the less amiable traits of Odette's daughter is revealed when her father Swann dies, and she takes the name of her mother's third husband, Forcheville, because its nobility (albeit of a minor kind) enables her to include the particle *de* in her name, and because it lacks the Semitic associations of the name Swann. But she cannot bring herself to the depth of entirely renouncing her real father, and so she compromises by subscribing herself G. S. de Forcheville, the innocuous initial "S" standing for Swann. At this point, Proust makes the brilliant observation that the real dishonesty of the signature lay not so much in the suppression of the name Swann as in the parallel suppression of the name Gilberte, for the latter omission implied that the former one was no more than a consequence of hurry and lack of time, while its real cause was to be found in Gilberte's snobbery and absence of feeling for the memory of her father.

[13] *Within a Budding Grove,* Part 2, pp. 234–35.

### HUMAN INSTABILITY

Perhaps the most basic insight of Proust into the nature of the human personality is how unstable it turns out to be when examined in the finest detail. The stability of people is mostly a fiction. What Proust has done for the personality is analogous to what the physicists have done to our tables and chairs. He has atomized it, showing that what had previously appeared to us as a continuous reality without interruptions is composed not only of contradictory particles but also of more space than solidity. He is to psychology what the pointillistes are to painting: he composes the large figures of his canvas with an infinity of tiny dots of the most varying shades. Or, to say the same thing through a figure suggested by one of Proust's own images, he photographs an action with a slow-motion camera which reveals numerous postures inside an action that had seemed to contain only two or three.

But just as the physicist atomizes our tables and chairs in theory and yet manages to return them to our senses in their familiar shapes, just as Seurat and his school combine their crowds of individual dots to compose the usual forms of the world which surrounds us, just as the slow-motion camera need only be speeded up a little to give us back the actions that had been so carefully analyzed, so Proust admits the gaps, contradictions, and instabilities of character while he manages to show that the series composes a curve which makes people predictable when viewed from a sufficient distance. It might perhaps be said by the skeptical that his discovery of the most infinitesimal subdivisions of time, due to the immense attentiveness of his self-analysis, has, then, merely an academic or, as some appreciators of Proust say, a technical interest. Even if this were true, his accomplishment would still be extraordinary, for he has provided literature with a most sensitive precision instrument for psychological analysis. Its importance, however, goes beyond this realm of science into that of art. The great changes in character which even in the best classical novelists like Dostoyevsky have to be accepted on the novelist's word alone and checked against our own intuitive realization of the limits of the credible are much more securely demonstrated by Proust's analytical method. It is the extraordinarily sudden upheavals, which make of the supposedly stable personality an ocean of uncertainty, that convincingly explain those large-scale, long-term changes of formation in the personality, visible even to the grossest eyes. It is when we are convinced by Proust of how close together the most contradictory feelings lie in the same personality, that we are better prepared to accept the fact that Swann, who a hundred pages earlier had cared nothing for her, now loves Odette to the point where he wishes that a protuberance on his body might be the sign of some fatal physical disease which would release him from his torment.

Proust epitomizes his theory of personality in the following remark about his character Albertine:

> It was incredible how spasmodic her life was, how fugitive her strongest desires. She would be mad about a person whom, three days later, she would refuse to see. She could not wait an hour while I sent out for canvas and colors, for she wished to start painting again. For two whole days she was impatient, almost shed the tears, quickly dried, of an infant that has just been weaned from its nurse. And this instability of her feelings with regard to people, things, occupations, arts, places, was in fact so universal that, if she did love money, which I do not believe, she cannot have loved it for longer than anything else.[14]

[14] *The Captive,* p. 556.

It must not be thought that this is a peculiarity of Albertine, who is a giddy little girl, more quickly changeable than other people. Proust makes generalizations which show that Albertine is only a particular example of a law which holds for everybody. Human instability extends from individuals themselves to the institutions which they build up.

We must bear in mind that the opinions we hold of one another, our relations with friends and kinsfolk are in no sense permanent, save in appearance, but are as eternally fluid as the sea itself. Whence all the rumors of divorce between couples who have always seemed so perfectly united and will soon afterwards speak of one another with affection, hence all the terrible things said by one friend of another from whom we supposed him to be inseparable and with whom we shall find him once more reconciled before we have had time to recover from our surprise; all the the ruptures of alliances, after so short a time, between nations.[15]

Contradictory mental states are so closely juxtaposed to each other in our ordinary experience that we cannot remember them with sufficient clarity, except with the most extraordinary effort.[16] Closely observed, Proust finds in normal people the germs of the schizoid, and their stability of nature "is purely fictitious and a convenience of speech." [17] A wonderful illustration of this is the description of the narrator's oscillation between love of Albertine and love of her friend Andrée.[18] Proust finds such instability characteristic of all the ages of man, but especially so of adolescence, and it is this which seems to him to constitute one of the principal charms of that period of development.[19]

What we possess in relation to other people is only a discontinuous *series of snapshots*,[20] with incalculable abysses

[15] *The Guermantes Way*, Part 1, p. 370. [16] *Swann's Way*, p. 236.
[17] *The Captive*, p. 78. [18] *Cities of the Plain*, Part 2, pp. 360 ff.
[19] *Within a Budding Grove*, Part 2, pp. 285–87. [20] *The Captive*, p. 196.

between the different attitudes, which present no problem of filling in so long as we are uninterested in a person but which become insoluble as soon as we are interested. It takes a phenomenon like jealousy to reveal what a trackless world of possibility we are continually liable to lose ourselves in. It is an uncontrollable complexity even to the most conscientious mind. To denote the overwhelming and hopeless task which proud men are always setting for themselves in managing an unmanageable task, the image of the sea returns over and over again in Proust's pages. "She had entered, in my life, upon that lamentable period in which a person disseminated over space and time is no longer a woman but a series of insoluble problems, a sea which we absurdly attempt, Xerxes-like, to scourge, in order to punish it for what it has engulfed." [21] The narrator had first seen Albertine outlined against the sea at Balbec, and she remains for him, throughout their relationship, like the sea.[22] But if the sea in its eternal, tormented restlessness and mobility is especially well suited to be the symbol of that wild girl's nature, its instability is at the same time emblematic of human nature in general.

What adds to the difficulties and embarrassments of the analyst of human behavior is his realization of the trifles which set off great chain reactions, perfect avalanches of feeling. The more obtuse or callous do not even realize the triviality of the reasons that have set them into motion, while the more attentive and observant do realize their own pettiness but are powerless to act otherwise. As he so often does with his most tragic comments upon human nature, Proust edges this with his sarcastic wit:

[21] *The Captive*, pp. 134 ff. [22] *Within a Budding Grove*, Part 2, p. 346.

As soon as she entered my room, she sprang upon my bed and sometimes would expatiate upon my type of intellect, would vow in a transport of sincerity that she would sooner die than leave me: this was on mornings when I had shaved before sending for her. She was one of those women who can never distinguish the cause of their sensations. The pleasure that they derive from a smooth cheek they explain to themselves by the moral qualities of a man who seems to offer them a possibility of future happiness, which is capable, however, of diminishing and becoming less necessary the longer he refrains from shaving.[23]

But the same thing happens to her lover, too, though he certainly does not lack self-consciousness. At one moment of his life, his jealousy, which constituted almost the whole of his existence then, is suddenly cooled by a trifle perhaps even smaller than the matter of shaving:

I think, however, that the chauffeur's explanations, which, by absolving Albertine, made her even more tedious than before, would not perhaps have been sufficient to calm me so quickly. Two little pimples which for some days past my mistress had upon her brow were perhaps even more effective in modifying the sentiments of my heart.[24]

### LOVE

It was through the relationship of sexual love that Proust achieved his most penetrating insights into the powers and limitations of the mind. To systematize these insights, however, is like trying to marshal a series of separate lightning strokes in order to achieve a steady illumination over the area which they are intended to reveal.

The primary step in Proust's line of reasoning is that love is a subjective phenomenon. For Proust, love is not created by something outside of a man but mainly by a certain need within himself, even if this need turns out to be only a curi-

[23] *The Captive*, pp. 14–15. [24] *Ibid.*, p. 175.

osity about the life which lovers lead, or, to recall La Rochefoucauld, a desire to imitate a literary pattern of love because of its high reputation. It is characteristic of the Proustian love affair that it usually takes place between a rich man (and an idle one, professionally speaking, because, as Balzac indicated, leisure is a necessity for allowing the feeling to unfold freely) and some poor opportunist. Besides more minor affairs, five major ones occupy the attention of Proust and his reader—the ones, that is to say, between Swann and Odette, between the narrator and Gilberte, between Saint-Loup and Rachel, between Charlus and Morel, and between the narrator and Albertine. Only one of these affairs (that between the narrator and Gilberte—and yet even here the woman is slightly lower in social esteem, because we see that the parents of the narrator will not speak to Gilberte's mother) involves those who are almost social equals. All the others are concerned either with men who keep women, or (in the case of Charlus and Morel) with a man who keeps another man. In every case, it is the woman (or the man playing the feminine role) who makes her lover suffer terribly, and in every case, the cause of this suffering is the same, jealousy. If we put these facts together, it seems probable that to Proust it must seem that suffering is precisely what a man seeks in love, what he pays for, and why he originally falls in love. It may be useful to examine the hypothesis that such jealous love is created by the need of self-punishment in a rich, spoiled child.

The theme of the subjective nature of love, the very foundation of its psychology, is already present—in disguised form it is true—in the first pages of the book, in which, describing his troubled sleep, the narrator tells us: "Sometimes, too, just as Eve was created from a rib of Adam, so a woman would come into existence while I was sleeping, conceived from some strain in the position of my limbs. Formed by the appetite that I was on the point of gratifying, she it was, I imagined, who offered me that gratification."[25] It might be said that Odette, Albertine, Gilberte, Rachel, and Morel are creations, in the sense that they are loved, of the minds of their lovers, just as the dream woman was the creation of the mind of the sleeper. They are all eventually proved as accidental and as subjective as she is.

Perhaps this oblique and veiled way of stating the theme is even more satisfactory to the imagination of the reader than the more explicit statements of it. Of the latter, there are numerous examples to choose from:

> I had guessed long ago in the Champs-Elysees, and had since established to my own satisfaction, that when we are in love with a woman we simply project into her a state of our own soul, that the important thing is, therefore, not the worth of the woman, but the depth of the state; and the emotions which a young girl of no kind of distinction arouses in us can enable us to bring to the surface of our consciousness some of the most intimate parts of our being.[26]

The same thought occurs in a discussion of Swann's surprising marriage to Odette:

> No doubt very few people understand the purely subjective nature of the phenomenon we call love, or how it creates, so to speak, a fresh, a third, a supplementary person, distinct from the person whom the world knows by the same name, a person most of whose constituent elements are derived from ourself, the lover. And so there are very few who can regard as natural the enormous proportions that a creature comes to assume in our eyes who is not the same as the creature that they see.[27]

[25] *Swann's Way*, p. 3. [26] *Within a Budding Grove*, Part 2, p. 184.
[27] *Ibid.*, Part 1, pp. 55–56.

Proust has an ambiguous attitude towards this power of transformation possessed by the mind. Admiration of the enchanter and contempt for its objects, and the progress in Proust, if there is any, is the same as the one we find in *Don Quixote,* from enchantment to disenchantment. That is why Proust's pages are so filled with unhappiness, for happiness, as Swift tells us, is "a perpetual possession of being well deceived," and none of Proust's people are so permanently possessed, for, sooner or later, like Cervantes' amiable Don, they awaken from their dreams to the accompaniment of shame and torment. Proust does take a certain pride in the lover's poetic ability, which might be compared to Rimbaud's voluntary derangement of his senses so that he should be able to see a romantic mosque in place of plain, prosaic brick buildings. This pride is present in his pointed comment on the disillusion so plainly printed on Saint-Loup's face when the narrator shows him the photograph of his mistress: "Let us leave pretty women to men devoid of imagination." [28]

It is the subjective nature of love, its growth in the soil of mind alone rather than in any external, material realities, that makes its bodily realization the least important of its phases. When Albertine leaves the narrator, it is not as a woman that he mourns for her. She would have been very innocuous to his peace of mind if he had been able to think of her physically, for he knows intellectually that she is not remarkable in that sense. She brings anguish with her because she is an image of frustration:

To carnal pleasure I did not even give a thought at this moment; I did not even see with my mind's eye the image of that Albertine, albeit she had been the cause of such an upheaval of my existence,

[28] *The Sweet Cheat Gone,* p. 31.

I did not perceive her body and if I wished to isolate the idea with which it was bound up with my suffering, it would have been alternately, on the one hand, my doubt as to the intention with which she had left me, with or without any thought of returning, and, on the other hand, the means of bringing her back.[29]

The idea that there is a necessary connection between love and physical beauty is a prejudice that is ingrained into us very early in our lives, and consequently to give up our notion of the inseparability of the two is often difficult and painful. In Proust, however, it is not good looks which beget love. Anxiety is the moving force:

Generally speaking, love has not for its object a human body, except when an emotion, the fear of losing it, the uncertainty of finding it again have been infused into it. This sort of anxiety has a great affinity for bodies. It adds to them a quality which surpasses beauty even; which is one of the reasons why we see men who are indifferent to the most beautiful women fall passionately in love with others who appear to us to be ugly. To these people, these fugitives, their own nature, our anxiety fastens wings. And even when they are in our company the look in their eyes seems to warn us that they are about to take flight.[30]

It is this hallucinatory quality of love, making us see things as no one else in the world would see them, that causes Proust to refer to love continually as a disease, a compulsion, a poison.[31] Whether a given person who has caught it ever recovers from it depends on his reserves of resistance, the strength of his mental constitution, and the seriousness of the original infection. There is no way of saying in advance whether it is going to be fatal or not. Once the recovery is complete, however, the sufferer himself (that is to say, literally, the *passionate* man) can see the world

[29] *Ibid.*, p. 21.
[30] *Ibid.*, pp. 117–18.
[31] *Within a Budding Grove*, Part 1, pp. 277–78.

once again in the same light as everybody else does, and then it is clear that it was something within himself which he called his love and not something outside. So after Swann expends his time, his fortune, and very nearly his life itself in his vain (and necessarily vain, for love cannot be compelled, and the effort to compel it only alienates it still further) pursuit of Odette, he, who had compared her with a masterpiece by Botticelli, who would have said in the manner of the elders of Troy when they beheld Helen, "All misfortunes are worth less than a single glance of her eyes," who had desired death as a relief from the intolerable pain of unrequited love, suddenly, luckily reaches the opposite shore of sanity and looks back in wonder at the Fata Morgana that had nearly proved his undoing. Then there follows the famous coda of the chapter called "Swann in Love," which recounts his reawakening to reality, accomplished ironically through the agency of a dream!

He saw once again as he had felt them close beside him Odette's pallid complexion, her too thin cheeks, her drawn features, her tired eyes, all the things which—in the course of those successive bursts of affection which had made of his enduring love for Odette a long oblivion of the first impression he had formed of her—he had ceased to observe after the first few days of intimacy . . . and he cried out in his heart: "To think that I have wasted years of my life, that I have longed for death, that the greatest love that I have ever known has been for a woman who did not please me, who was not in my style!" [32]

If we turn to the other half of the team of love, the part represented by Odette, Rachel, Gilberte, Albertine, and Morel, we find that they are the ones who only let themselves be loved. They are carriers of the disease but are not themselves infected by it. They see the world only too clearly and

[32] *Swann's Way*, p. 494.

too well to mistake their dreams for reality. They are hard-headed Sanchos, who look for their rewards in the governorship of some island promised them by their crazy masters, except that, being shrewder than Sancho was, they choose to follow men who already possess islands to give away instead of one who is only planning to conquer them. The connections which Proust traces between love and the opportunity to enter society, to acquire money, to advance one's career, and in general to gain material advantage, would appear to be extremely cynical, were it not for the fact that the circumstantial details which he supplies show very clearly that he knows what he is talking about.

To Proust, there seems no real possibility for the development of all the potentialities of love which shall illustrate his laws, where there is an absence of money, position, or other advantages. In the latter case, the affair is doomed even before its growth, for an adequate soil and means of nourishment are lacking for it. Where there is no leisure, their may be a simulacrum of romantic love, there must be simple sex, but not love in the involved, fully developed Proustian sense. Love is a luxury, and sex only a necessity; consequently, while everyone can enjoy the latter, few can afford the former. Quite seriously, Proust quotes the aphorism of La Bruyère: "It is a mistake to fall in love without an ample fortune." [33] That is a mistake which Proust's characters never make. But Proust amended the ironic observation of La Bruyère with still more irony: "It is a mistake," he seems to say, "to fall in love at all—unless one seeks there the suffering which may startle our lazy, comfort-seeking minds into undertaking the creative task which we have evaded for so long and which most people seem to be

[33] *Within a Budding Grove,* Part 1, p. 281.

happier in never finding at all." Love to Proust is a self-sought laceration for one side, for the rich or the noble, and it is a golden opportunity for the other side, for the ambitious beggar. For the latter, love is quite often the key which provides an entry into a new and delightful world. "A young king or a crown prince may travel in foreign countries and make the most gratifying conquests, and yet lack entirely that regular and classic profile which would be indispensable, I dare say, in an outside broker."

All the lovers in Proust are conscious of the advantage which is gained for them by their titles or wealth. And they are continually uneasy about the sufficiency or continuation of these advantages. So we find Saint-Loup, for example, looking forward without much delicacy to the prospect of a rich though loveless marriage in order that he might be able to afford keeping his mistress, Rachel.[34] For though he drugs his pain occasionally with the optimistic self-assurance that it is himself and not his money that she loves, really he is at bottom quite aware that his little friend suffers him "only on account of his money, and that on the day when she had nothing more to expect from him, she would make haste to leave him." Nor does the narrator feel any more confident about his own relations with Albertine. "Pecuniary interest alone could attach a woman to me," he confesses.[35] Swann, too, had been aware of the degrading reality that underlay his romantic dreams, and once, in a conversation with the narrator, he makes the following generalization: "Nervous men ought always to love, as the lower orders say, 'beneath' them, so that their women have a material inducement to do what they tell them." [36]

[34] *The Guermantes Way,* Part 1, p. 269.
[35] *Cities of the Plain,* Part 2, p. 374.
[36] *Within a Budding Grove,* Part 1, pp. 192–93.

It is to be noted, however, that Proustian love is never inspired by outright prostitutes. Even when the woman has sold herself in the past for a definite sum (as is the case with Rachel), that fact is not known to her great lover, though it may be known to all his friends. Saint-Loup never finds out the truth about Rachel, nor does Swann about Odette (until it is too late for them to be interested in it), because, as Proust so excellently shows (and it is one of his best observations), around every lover there is woven necessarily a conspiracy of silence, either by the consideration of other people towards him or their cruelty. If it is obvious to the reader that Swann, Saint-Loup, and the rest are also purchasers of the favors they receive, they have nevertheless been convinced by a very artful process that they are quite exceptional, and that their virtuous mistresses have been seduced and corrupted by them. If it sounds funny to put it in this way, that is because it is actually funny, though the dupe is not expected to appreciate the joke. Proust theorizes more than once on the fact that known prostitutes do not inspire love,[37] and he thinks that that is because there must always be "a risk of impossibility" standing between ourselves and our object in order to lend its possession savor. Therefore, says Proust, difficult women alone are interesting,[38] and love is always born of uncertainty.[39] But, on the other hand, completely virtuous women are without power to inspire love either. When the narrator is repulsed by Albertine at Balbec and draws the erroneous conclusion that she is impossible to seduce, his interest in her vanishes with startling suddenness. It is those women who are doubtful in their morals, very difficult perhaps but not impossible to

[37] *The Captive*, p. 186. [38] *The Guermantes Way*, Part 1, p. 73.
[39] *Within a Budding Grove*, Part 2, pp. 132–33.

corrupt, who are capable, in the presence of other favoring circumstances, of exercising a fatal attraction upon men. Women who seem to be wavering in their allegiance to virtue, without being yet committed to vice. Women who *this time only* seem capable of succumbing to the lure of money or position, who have never yielded to their weakness before.

The connections beween love and guilt are both subtle and manifold. Essentially, it is a nameless guilt of which the sufferings caused by jealousy are the expiation. For example, Swann's grief over his love and his need continually to speak of it to anybody who will listen is compared by Proust to the murderer's need to confess.[40] This "figure of speech" is far from accidental, as I hope to make clear by other examples soon. It is not *we* who seek love, but the albatrosses that hang round our necks. The proof of the morality of Proust's vision of the world, if any were needed, is that pain seems to him a retribution—ultimately, it may be as his language suggests, of original sin. The merit of love is that when its torture has reached the most excruciating point, it may lead us to a re-examination of our festering conscience. A man unfortunate enough to fall into the hands of a woman like Odette must ask himself at some time—what did he do to deserve this? The answer that Proust himself gives to the question is "Enough!" In that tremendous scene at the end of *Cities of the Plain,* in which Albertine finally confirms her grip upon the heart of the narrator, by the silly accident of her false claim to an intimate friendship with the perverse daughter of Vinteuil (a perversion of which the narrator is aware but Albertine is not), he reveals under the shock of being struck into the nethermost despair the burden of guilt which he had carried

[40] *Swann's Way,* pp. 442–43.

concealed from himself for so long. His jealousy then appears to him

> as a punishment, as a retribution (who can tell?) for my having allowed my grandmother to die, perhaps, rising up suddenly from the black night in which it seemed forever buried, and striking, like an Avenger, in order to inaugurate for me a novel, terrible, and merited existence, perhaps also to make dazzlingly clear to my eyes the fatal consequences which evil actions indefinitely engender, not only for those who have committed them, but for those who have done no more, have thought that they were doing no more than look on at a curious and entertaining spectacle, like myself, alas, on that afternoon long ago at Montjouvain, concealed behind a bush where (as when I complacently listened to an account of Swann's love affair), I had perilously allowed to expand within myself the fatal road, destined to cause me suffering, of knowledge.[41]

So here, many volumes later, we have the logical conclusion of that Biblical image in the opening pages in which a woman was created by the strain in a sleeper's limbs "just as Eve was created from a rib of Adam." Woman, the cause of man's transgression, is also the instrument with which he is punished. Love seems to Proust another name for fate.[42] There is "no peace of mind in love" but instead "a permanent strain of suffering." [43] What the narrator means by his phrase about causing the death of his grandmother, the reader can only guess at. The death of the grandmother, as it had been described in the book, was not only the inevitable result of a physical disease, but she had been surrounded with all the marks of consideration and respect of her family, and especially of the narrator. Nevertheless, he keeps torturing himself with scruples that he had not cared

[41] *Cities of the Plain,* Part 2, p. 362.
[42] *Within a Budding Grove,* Part 1, pp. 102–3. [43] *Ibid.*, pp. 219 ff.

enough for her, that he had caused her much needless anguish. This feeling becomes symbolic of all the dread and nameless guilt which he feels, and faced with the gravest crisis of his spiritual life, it arises from his memory at once to taunt him. Long ago, he had suffered conscience pangs because of what he considered his inadequate grief for his grandmother.[44] His sufferings at the hands of Albertine merely crystallized these feelings which were already present in him.

But the narrator does not feel himself absolved of his old guilt by his new suffering. On the contrary, he feels like a criminal who goes on compounding his crimes. Each instrument of his castigation, after it has served its purpose, becomes the source of fresh blame of himself. Thus, after Albertine runs away from him and is killed in an accident before she can return, he does not think of the pain she had caused him, but, as in the case of the grandmother, whom he had better reason to love, of his own failures of sympathy with his tormentor. This is delicacy carried almost to the point of self-destruction. "In these moments, thinking at once of my grandmother's death and of Albertine, it seemed to me that my life was stained with a double murder from which only the cowardice of the world could absolve me." [45] The same thought occurs in other forms: "It seemed to me that, by my entirely selfish affection, I had allowed Albertine to die just as I had murdered my grandmother." [46] His guilt seems both active and passive. Either he *lets* a person die or he actually *commits murder.*

*We instinctively love what will make us suffer.* "We are wrong in speaking of a bad choice in love," says Proust,

[44] *Cities of the Plain,* Part 1, pp. 234–35.
[45] *The Sweet Cheat Gone,* p. 111. [46] *Ibid.,* p. 118.

"since whenever there is a choice it can only be bad." [47] And in another place: "It is human to seek out what hurts us." [48] The inseparableness of love and suffering had been one of Proust's earliest ideas, and had occurred in his earliest stories in *Les Plaisirs et les jours,* where he had said of one of his characters: "She did not yet know love. But it was not long before love made her suffer, which is the only way one ever comes to know it." [49]

And when we consider all the *good* that accrues to us through our suffering, says Proust, we conclude by being grateful for it, and seeing that we have chosen right after all. "A woman is of greater service to our life if she is in it, instead of being an element of happiness, an instrument of sorrow, and there is not a woman in the world the possession of whom is as precious as that of the truths she reveals to us by making us suffer." [50] And later on in the same volume: "Desire, going always in the direction of what is most opposite to ourself, forces us to love what will make us suffer." [51]

Suffering is so valuable to Proust because without it, he thinks, we must always remain strangers to ourselves.[52] Without suffering we are "ignorant of ourselves." [53] "How much further," says Proust, "does anguish penetrate in psychology than psychology itself!" [54] By the second term, he makes it clear that he means cold, intellectual analysis. But the innermost nature of life for Proust as for Schopenhauer is something much more akin to feeling than it is to reason—consequently, thought can work best when it is

[47] *Ibid.,* p. 268. [48] *Cities of the Plain,* Part 1, p. 325.
[49] *Pleasures and Regrets,* trans. by Varèse, p. 91.
[50] *The Sweet Cheat Gone,* p. 111. [51] *Ibid.,* p. 267.
[52] *Cities of the Plain,* Part 2, p. 33. [53] *The Sweet Cheat Gone,* p. 1.
[54] *Ibid.*

roused by the keenest of all feelings which is pain. Schopenhauer says of death that it is the muse of all philosophy, and Proust makes of frustrated love the inspiration of all art. This earliest of Proust's ideas was also his latest. It had been expressed in *Les Plaisirs et les jours* in the following way:

> When life is happy the fate of our fellow-creatures does not appear in its true light, either masked by self-interest or transformed by desire. But in the detachment that in life comes to us with suffering, and from the sensation of sorrowful beauty on the stage, the fate of other men and even our own awakes our soul at last, the unheeded and eternal voice of duty and of truth. The sad works of a true artist speak to us in the tone of those who have suffered, making all men who have suffered cast aside everything else to listen.[55]

Suffering for Proust, in other words, is the begetter of sympathy, and without sympathy there can be no real understanding or communication among men, and therefore no art either.

Love attaches itself to cruel people because it fulfills the need of suffering in lovers. The lover in Proust has "an excess of good nature," the loved one "an excess of malice." [56] We have a very wide latitude of choice, for Proust thinks that people in general tend to be cruel and cowardly at the same time; one of his most striking aphorisms on human nature is that we all enjoy tormenting others but hesitate to put ourselves clearly in the wrong by going to the length of killing them outright.[57] Morel, Rachel, Gilberte, and Odette are exhibited in the most hideous postures of willful torture, sometimes of their lovers, sometimes of other innocents. The Rachel who arranges that her coterie

[55] *Pleasures and Regrets,* trans. by Varèse, p. 137.
[56] *Within a Budding Grove,* Part 1, p. 266.
[57] *The Past Recaptured,* p. 363.

shall hiss a rival actress off the stage [58] is the same Rachel who taunts Saint-Loup. Morel is seen in perhaps the greatest variety of such acts, possibly because homosexuality, being itself the quintessential perversity, attaches itself sometimes to creatures more obtuse morally than any that can be found among normal lovers. Morel's public rebuff of Charlus, after the concert which the latter has arranged to introduce him to smart society, is one of the most painful scenes in literature. He is brutal to the poor coachman of the Verdurins, whom he plots to have discharged because he wants the post for one of his own friends. As for Gilberte, she is cruel without provocation not only to Marcel but to her own father as well. And in this respect, she shows herself worthy of her mother Odette, the depths of whose inconceivable depravity are sounded by Swann when he suspects her of being capable of hiding a lover in her room in order to inflame his senses or to torture him by allowing him to witness her lovemaking with Swann. Albertine seems to the narrator the heaven-sent instrument of his castigation—he speaks of "the contrary, inflexible will of Albertine, upon which no pressure had had any effect." [59] These are ideal objects of love, because sensitive men "need to suffer." [60]

In one passage, which is about no character in the book in particular but rather deals in the abstract with those qualities of women which we find most attractive in them, Proust uses phrases which unmistakably show, by the isolation of certain traits of physiognomy and of posture, that it is those external signs which seem best to denote an inward coldness and cruelty that are the most compelling—I mean such expressions as "haughty calm," "indifferent," "insolent,"

[58] *The Guermantes Way*, Part 1, pp. 233 ff. [59] *The Captive*, p. 122.
[60] *Ibid.*, p. 275.

"the proud girl," "the beauty of stern eyes." [61] Perhaps an instance of the working of the same law, though not as between lovers, happens with Aunt Léonie and her servant Françoise, whom she inspires with such terror while she lives that everyone in the family thinks Léonie must be hated, but they discover when she dies that, instead of hate, she had inspired her maid with more love for her than anybody else in the world had.[62] Only people capable of making us suffer have the power to bring us the blessing of calmness, too.[63]

Proustian love is a passion to which the consent of the sufferer is necessary—at least at first; after that, it acts like the spring of a trap which has been released. If the femme fatale did not exist, according to Proust, the romantic would have to invent her, for she corresponds to his need to suffer, and necessity is the mother of invention. In the respect that consent is necessary at the beginning, love is like hypnosis, because no one can be hypnotized against his will, nor be made to do anything while in that state which runs counter to his basic character formation. So, no one who is not at least potentially a criminal to begin with can be made to commit a crime by suggestion. But though the consent of the patient is needed at first to induce the state (of love or of hypnosis) once the state is fully established and fixed, one may be influenced to do many painful things, and the process of awakening, unless managed very skillfully by a physician (but in love, the cause is not a physician, says Proust, but a disease), may be very difficult and disturbing. This matter of consent and foreknowledge of the passion of love before it can come is important to understanding Proust. It indicates that love is something which, in spite of

[61] *Ibid.*, pp. 186–87. [62] *Swann's Way*, p. 196. [63] *The Captive*, p. 89.

all its torments and anguish (more likely because of them), is sought as an expiation of some dread or guilt, which is even more serious to face—just as some types of mental illness can apparently be cured only by the artificial stimulation of such high fevers as are themselves eventually dangerous to life. We are forced, like Ulysses, to choose between evils, and, if we choose love, it must be because unconsciously we regard it as the lesser evil in comparison with some other, the very name of which we suppress from our own knowledge, though it may be sometimes unearthed by a skillful analyst. Charlus makes the brilliant observation that homosexuality is perhaps a disease which prevents a man from suffering an even more dangerous one.[64]

Swann had been cautious with his heart before he met Odette. He had stayed within easy sight of the shore, so he could get back when he wished. He had never given himself deeply to any of his female friends, or lost that mastery of himself, which, so long as it is retained, keeps him from being a lover in the Proustian sense—that is to say helplessly, compulsively, perhaps even convulsively. In general, Swann is a man whose awakenings to the fundamental realities about himself come very late—that was true not only of his great love for Odette but of his discovery of his Jewish identity under the impact of the Dreyfus Case. The motivations which make him *consent* to become involved with Odette as he had successfully avoided becoming involved with anyone before that are multiple—curiosity about the life which lovers lead of which he had read and heard and dreamt so much though he had lacked the courage to try it (in which caution he was well-advised, for it very nearly kills him when he does experience it), respect for the

[64] *The Guermantes Way*, Part 1, p. 399.

nobility of self-sacrifice in love, and finally his own lack of fulfillment as an artist which he may have associated with his lack of inspiration by love. In the middle stages of his affair with Odette, Swann took delight in exhibiting himself before all his friends in the traditional role of the lover, and he would imagine their comments upon him in that light:

To be frank, as often as not, when he had stayed late at a party, he would have preferred to return home at once, without going so far out of his way, and to postpone their meeting, until the morrow, but the very fact of his putting himself to such an inconvenience at an abnormal hour in order to visit her, while he guessed that his friends, as he left them, were saying to one another: "He is tied hand and foot, there must certainly be a woman somewhere who insists on his going to her at all hours," made him feel that he was leading the life of the class of men whose existence is colored by a love affair, and in whom the perpetual sacrifice which they are making of their comfort and of their practical interests has engendered a spiritual charm.[65]

The narrator, reflecting upon his own successive infatuations with Gilberte, with the Duchesse de Guermantes, and with Albertine, uses a phrase which illuminates the whole subjectively compelling necessity that is fulfilled by love: "our need of a great love." [66] That is to say, not a love lightly taken or trivial, but profound and exhausting. "Slight" love affairs in Proust's pages serve as relaxations between more serious ones.[67] The source of much tragedy in the world and almost all in the pages of Proust is that the nature of things makes it inevitable that there are very few beings who correspond to "our need of a great love" and only too many to take advantage of it. Proust makes it clear

[65] *Swann's Way*, p. 305. [66] *The Guermantes Way*, Part 2, p. 112.
[67] *The Past Recaptured*, p. 332.

in relation to the narrator, through the use which he makes of the Mme de Stermaria episode, that at a given moment of life, *a man is simply ready for his great love.* The object of his feelings is certainly secondary if not entirely accidental. He is *determined* to let himself fall into the deadly grip of love.

Love is the ultimate test of life in Proust. The analogy which he makes with war has been used before, but it is given new force by him. Like war, love is a test from which we do not always come back alive. Like war, it is a situation in which the control of our destiny is committed to the hands of another. And like war, too, it terrifies and thrills us simultaneously with a feeling of our insignificance and helplessness. There seems to be a carnal attraction to danger.[68] That all of the greatest love affairs of literature and history—Antony and Cleopatra, Paolo and Francesca, Heloise and Abelard, Tristan and Isolde, Romeo and Juliet, Launcelot and Guinevere, Hero and Leander, Dido and Aeneas—seem to have been in some manner illicit or surrounded by danger is not an accidental coincidence.

It is characteristic of Proust's lovers that they know *in advance* the path that their love is bound to follow *or think they do.* Thus, from the moment that he is irrevocably taken in the toils of Albertine, the narrator makes an analogy between his own situation and that of Swann which he had heard about.[69] Yet this intellectual knowledge is without visible effect upon his actions. The pattern which all the different affairs in Proust follow is their nonreciprocity: "I felt even then that in a love which is not reciprocated—I might as well say in love, for there are people for whom there is no such thing as reciprocated love." [70] We may add that

[68] *The Captive,* p. 101.
[69] *Cities of the Plain,* Part 2, p. 374.
[70] *Ibid.,* Part 1, p. 327.

the people for whom there is not reciprocated love are all the people in Proust, for, if there are any others, he either did not observe them or describe them, though his phrasing carefully leaves open the possibility that somewhere they may exist.[71]

The initial condition of love, then, is the expectant, perhaps even eager, condition of the organism that awaits it (if I use such scientific verbiage it is because Proust's clinical treatment of the subject suggests it). The immediate cause of love, in the presence of this weakened and assenting state, is, as I have said before, less than nothing in comparison with the vast turmoil that follows. The cause of love Proust compares to an "insignificant bacillus" which might nevertheless make the proudest of men die.[72] Charlus says very well that it is not whom or what one loves that is important, but the fact of loving.[73]

I have spoken of the cruelty of those who cause the most lasting passions in Proust—sometimes this is not an intentional cruelty, but rather the product of thoughtlessness, carelessness, or stupidity. The thoughtlessness of Odette is invaluable to her in bringing about Swann's most violent paroxysms of love.[74] "A person," writes Proust, "has no need of sincerity, nor even of skill in lying in order to be loved." [75] Swann clearly realizes Odette's lack of intelligence.[76] In fact, we might put Proust's thought in the following way, exaggerating his pessimism a little perhaps but not being basically unfair to him—the more moral worth a person has, the more sensitive he is, the more intelligent and considerate, the less are his chances of inspiring that

[71] Maurois, in his biography, *Proust: Portrait of a Genius*, supplies certain passages which Proust cut out of his book finally in which he had asserted that there never could be such a thing as reciprocated love.

[72] *Swann's Way*, p. 444. [73] *Within a Budding Grove*, Part 2, p. 85.

[74] *Swann's Way*, p. 383. [75] *The Captive*, p. 142.

[76] *Swann's Way*, p. 312.

great love which we need as an expiation. The more worthless the object of love the better, for in that case we are bound to suffer more, and that is what we are really seeking, without clearly knowing it at the beginning, or admitting it to ourselves perhaps. A sensitive, moral, intelligent person would hesitate, after all, to drive us into such a tormenting situation to begin with, and, once he realized what was happening, he would do his best to alleviate the pain he had unintentionally caused. A good, strong, and wise person is therefore constitutionally unfitted to do the work which is left for the *insignificant bacilli,* Odette, Rachel, Gilberte, Albertine, and Morel.

Jealousy is the inseparable shadow of love,[77] and just as a man or any material body which cast no shadow would be impalpable or unreal, so Proust would doubt the existence of any love which did not find any counterpart in jealousy. To Proust, there seems to be an absolute necessity for jealousy in the pattern of love.[78] And it seems very often that we are jealous not because we are in love, but that we are in love in order to be jealous:

> My bitterest grief would not have been to be thrown over by whichever of the girls I liked best, but I should at once have liked best, because I should have fastened on to her the whole of my melancholy dream which had been floating vaguely among them all, her who had thrown me over.[79]

The women in Proust who are the most successful in arousing love are those who recognize instinctively its connection with the personal insecurity and anxiety of the lover. Albertine knows how to exploit the narrator's jealousy, just as Odette had exploited Swann's—in their own persons, these

[77] *Ibid.*, p. 357. [78] *Cities of the Plain,* Part 2, pp. 378 ff.
[79] *Within a Budding Grove,* Part 2, p. 341.

women bore their lovers; what gives them power is the desire which they arouse in others.[80] Women enchain us in direct proportion to the suffering they cause.[81] The initial shock of anxiety is sudden and knocks down a lover who had not thought himself so weak till then. Thus Swann, who had not even kissed her till then, has only to miss Odette from her accustomed place at the Verdurins in order to be rendered frantic and to "ransack" the streets of Paris through the night till he finds her. It is at this point that Proust writes one of his most suggestive comments on the mystery of the origin of love:

> Among all the methods by which love is brought into being, among all the agents which disseminate that blessed bane, there are few so efficacious as the great gust of agitation which, now and then, sweeps over the human spirit. For then the creature in whose company we are seeking amusement at the moment, her lot is cast, her fate and ours decided, that is the creature whom we shall henceforward love. It is not necessary that she should have pleased us up till then, any more, or even as much as others. All that is necessary is that our taste for her should become exclusive. And that condition is fulfilled as soon as—in the moment when she has failed to meet us—for the pleasure which we were on the point of enjoying in her charming company is abruptly substituted an anxious, torturing desire, which the laws of civilized society make it impossible to satisfy and difficult to assuage—the insensate, agonizing desire to possess her.[82]

If the power of women over men, as Proust illustrates the truth in a hundred variations (so that his demonstration assumes gradually the rigor of mathematics), grows with each pang of suffering they cause and in proportion to the strength of each pang, that is because, like Baudelaire and Poe, Proust believes that in human nature there is some

[80] *Swann's Way*, p. 351. [81] *Within a Budding Grove*, Part 1, pp. 281 ff.
[82] *Swann's Way*, p. 299.

"demon of perversity." [83] It is this demon of perversity which explains why the most senseless and harmful habits of human life are also the hardest to rid ourselves of.[84] The human condition, for Proust, is both very sad and very futile. The least unkind thing that he has to say for love is that it is "a sedative." It feeds the silliest element of human nature, our vanity, and it results in at least the temporary appeasement and satisfaction of our insatiable egos, by giving to us an illusory, imaginative triumph "over countless rivals." [85]

We can see how this whole psychological structure of love is based upon his conception of the human personality as I outlined it at the beginning—its general instability and changeableness, its shifts of mood and key. Whoever relies on human beings composed of such fragmentary elements steps upon a spiritual quicksand. Since the relationship of love implies the heaviest reliance upon the personality of another, it is liable to sink the deepest into the quagmire. The safest course for a human being sentenced to this world is to be alone. Proust rejects friendship and society along with love.

If, as Proust repeatedly says, we must remain in perpetual ignorance even of ourselves,[86] just as the kaleidoscope is ignorant of what its own pattern will be after the next shake, we are condemned to an even darker ignorance of the character and doings of our mysteriously moving neighbors in life. Love is so torturing, because the more we are interested in other people the less, it seems, we can find out about them. It is when we no longer care that the truth about them, so carefully concealed from our eyes while we gazed so fixedly at them, suddenly appears. Thus it is only years after the

[83] *Cities of the Plain,* Part 1, p. 148.
[84] *The Captive,* pp. 84–85.
[85] *Ibid.*
[86] *The Sweet Cheat Gone,* p. 1.

end of his affair with Gilberte that her double life at the time when Marcel loved her becomes known to him.[87] But when he would have given his life for the knowledge of her infidelity it was denied him. It is not to Swann that his friend Charlus reveals that he had introduced Odette to him in order to get rid of her.[88] And it is after Marcel is hopelessly enmeshed with her that Albertine tells him that the first and fatal step into the abyss for him (his thinking that she knew Mlle Vinteuil and was, therefore, a Lesbian) had been based on a lie.[89] Nor does thinking things through seem to help any, for there are an infinite number of hypotheses possible about the intentions of other people.[90] The sources of all events in life, like the sources of great rivers, says Proust, are sought in vain.[91] We can trace them step by step, but one more step is always possible after the last discovery we have made. It is an inflexible law of nature that, as one subdivision of our vast and total ignorance of life, we must also be ignorant of those we love best.

### PARALLELS WITH FREUD

The pattern of ideas which I have traced in the preceding section has certain resemblances to the system of Freud which I should like to indicate.[92] In the relationship of

[87] *The Captive*, pp. 175 ff. [88] *Ibid.*, p. 405. [89] *Ibid.*, pp. 461–62.
[90] *Ibid.*, pp. 493 ff. [91] *The Sweet Cheat Gone*, p. 12.
[92] F. L. Lucas suggests (*Lindner, Marcel Proust—Reviews and Estimates*, p. 191): "The answer to many of Proust's general problems is to be found not in Proust but in Freud." I am not sure of his exact meaning, but he seems to go too far in implying that Proust's awareness has to be supplemented with Freud's in order to derive the maximum meaning from his work. That concept of the relation of science to art seems to me radically false (I mean the idea that science can, in any sense, be the *key* to art). Rather, as I have tried to suggest through my own treatment, there are numerous analogies between the insights of Proust and those of Freud. Proust himself knows quite enough, as an artist, not to need the "help" of Freud. Perhaps that is why Proust abandoned his own psychotherapeutic cure soon after he embarked on it.

sexual love, Proust emphasizes the subjective element just as the psychoanalysts do—that is, that our passions arise from something within ourselves rather than from the outside. Proust sees the guilt which is in the background of every love affair, and, like Freud, he sees the analogy between the pattern of an individual's love and the nature of his relationship with his parents. Over and over again, so that it cannot possibly be accidental, the narrator compares the kisses and caresses of Albertine with those he had received from his mother when he was a child.[93] Swann, too, unfortunately regains his confidence in the perfidious Odette when he thinks that a certain look on her face reminds him of the expression on his mother's face.[94] In fact, a whole chapter could be written on the Proustian topic—Mothers and Mistresses. In perverted lovers like Charlus and Mlle Vinteuil, Proust emphasizes the concern with insulting the parental image. The first approach of Charlus to the narrator is with the suggestion that he dislikes his grandmother, and later the Baron rouses Marcel's suspicions of his sanity by desiring to see Bloch thrashing his old mother. Proust once promised his readers a section on what he calls "The Profanation of the Mother," [95] but this was one of the things unfortunately which he left unfinished in his work. Mlle Vinteuil's case is perhaps the most flagrant along this line, because she can derive no pleasure save when her Sapphic friend brutally spits upon the image of her dead father.

Other analogies between Proust's description of love and Freud's are contained in his tracing back its inception to a period of intense anxiety, and I think too in his seeing the

[93] *The Captive*, p. 2; *Swann's Way*, p. 238. [94] *Swann's Way*, p. 347.
[95] *Cities of the Plain*, Part 2, p. 75.

pains of love as an expiation of some kind, and the consequent tendency which lovers have for attaching themselves to cruel people.

But the most remarkable analogy between Freud and Proust, I think, is that which can be made between the form of the novel as a whole and a typical psychoanalytic case history. When we consider the opening section of the book (from the beginning to the cup of tea which summons up the image of Combray to the narrator) this becomes apparent. Let me recall the most important things from that section. It tells how the narrator as a boy was unable to go to sleep without a good-night kiss from his mother, how very delicate nervously he already was at that age, and how he was being subjected to a calculated disciplinary regime by his mother and grandmother who realized the importance of a principled training to strengthen his character and will. The father, who was insensitive to his son's nature, would often undo the good patiently brought about by this maternal training by treating him with a summary arbitrariness, sometimes indulging him with excessive leniency when he should have been curbed, sometimes treating him with rigor and excessive severity when he needed a more gentle approach. On the particular evening which is described at length in the beginning of the book, a neighbor, Swann, is the guest at dinner, and the father unthinkingly sends his son off to bed without the usual sedative good-night kiss from his mother. The child is unable to rest upstairs, devises all sorts of futile stratagems to make his mother come up from the party to his room, but fails until, in desperation, he leaves his room, waits for his parents on the stairway, and "throws himself upon" his mother for her blessing, whereupon his father, realizing for the first time apparently how unhappy his son has become, instructs his wife to spend the night in their son's room. This abdication by his mother was the beginning of the narrator's difficulties in life. The night which he calls "the sweetest and saddest night of my life" [96] marked the "decline of his will." In other words, his conditioning to so easy a victory on so important a matter by the mere exercise of his whim unfits him later on for meeting on its own terms a world which is bound to treat him more coldly than his parents have done. The mother, who apparently senses all this, is absolved from blame by the son, so that the whole onus of guilt in the ruin of his character is placed on the father. It could be said with complete justice, it seems to me, that this classic Oedipal situation acts as the traumatic experience, which illuminates everything that happens to him later. This opening panel of Proust's story, in other words, is precisely the sort of primary memory which the psychoanalyst tries so patiently to find, and which is so often sought in vain. It is not an easy memory to call up; it seems too full of shame. We see now, from the nature of this primary experience, the meaning of the numerous analogies between Albertine's kisses and his mother's. We see more clearly the reason for his necessary failure in the relationship of love. We understand why he is so often reduced by the refusals, resistances, and rejections of his mistresses to the point of childish tears, as he had been reduced on that fatal evening at Combray. But his mistresses are not as kind as his parents were. They cannot be moved by his distress to depart from their own inflexible and selfish purposes in life. Had his father not given up his conjugal prerogative to his wife's company on that night, the child might have been spared the cruelty of those

[96] *The Past Recaptured,* pp. 214–15.

later rebuffs by building early his preparations and defenses against the self-assertion and indifference of others. We see, too, the nature of the guilt which he felt he had to expiate through his own sufferings later. He had taken away his mother's love from his father, and had compounded the crime by feeling contempt for his father's callousness, insensitivity, and lack of principle. This is the basic source of all those anxieties which trussed him up so helplessly as a sacrificial lamb who has to endure the sensual fury of his pitiless mistresses.

It would not be too much to say that if Proust had intended to transmute the findings of Freud into an artistic pattern, he could hardly have done so more efficaciously than by the construction of the book in the form that we now have it. We know that Proust, after his mother's death, entered the sanatorium of Dr. Sollier, and, in a letter to Georges de Lauris,[97] he speaks of "my psychotherapeutic treatment." The exact nature of his treatment has not been disclosed by anyone to my knowledge—it constitutes a fascinating gap in his biography. We know, however, that whatever the nature of the treatment used in Dr. Sollier's sanatorium, Proust did not stay with him very long.

There is one signal difference, of course, between Proust and Freud. The scientist is hopeful, while the artist is not, though even this distinction is perhaps more true of the earlier Freud than of the later one. The later Freud discovered the death wish, while the younger one had concentrated on the pleasure principle, and the later Freud, too, reading Schopenhauer extensively for the first time, found the ideas expressed there very agreeable to his own way of thinking. It is interesting to note that the three principal

[97] *Letters of Marcel Proust,* ed. by Curtiss, p. 197.

thinkers, whose ideas I have analogized with Proust's, namely Wagner, Schopenhauer, and Freud, were mutually congenial to each other in an intellectual sense. The original pattern in which Proust unites their various insights into art, life, and the mind constitutes his own intellectual integrity. Freud, as a physician, was concerned with cures, but Proust, as a patient, despaired of them. Proust is always derogatory in his references to medicine and to doctors (his character Cottard is only the most flagrant example of his contempt for members of that profession). In this connection, we should remember that Proust's own father and brother were both physicians, though the father's profession is changed to that of diplomat in the pages of the book.

But Proust saw his own disease as only a particular variant upon the general curse of mankind. The final moral of Proust's psychology is not so different from the conclusion of Socrates—the greatest wisdom is to know that one knows nothing. Even with the utmost subtlety and patience which Proust continually exhibits, it is hopeless to come to any real understanding of other people or of ourselves. At best, reality appears to Proust with all the insoluble complications of a Gordian knot. It can be cut, but it can't be unraveled. The cutting of the knot can be brought about only by what Pavlov would have called "the reflex of purpose" in the human being—such a purpose as is represented in the highest degree by the construction, in spite of all of Proust's neurotic handicaps or perhaps because of them, of *Remembrance of Things Past.*

# The Sociology of Proust

*People foolishly imagine that the vast dimensions of social phenomena afford them an excellent opportunity to penetrate farther into the human soul; they ought, on the contrary, to realize that it is by plumbing the depths of a single personality that they might have a chance of understanding these phenomena.*[1]

PROUST as a social reporter seems to have attracted much attention; but he is obviously much more a poet than a reporter, and though he himself aspired to the title of social historian, his history belongs to art rather than to journalism. Therefore, almost all discussions of Proust as a social observer seem to miss the point for the same reason basically—his sociological critics see his work through Marxist eyes. To do that is to invite a double distortion, for to the natural imperfections of the critic's own understanding is added the obstruction of a specially colored pair of spectacles. If I have said in earlier chapters that Proust's philosophical ideas resemble those of Schopenhauer and probably stem from him, that his aesthetics owe much to Wagner, and his psychology has parallels with Freud's, I

[1] *The Guermantes Way,* Part 2, pp. 26–27.

was simply recording observations which suggested themselves to me after I had defined as sharply as I could Proust's own ideas. But sociological critics approach Proust, it seems to me, looking for confirmation of their own theories, and they occasionally seem to twist the facts to serve this purpose.

The first question that seems important to me about the social aspect of Proust's work is the one which Albert Thibaudet raised in his notice of Proust's life in the *Encyclopaedia Britannica.* Is it possible that a cast of characters so special in their lives and ambitions as Proust's can be of permanent interest to mankind? The answer seems to me to be that Proust makes the drama of the rise in society both of the narrator and of his other characters universally significant by endowing each successive tier above him with the luster of the unattainable, and then showing how the luster fades with the attainment. Thus he illustrates a philosophy of disillusion which each man, by substituting his own ambitions, whatever they may be, for those of Proust's characters, may share. The vital quality of literature is that the author's treatment of his subject may allow for such substitutions. His characters and situations can then be transformed into the lives of his readers. From a superficial point of view, what situations could be more circumscribed than those of Hamlet, or Othello, or Oedipus, or Agamemnon? What is important is that the dramatist permits the reader to identify the paralytically scrupulous side of his own personality with Hamlet's, the unscrupulously ambitious though perhaps suppressed side of himself with Macbeth, the fiercely sensitive lover in himself with Othello, the subconscious parricide and incestuous husband that fate might have made him with Oedipus, and so on.

Proust's work allows for imaginative translation far removed from the specific concerns of Swann, Charlus, the narrator, Legrandin, Bloch, the Duchesse de Guermantes and the other characters whom he has created. If the arithmetical common denominator of most of their social strivings is *snobism,* its more general algebraical character is that of the eternally striving human will to change the framework of a way of life into which we are born. Furthermore, even in its portrayal of the more specialized manifestation of this will, which Proust calls snobbery, we must not make the error of thinking his subject matter to be either parochial or unimportant. As we shall see later on, Proust believed that there is something in human nature which might well go under the name of *universal snobbery.*

Part of the broadening poetic effect in Proust is due to the wisdom of a choice which has not been sufficiently credited because it has hardly been noticed. Most of his critics with Marxist dispositions assume naturally that Proust is describing the real world, instead of *a world which is real only insofar as the imagination of man is real.* Scholars like Spagnioli [2] have pointed out that Proust's social world is a literary construct with at least as many resemblances to the novels of Balzac as to the actualities Proust observed around him, but even Spagnioli has not drawn the right inferences which follow from this assumption, it seems to me. It is of the greatest significance, I think, that the Faubourg Saint-Germain is the social cynosure in Proust's pages. For we must ask ourselves—what is the Faubourg Saint-Germain and what can it represent? If present-day constitutional monarchies like England's and the few like it that survive in Europe are mere shadows of a

[2] *The Social Attitude of Marcel Proust* (New York, 1936).

vanished reality of power, what must be said of aristocracies like those of Russia and France, which have had even their nominal titles taken away from them? Are they not *shadows of shadows?* It is hardly more than a generation now since the Russian aristocrats actively ruled their country, and yet see how pathetic their pretensions already seem! The soul of their sway—that is, their domain and authority in the eyes of their subjects—has gone out of them. What then of the Bourbon aristocracy of the Faubourg, which for more than a century has been deprived of its powers and prerogatives? If the Faubourg possesses any real power, it does so through the same means employed by the other classes of French society. In the pages of Proust, imaginary titles are always being traded for money. There must be a reality of the imagination, since even the hardest-headed and most unimaginative bourgeois is willing to recognize it and pay for it. Proust was very early aware of the intimate connection between snobbery and imagination, as is shown by this description of a character in *Les Plaisirs et les jours:* "Her snobbery was all imagination, and was moreover all the imagination she had." [3]

Proust's characters are dukes who do not lead anybody, princes who rule over nobody, barons who are robbed perhaps but are thoroughly inoffensive themselves. From Proust's point of view, it does not matter if social distinctions are real or imaginary—in a subjective sense, in fact, nothing is real unless it is imagined first of all. The last phase of the Faubourg Saint-Germain took place almost purely in the imagination of Proust and in the pages of his books. He naturally gravitated, not to the actual centers of social power in our time (which would have taken him, as it has taken Jules Romains, John Dos Passos, and other

[3] *Pleasures and Regrets*, trans. by Varèse, p. 51.

writers to the contemplation and portrayal of politics and trade unionism and the stock exchange), but to a sphere created almost entirely out of his imagination, because he was a poet rather than a social scientist, and though some of his insights may have value for the historian, it is the poet in Proust who has supplied them.

He understood this limitation (if it is one) better than any of his critics, and he speculated—very brilliantly, it seems to me—that ultimately imaginary forms, without any "local habitation," might become forces more compelling than those of the material world itself. These speculations of Proust seem to have more point with the passing of time rather than less, but they are not Marxist speculations, and the weakness of Marx, aside from his great strength and insights which are now universally recognized, is that he did not take into sufficient account the power of ideas which Proust speaks of. Marx did not credit the imagination and poetry enough, it seems, even in terms of purely social results. The following passage from Proust is not simply a pretty paradox, but presents a very serious and substantial truth:

> Would not society become secretly more hierarchical as it became outwardly more democratic? This seems highly probable. The political power of the Popes has grown enormously since they ceased to possess either States or an Army; our cathedrals meant far less to a devout Catholic of the seventeenth century than they mean to an atheist of the twentieth, and if the Princesse de Parme had been the sovereign ruler of a state, no doubt I should have felt myself impelled to speak of her almost as I should speak of a President of the Republic, that is to say not at all.[4]

The same thought essentially occurs in a letter to a friend of his mother in which he says: "Physical force is a small

[4] *The Guermantes Way*, Part 2, p. 203.

thing; the Pope has never been so powerful as when he lost possession of his army and territory, and this is true of him even in France, where he held the least sway in the days of his greatest material power." [5] Proust thinks that such figments of the imagination as the Faubourg Saint-Germain are perhaps the "realest" of realities.[6]

The position of the Faubourg in the world of reality is almost entirely due to the power of suggestion. Of course, it may be argued that there has always been a small royalist party in France, and that there is consequently a chance that the old monarchy might be restored and the titles have substance again. But very few people, even in the Faubourg itself, credit that possibility, and in the whole of Proust, I do not recall that it is ever mentioned by anybody. Some of his aristocrats, like Charlus, might even be disappointed if such a resurrection of their worldly authority took place. Where would be the proper field for the exercise of his extraordinary imaginative powers? People with such a superb gift of seeing visions do not enjoy the intrusion of the real world upon their dreams. The nobility described by Proust is a perfect illustration for that great saying of Rabelais: "So much is a man worth as he esteems himself." It is the conviction inbred in the aristocrat of being "better than other people" that prevents all manifestations of the usual efforts, born of feelings of inferiority, to show that one is "just as good" as others—it is this latter effort "which mars with so much ugliness, so much awkwardness, the most sincere overtures of a plebeian." [7]

Some dreamy and poetic minds like Proust's own are especially amenable to such a power of suggestion, and

[5] Marcel Proust, *Lettres à Mme C.*, pp. 85–86.
[6] *The Guermantes Way*, Part 1, pp. 31–32.
[7] *Within a Budding Grove*, Part 2, p. 49.

over them its influence is truly hypnotic. But even more prosaic minds are bound to be affected by the presence of a steady, unfaltering self-esteem, which only a self-acclaimed aristocracy can have. The Faubourg fascinated Proust because it was "a little world apart," carrying on all of its inconsequential activities "behind a barred threshold." [8] In this sense, it is contrasted with even the loftiest bourgeois, the great financiers, whose aggressive insolence to subordinates and inferiors is only the outward sign of their basic lack of confidence in their own worth. The Faubourg suffers from no such doubts. And society as a whole seems to conspire to allow it to keep up appearances, for the world is too humdrum and dreary a place not to need such distraction. And in all human nature, there is a deep insecurity which makes people fearful of calling into question even the most flagrant delusions, when they are stubbornly held and sufficiently harmless. There is a "will to believe" on both sides of the footlights—actors and audience are joined in a common bond. The slightest hold on reality is used to justify the most fantastic claims. The fact that the ancestors of these aristocrats *did hold power at one time,* and that many of them are still very rich, is sufficient excuse for self-aggrandizement. The boundary line dividing such inflation from megalomania is difficult to determine at times, but it is clear to Proust that nobles like Charlus have crossed it.

Proust tells us that among his favorite books were the *Memoirs of Saint-Simon* and the *Arabian Nights,* and he also informs us on one occasion that it was the height of his own ambition to write the contemporary equivalent of these two classics. It seems to me that he has done so, and that furthermore he has united the two books into one. Into the

[8] *The Guermantes Way,* Part 1, pp. 40–41.

*Memoirs of Saint-Simon* he has introduced the magical atmosphere of the Oriental masterpiece, while he has reversed the process for the latter—he has succeeded in giving the fantastic genie and Caliphs of Baghdad a habitation in Paris so localized that he has fooled his critics into confusing it completely with reality and so writing sociological treatises upon it. It must not be forgotten that the *Memoirs of Saint-Simon,* fantastic as some of them are, were yet only embroideries upon the margins of a very natural world—for the French nobleman was writing of the Court of Louis XIV, when France occupied the center of the European stage and that Court was the magnetic center of France. Time, by changing both these circumstances, suddenly cuts the supports of Proust's similar creatures in the world of fact, and at the same time wraps them in a kind of sorcery as if their pageant had materialized at the summons of a magician.[9]

But if critics with astute intellects have accepted for reality what was never intended except as an illusion, it is because the resemblances between the two are very great, and it may be worthwhile to examine the articulation of Proust's fictitious society as it is drawn in his books. Proust opens his story with an outline of what he calls the Combray caste conception of society,[10] which he jokingly compares to that of India. This is the point of view of his family and of the whole environment in which he is brought up. Briefly, as its name indicates, it is the view that society is divided into

[9] Maurois, *Proust: Portrait of a Genius,* p. 283, recalls to me that the French critic P. Abraham has made a similar reflection: "Pierre Abraham points out that if, like Proust, Saint-Simon concerns himself with a world of limited extent, the world of the Court, he does, at least, show it in action, and at a time, too, when that world was the scene of great happenings. Saint-Simon's courtiers are men with a career, men who have set out to achieve power, and from whose ranks ministers and military commanders are recruited."

[10] *Swann's Way,* p. 17.

several classes, among which only the slightest communication is possible. A man is born into a certain class, it is said, and, except for the unlikely contingency of "a brilliant career or a good marriage," he dies in that class. If one has known the father, one knows the son as well, at least in his social aspect. One knows the people with whom "he is in a position to associate." Here is a conception which is suitable for an old and stable society with a rigid framework. The suspicions of Proust's critics should have been aroused at the very beginning about the directness of the connection of his picture with reality. Is it possible, they might have asked themselves, that the narrator was brought up into a Hindu caste conception of society? Proust was born in 1871, the year of the Commune and the year after the defeat by the Prussians. He reached his manhood a century after the great French Revolution, and that century had been filled with turmoil, usurpers, anarchy, and reaction. Is it possible that anyone in France at that time thought of class boundaries as firmly fixed and unbreakable? If Proust puts his family's point of view in this way, it is because he finds it convenient to exaggerate certain features in order to achieve a dramatic contrast with some of his own social discoveries which come later on.

The application of the caste point of view is seen in his family's reaction to Charles Swann, the "young" Swann, who, while living another life in Parisian high society in which he is a member of the ultra-exclusive Jockey Club and of what, in newspaper language, would be called the "international fast set," keeps up relations with people like the narrator's family—that is, middle class friends of his father who know nothing of his other life. Without knowing who his other friends were, the narrator's family thought that they knew the *kind* which they were likely to be: sons of other rich stockbrokers like Swann himself. So strong a hold do habitual expectations have upon people that they reject the evidence of their senses when these suppositions are contradicted—

> One day when he had come to see us after dinner in Paris, and had begged pardon for being in evening clothes, Françoise, when he had gone, told us that she had got it from his coachman that he had been dining "with a princess." "A pretty sort of princess," drawled my aunt, "I know them," and she shrugged her shoulders without raising her eyes from her knitting, serenely ironical.[11]

There is more irony than Proust perhaps intended here, for even after we have found out that it is indeed a woman of title instead of a nameless hussy that Swann had been to see, we might still echo the aunt's comment: "A pretty sort of princess!"—one who ruled over no domain outside of the imagination of her romantic guests.

This static conception of society, which Proust uses as a contrast with his own more mobile and dynamic conception, nevertheless seems to be essentially similar in certain respects to his own view. When he speaks of the servant Françoise as a "survival of the Middle Ages," [12] and notes in her what seems to be an innate and almost hereditary respect for the old nobility,[13] he is saying, in a more imaginative and roundabout way than his parents it is true, that in spite of superficial appearances society really alters very little from one generation to another or even over a period of many centuries. There is a stability in the underlying framework which survives changes and even revolutions. When the same wisdom is transposed to the lips and the mentality of the servant Françoise herself, it emerges in her

[11] *Ibid.*, p. 20. [12] *Ibid.*, p. 193.
[13] *The Guermantes Way*, Part 1, p. 37.

embittered social comment that no matter what else happens in the world, there will always be masters in it and there will always have to be servants.[14]

I suppose that what has tempted the Marxian critics in Proust's case has been the dynamism of his social outlook. But there are dynamisms of all kinds. Proust's vision is certainly not of an ordered and progressive change in the structure of society, which would seem to be the essential and distinguishing feature of the Marxist view. Marx believes that society is going somewhere desirable. I find no such conviction in Proust. He certainly is aware that society does not stand still, but he is not sure that it is getting anywhere worthwhile. Proust, in general, is either nonpolitical or antipolitical. There are many sideswipes at politics and various breeds of politicians throughout his work. In one place in the novel, he alludes in a felicitous phrase to "the short memory of politicians." In another, he speaks of "the stupidity of the nationalists," but even so prefers them as the lesser evil when he considers the crimes of the Bolsheviks. In an article on Baudelaire,[15] he equates (in a figure of speech) politicians and madmen!

The image which best conveys Proust's conception of social change and at the same time precludes all notion of scientific progress or even of rational explanation is that of the kaleidoscope.[16] Society, like an amusing toy for children, continually rearranges its patterns to the delighted astonishment and amusement of an observer like Proust, but nothing significant is really accomplished by the succession of patterns. The transformation of the bourgeois vulgarian Mme Verdurin into the Princesse de Guermantes, or of simple Gilberte Swann into the Marquise de Saint-

[14] *Ibid.*, p. 27. [15] Marcel Proust, *Chroniques*, p. 218.
[16] *Within a Budding Grove,* Part 1, p. 125.

Loup is not significant, as some critics have pretended, of a "fusion" between the middle class and the aristocracy; still less does it foreshadow the absorption of the nobility by the bourgeoisie as others have said. What it indicates is that another shake of the social kaleidoscope has taken place and that it has resulted in an amazing change of identities. This is the *Arabian Nights* aspect of Proust, so to speak.

On a larger scale, it is the same phenomenon which we witness at the beach hotel in Balbec, where in the last few dreary days of the season the weather accomplishes a complete change in the social relationships of the guests, so that meetings take place which seemed completely impossible at the beginning of the summer.[17]

Social weather, in fact, is a favorite topic of Proust's observation, just as an interest in the barometer had been characteristic of the narrator's father. Mme Verdurin and Gilberte Swann enter the Faubourg Saint-Germain by what has almost become a legitimate door, so usual has it become over the centuries—namely, the possession of great sums of money, the transfusion of which into the financially dwindling veins of an aristocratic family renews its lease on life. But there are other ways of achieving the same results. Fashions in politics and in art are almost as good passports to social distinction as money. Proust shows how the Dreyfus Case, for example, gave a very violent shake to the social kaleidoscope. Rich Jewesses, who had been welcome in certain exclusive salons before, were now on the "wrong" side of the "Case," and found themselves excluded, while various other obscure ladies, who had been knocking vainly at various doors for years, welcomed a heaven-sent opportunity of exploiting nationalistic sentiment, though they

[17] *Ibid.*, Part 2, pp. 352–53.

had, of course, no interest in or understanding of nationalism itself.[18] Such a change, for Proust, is entirely the result of fortuitous circumstances which no one could have foreseen. If, says he, instead of the Dreyfus Case, there had been a war with Germany, the Jews, having shown themselves to be patriotic Frenchmen, would have been welcomed everywhere in society in larger numbers than before, while the smartest drawing room in Paris, that of an Austrian prince, would have fallen so completely from favor that nobody would have admitted ever having gone there. Astute hostesses also know how to make use of artistic fashions in order to make their own way in the world. It is not necessary, in order to do this, that they really understand and respond to art or know anything about it. What is necessary is that they be in a position to capitalize on the new rage for Russian Ballet, for example,[19] or that they "corner" some promising artist or writer or musician of the current season, so that people who would not otherwise set foot inside their door, will be drawn by curiosity about the celebrity into allowing an introduction.

Proust compares social mobility with the mobility of individual character,[20] and we have seen how extreme that can be. We observe many analogies between the behavior of society as a whole, as Proust draws it, and the behavior of his individual characters. Thus, it seems to be a law no less true in Proust's sociology than, as has already been shown, in Proust's psychology that there is a great demand for those who withhold themselves.[21] The attitude of a hostess to her drawing room is compared by Proust to the attitude of a lover to the mistress of whom he happens to be jealous. We

[18] *The Guermantes Way,* Part 1, pp. 325 ff.
[19] *Cities of the Plain,* Part 1, pp. 198 ff. [20] *Ibid.,* p. 197.
[21] *The Guermantes Way,* Part 2, pp. 186–87; *The Captive,* pp. 505–6.

begin to perceive what Proust means when he advises us, if we wish to understand vast social phenomena, to study the units of which such phenomena are composed. We see that individuals behave with the same perverseness towards their group, as we have seen them behaving towards other individuals. A Marquise who obstinately spurns society when she has it at her feet, will spend years of her life trying to regain the position she has frittered away, after society has turned its back upon her and treats her with contempt.[22] Proust's society, like his characters, seems capricious. There are always surprising developments, like the one which Gilberte calls "the unforeseen accident" of the Russian Revolution.[23]

When he had visited Venice in the later part of the story, news of the marriage of Saint-Loup to Gilberte had made the narrator point out to his mother how shocking such an alliance would have been from the Combray caste point of view of his dead grandmother. But the full extent of the change in the whole social setup is not evident to him until he visits the Faubourg after the War, and finds the world of his youth completely upset. Everybody is there who, according to the old standards, should not be there. In a passage from his last volume which has often been quoted, Proust says:

> the distinguishing characteristic of this social set was its prodigious aptitude at wiping out social classifications. Whether relaxed or broken, the springs of the protective apparatus no longer functioned and much foreign matter was getting in and destroying the homogeneousness and the distinctive appearance and color of the group. Like a senile old dowager, the Faubourg Saint-Germain replied only with timid smiles to insolent servants who invaded its draw-

[22] *Cities of the Plain,* Part 1, p. 148. [23] *The Past Recaptured,* p. 307.

ing rooms, drank its orangeade, and introduced its mistresses to it.[24]

But Proust did not think this observation as significant as his critics have made it seem. He introduced scrupulous qualifications which make it less startling than at first sight it appears to be. He saw upon reflection that the transformation of Mme Verdurin into the Princesse de Guermantes was not as novel or revolutionary a phenomenon as he had at first assumed. Actually, society had always been undergoing changes like that, but people either did not notice them or did not care to notice them. The reason why this particular change seemed so unheard-of and earth-shaking to him was that, whereas he had only read about the others, he actually lived through this one.

Even in that past to which I traced back the Guermantes name in order to give it all its grandeur (and with good reason, by the way, for under Louis XIV the Guermantes, being almost a royal family, occupied an even more prominent position in society than today) the phenomenon that I was witnessing used also to occur. Do we not find them at that time allying themselves by marriage, for example, with the Colbert family, which today seems to us of very noble rank, it is true, since marrying a Colbert is regarded as a fine match for a la Rochefoucauld? But the Guermantes did not ally themselves with the Colberts on account of the latter being noble, for they were simple bourgeois at that time, rather it was through their alliance with the Guermantes that they became noble.[25]

If there is any difference between our age and earlier ones, Proust thinks that it may perhaps be that the changes which have always been occurring are speeded up in our time. Transformations, which once took a century, seem now to be accomplished in the space of a generation.[26]

[24] *Ibid.*, pp. 297–98. [25] *Ibid.*, pp. 309–10. [26] *Ibid.*, p. 294.

In other words, from one point of view the Combray caste conception had always been wrong, because there never had been such rigid walls between the classes as it had assumed, and yet, in another sense, society really was unchanging. There had always been an aristocracy and commoners (or, as Françoise would say, masters and servants) and the former had always made use of the latter when they wished to do so. It is not the bourgeois that absorbs the nobility, but the other way about, according to Proust. A bourgeois, like Gilberte Swann, falls in love with the Faubourg because it insults her (as a man will sometimes succumb to an insulting woman). But upon entering its sacred precincts, the unfortunate climber must quickly slough off any remaining sympathy he has had for his fellow bourgeois. He is now a part of the great Faubourg, a captive of it (though a willing one perhaps), who sees the world through its eyes, judges people by its standards. To speak of this process, as Edmund Wilson does, as one in which the bourgeois absorbs the nobility is the same as if we would regard the monuments of the ancient Egyptians, because they were often made literally out of Israelite flesh and blood, as being Hebrew and not Egyptian for that reason. The bourgeois "ennobled" will show scant sympathy for the bourgeois unredeemed, no matter how rich, though he will regard an impoverished Queen of Naples with the same benevolence and respect which the rest of the Faubourg thinks is her due. And Proust must think that this system has the vitality to endure because at one point of his story he speaks of "the countless Princesses de Guermantes to come in the future." [27]

[27] *Ibid.*

## THE SYMBOLISM OF THE FAUBOURG SAINT-GERMAIN

Proust has been accused of being a snob and defended against the charge. He himself was early aware of the possibility that such an interpretation might be put upon his interests, and he defended himself against it. For example, in a letter to his friend Georges de Lauris, written in 1908, he says: "Being all alone I have read a lot. But I mostly occupy myself with nonsense, such as genealogy, etc. I swear it isn't snobbishness, it amuses me immensely." [28] More writers have thought him a snob than have agreed with his own estimate of himself. Some of those who knew him personally (though not very well it seems) thought that his primary interest in life lay in social advancement, and that, like some of the hostesses he describes in his book, he was ready to use his rather minor artistic talents for the achievement of his major social ends. In his letter of apology to Proust for turning down the manuscript of his novel when it was submitted to the *Nouvelle revue française*, André Gide confessed that after having met him in some of the fashionable drawing rooms of the 1890's, he had written him off as a snob, who was never destined to go beyond a small amateur competence in the arts. But Gide, at least, in a characteristically conscientious manner, has confessed his error after the decisive evidence of the great book itself came in to disprove him, while some other critics have continued to regard Proust as a snob of great talent, which he was willing to exploit to further his social ambitions.

On the other hand, there have been some scholars and critics who have thought of Proust as almost exclusively artistic in his real interests, with his worldly subject playing

[28] Marcel Proust, *Letters to a Friend*, pp. 113–14.

a subordinate and distinctly unimportant role in his work. Fashionable society, they say, was not a consuming ambition of Proust's life; it was simply a colorful spectacle which enabled him most impressively to display and exercise his own literary talent. The distinction of an artist, according to this view, lies not in his subject matter, but in the formal treatment which his talent enables him to bring to it. Spagnioli and Clermont-Tonnerre make this vivid comparison—smart society, they say, was for Proust what the ballet stage was for Degas. In a similar vein, Lucien Daudet says that Proust's interest in the flora and fauna of society was that of the botanist and not of the florist.

The truth seems to me to lie somewhere between these two extremes. Proust was certainly not so much of a snob as unsympathetic critics have pictured him, nor was he so complete an artist as excessively devoted admirers believe. If Proust had been a great snob, he would never have found the time or the energy with which to construct his great work of art, for he shows us that real snobbery involves as much strenuous effort as any mere human being can give to a serious undertaking in this world. But if he had been exclusively an artist, he would never have found a key to the heart. We must not lose sight of the fact that it is always life and humanity which are transmuted into even the highest and purest art. The fashionable world did not represent the height of Proust's spiritual reach, but it was something more for him than an icily distant and opportunistically sought artistic subject. The fashionable world was a powerful human interest for Proust, and it is this which has enabled him to make it so engrossing for us. The artist must be touched very near the core of his own being before he can affect his audience. The Faubourg Saint-Germain was the object of Proust's greatest love affair in life. He was more elated and depressed by it than by anything else except, perhaps, the death of his own mother.[29] And he has made it significant to us because it was first of all significant to himself. But, as in all of his deepest and most painful love affairs, Proust came to realize eventually that it was something primarily in himself which had made him seek out and become attached to an object. And when he realized that, he could hold the famous Faubourg as he had held his friends and his sweethearts off at arm's length and he was able coolly, philosophically, and aesthetically to describe it not in its transitory shape or fashion but in its permanent symbolic form. By making a myth of the Faubourg and of his experience with it, he made it translatable into the experience of the whole of mankind.

But it must be determined precisely what kind of a symbol Proust found in the Faubourg. Proust, though he spent a long time fleeing from contact with his fellows, trying first to immure himself behind the "barred threshold" of the aristocracy, and later, with more success, in his own cork-lined chamber, realized finally (just as he realized that he had not been the only or even very exceptional bourgeois in breaking into high society) that his own was only a special variant upon a discernible streak in human nature,

[29] It is tempting to connect Proust's interest in high society with his mother's. In the novel, we see the narrator's mother and grandmother both interested in aristocratic memoirs. In life, we find Proust passing on society news to her. Did he want to conquer society to please her originally? His father, according to Maurois, could not understand the reasons for Marcel's popularity. After his mother's death in 1905, pleasing her with his social conquests must have become meaningless and ironic for him, and it was then that he saw society for what it essentially was. His mother had wanted him to be an artist as well as a social success, but a man, even in the full possession of all his energies, which the invalid Proust was not, cannot divide himself up so easily. It may be really his mother's interests that Proust was acting out during his excursions into high society.

which could be observed both in its literature and its history. Such a realization is, of course, the beginning of a healthful restoration to the body politic. He needn't feel either guilty or superior any longer because of his snobbish interests, because they were only a proof that he was a man. He realized something more. Literature is the memory of the race, but this memory (like the individual memory) is not infallible and does not even fall always on the highlights of actuality. Rather, it is the point upon which the memory of literature falls that, whether so from the beginning or not, now becomes the focal point of history. For example, in his book he tells us how the drawing room of a certain Mme Leroi was one of the most fashionable of its time in Paris, much more so than that of the Marquise de Villeparisis, upon whom Mme Leroi looked with disdain which made itself felt. But it so happened that Mme Leroi herself was not a writer, while the Marquise was the author of some very interesting memoirs; and so, says Proust, the future is bound to think of the latter's as the great and representative salon of her time, while that of Mme Leroi will vanish without a trace. The power of literature, then, triumphs in the long run over the power of society, since the memory of the last can survive only through the other. But who are the people who are interested in this vain and subtle distinction between the drawing rooms of Mme Leroi and that of the Marquise de Villeparisis? Here we come to the heart and originality of Proust's answer. You and I are interested, you and I who are the readers of literature who have remained essentially the same in nature for thousands of years, you and I who are a part of "that posterity which has not changed since the days of Homer and Pindar, and for whom the enviable things are exalted birth, royal or quasi-royal, and the friendship of kings, the leaders of the people, and other eminent men." [30]

We have already seen that Proust thought that as long as there was humanity, there would also be hierarchy, and that it was even possible that as society became outwardly more democratic (if that was the trend) it might become secretly more hierarchical.[31] It was natural, furthermore, that those on the lower levels of this hierarchy should always be interested in what those of the upper levels were doing. In a journalistic age, the chronicles of John Gunther perform a function essentially similar to that of the *Memoirs of Saint-Simon*. Proust's difficulty and the greatest obstacle to his widespread popularity are not that he deals with an upper-class society, but that his upper class is not universally recognized as such. It is as difficult for the public to recognize Proust's aristocracy as it would be for a country nowadays to conduct its diplomatic negotiations with Russia through its émigrés. It requires a stage of sophistication more rarefied and refined to respond to Proust's insinuation that things do not exist apart from the imagination of man, and that the study of an imaginary upper class, therefore, may be as interesting and as fruitful in the long run as the study of a real one.

Mme de Cambremer, who calculates the number of years which it must take her to reach a certain drawing room—if, that is, the fatal disease which she knows she is suffering from does not strike her down first—is instantly recognizable as the blindly fanatical careerist in terms of any other social setup.[32] It does not really matter whether or not the goal of her strivings is worth such calculations. What goal

[30] *The Guermantes Way*, Part 1, p. 263.
[31] *Ibid.*, Part 2, p. 203.
[32] *Ibid.*, Part 1, p. 66.

is there that would be so worthwhile as to cause one to treat matter-of-factly the possibility of death? What is significant is that she has found something in life which is important to her. Of course, the goal of such striving is not irrelevant to ethics, nor is it altogether irrelevant to Proust, but he subsumes it under the more general heading of worldly ambition, and the essential difference between Mme de Cambremer and the novelist Bergotte, both of whom neglect the importance of death in the intensity of their interest in something else, is that the goal of the woman's striving lies in this world while that of the writer lies in a world of ideas beyond. And that is why I think that Proust implies that there is more truth than the speaker realizes in Legrandin's statement that snobbishness is "the unforgivable sin." [33] This sentiment lies with ill grace on the lips of the hypocritical country gentleman, who has worldly ambitions himself, and perhaps for this reason, the condemnation is somewhat exaggerated. In his own person, the narrator does not speak of "sin" in connection with snobbishness any more than (not being devout) he speaks of sin in other connections. But he does call it "a serious malady of the spirit." [34] Disease—the term he had already employed about love and about homosexuality, and the reason for the use of the same term in all three cases is equally clear. Snobbishness is one of those false and vain pursuits which, capable though they are of distracting a Mme de Cambremer from the thought of death, promise us something real, but leave us with nothing save an ashen taste.

It is the intensity of his disillusion which makes Proust's sociology shade off into philosophy:

[33] *Swann's Way*, pp. 83–84. [34] *The Captive*, p. 8.

One way among others of becoming reconciled to life is to realize through a near approach that the things and people which from a distance seem beautiful and mysterious are really devoid of beauty and mystery. Among the possible systems, this one perhaps is not to be recommended, but it at least gives us a certain equanimity that helps us through life and resigns us to death, since, by convincing us that we have known the best and that the best is not too much, it permits us to regret nothing.[35]

When one achieves the ultimate ambition in regard to the fashionable world (even as when one achieves it in love), there is nothing to do but turn aside in disgust, because there was nothing but a mirage to attract us there in the first place, while in a truly creative activity such as art, the more that one achieves, the more one desires to achieve, for there is something there to correspond to our innermost and truest desires.[36]

And Proust knows that such an exclusively and irrationally pursued aim as snobbery implies holds more than disappointment for ourselves alone. It may also do positive harm to other people, not only in the spiritual sense of the hurtful snubs and exclusions with which the pages of Proust are teeming, but more crudely still in a crude character like that of the doctor Cottard who, says Proust, would forego a social gathering at Mme Verdurin's which she referred to as her "Wednesdays" (a vulgar enough aim in life but one which suited the level of the low-born doctor) for a cabinet minister's cold but not for a workingman's stroke![37]

[35] Maxim 69, *Maxims of Marcel Proust,* ed. and trans. by O'Brien.

[36] Proust speaks of the vacuity of social life and attributes to its vacuity the inability of a great writer like Sainte-Beuve to convey clearly its most subtle and futile distinctions. *The Guermantes Way,* Part 2, p. 149.

[37] *Cities of the Plain,* Part 2, p. 36.

In the case of the most consummate snob in the book, the Baron de Charlus, there is less evil in his flights of fantasy than amusement.[38] He lives in a world so completely self-centered that were he not thoroughly harmless as well as witty and entertaining, he would undoubtedly have had to be forcibly confined to rather narrow quarters. By reducing the idea of snobbery to the dimensions of a Charlus, Proust satirizes it more effectively than he could have done in any other way. But in doing so he does not appeal to the reader's self-complacency. He seems to hold Charlus up for our inspection, while saying: "Here but for a grain of sand in his make-up might have been a poet!" Upon the thoughtful reader, this will have the effect not of making him feel superior to the quixotic nobleman but of asking himself if the things that engross his own attention have any more validity than this, and if we do not all (except for a chosen intellectual few) sacrifice on every day of our lives, under different pretexts, reality to appearance.

The poetry of the Faubourg Saint-Germain—Proust did not create it, but he has recreated it wonderfully well. Proust himself in a letter to Lucien Daudet says that he has written "from the point of view of whatever there may be of poetry in snobbery." [39] Principally, it is a matter of associations—historical associations and poetic ones (when the two are not the same, for Proust was attuned to what may be called the poetry of history, that is, of history divorced from politics and become pure spectacle)—associations which cluster magnetically around certain distinguished names.[40]

. . . The whole succession (of my social memories) making up a woven pattern of frivolities, yet full of poetry, despite their world-

[38] *Ibid.*, p. 326. [39] *Letters of Marcel Proust*, ed. by Curtiss, p. 290.
[40] *The Guermantes Way*, Part 1, p. 9.

liness, because the stuff is the stuff of dreams, is an airy bridge that joins the present to a past already very far away, and life to history, so that, because of it, history is made more living and life almost historical.[41]

The principal name which Proust projected upon the screen of his reader's imagination was that of Guermantes, for all of his principal characters become, in the course of the story, related to that family through ties of blood, marriage, or friendship. And it is the *name* of Guermantes, the family *name*, which Proust expends his artistic power most lavishly in making alive. There is a mystery in the name itself, Proust felt, and a great name almost creates the people who bear it. The magic power of the word is nowhere as evident or concentrated as it is in names. Proust is always finding glimpses of historic grandeur in those who bear the name of Guermantes. It gives an extra dimension in time even to such a nonentity as the Duc de Guermantes and it adds interest to a young man like Saint-Loup, who might otherwise seem fairly commonplace.[42] Proust insists that this quality is real; it is not simply an illusion created by the overactive imagination of Charlus (who finds all sorts of historical parallels between himself and his illustrious ancestors). And in the course of the novel, he pretty well convinces us of the reality of family and race, so that this new vision becomes one of the most palpable influences of Proust upon a sympathetic reader.

A great name, he says, "keeps those who bear it in the full light of day," [43] where both their merits and defects are underscored. He finds biological explanations for both in their lineage. Genealogy gives Proust an aesthetic pleasure

[41] Marcel Proust, *Selections from His Miscellaneous Writings,* p. 151.
[42] *The Guermantes Way,* Part 2, pp. 146 ff. [43] *Ibid.,* p. 320.

of peculiar vivacity, but it also satisfies a scientific curiosity to see the same quality in a family appear regularly over many generations. It is this pleasant interest that made him gravitate towards the aristocracy, for, as he points out, genealogical researches are feasible only when one can trace a family line with certainty and where most of the members have either handed down written records about themselves or have been the subject of records made by others. It would be absolutely impossible among members of the middle class where, after a few generations, ancestry runs into obscurity and conjecture. It is the marvelous echoes across vast chasms of time and of social history that makes the Duchesse de Guermantes as she talks "productive of literature" for Proust.[44] Noblemen and peasants, he says, are the last people from whom we can learn authentically about the past.[45] His servant Françoise is the shadow cast by the Guermantes upon history—she is the living witness of their former glory. The mobile middle and professional class into which he himself was born is too immersed in the present to be interested in the past, from which it has nothing to gain.

The aristocracy fascinated Proust, too, by its ability to make the most subtle, one may almost say invisible and non-existent distinctions, among the claims of men. It is the same great human mind at work here which (along other lines) made it possible for the medieval schoolmen to create such fine intellectual distinctions and for the modern scientists to harness matter. What ingenuity Charlus displays at observing differences within differences and at overwhelming with invective those who cannot recognize the use of his labors. He himself belongs to the old Bourbon nobility, the

[44] *Ibid.*, p. 257.

[45] *Ibid.*, pp. 330 ff.

only "legitimate" aristocracy, and he no more recognizes the titles of those families raised to the peerage by the two Emperors Napoleon than he would those of the nobility of Tahiti.[46] To what superb heights of withering scorn is he not capable of rising as he surveys all (the whole world it seems) whom he regards as beneath him. And Charlus, even more than his cousin the Duchesse de Guermantes, is "productive of literature" for Proust, because the amazing use to which he puts his superior mind continually feeds the imagination of the contemplative author. Facetiously, Proust compares the part played by Charlus for artists like himself to that of the reindeer among the Eskimos: "This precious animal plucks for them from the barren rocks lichens and mosses which they themselves could neither discover nor utilize, but which, once they have been digested by the reindeer, become for the inhabitants of the far North a nourishing form of food." [47]

But I don't suppose that anybody ever did so thorough a job of debunking the upper class as Proust did. If the French aristocracy had not been dead when he began his work, his merciless exposure would have killed them all over again—it would be enough, it seems, to touch off another French Revolution. Proust may be compared in quality to Watteau; yet the romantic and golden haze in which that painter wraps his figures is only an illusion of distance in the picture that Proust draws. Upon nearer view, he seems to have more in common with the brush used by Goya to portray the royal and noble families of Spain as a collection of imbeciles and degenerates. Here is Proust's own evaluation of the social implications of his story, in a letter to

[46] *Ibid.*, p. 350. [47] *Ibid.*, p. 356.

Marcel Boulenger: "In *Temps perdu* the class that is slandered, that is always wrong, talks only nonsense, the vulgar and hateful class is 'le monde.' "[48]

The disillusion of the narrator with the nobility proceeds relentlessly. It begins with appearances. The initial thrusts seem charmingly naive, but that is only a polite preface to the destructive strokes which follow. The first lesson is taught him by the physical appearance of the Duchesse de Guermantes. Before seeing her in the Church of Combray, she had been a figure in an imaginative tapestry for a sensitive child, like her ancestor Genevieve de Brabant. How could he have known that in the flesh she would resemble the ordinary prosaic wives of doctors and tradesmen with whom he was acquainted.[49] By a supreme effort of a powerful imagination, the narrator succeeds in finding her beautiful at last, but only because he wants to do so.[50]

Before the narrator had come into contact with the great world, the novelist Bergotte had provided him with a preview of the falsity of society, shocking to the young man at the time but later remembered as entirely characteristic of all his experiences. It happens that they are both guests in Swann's house, and, upon leaving, the novelist makes some very cutting remarks about their host to whose face he had just been so polite. The astonished young man says nothing.

But such instances of hypocrisy are trivial and are noticed only by the most uninitiated. Marriage, for example, is a useful instrument for Proust's dissection of the real, underlying motives of his characters. Even those (like the Princesse des Laumes) who take an intelligent interest in

[48] *Letters of Marcel Proust*, ed. by Curtiss, p. 343.
[49] *Swann's Way*, pp. 224–25. [50] *Ibid.*, p. 227.

things of the spirit and make some effort to educate themselves, when they come to marry unerringly gravitate towards name and money, though these (in the Duc de Guermantes upon whom the choice of the Princesse and her aunt, the Marquise de Villeparisis, falls) are associated with a very common nature.

But most members of society do not even pay their hypocritical tribute to virtue and make no pretense to spirituality at all. Proust was hurt by his first critics who labeled him as a "society writer." That wasn't true, he said, if it meant that he wrote for society rather than about it. Had he written for society, he says in his last volume, he would have had no readers, for he has been in the great world long enough to know that the real illiterates are to be found not among the workers of the General Confederation of Labor but among society people.[51]

Bad taste in art is not an exception but the rule in society.[52] And how could it be otherwise when the whole fashionable life is characterized by "idleness and sterility" which Proust contrasts with "true social activity." [53] Boredom, which is the great enemy of the idle socialites even as pain is that of the workers, makes it natural that the former go to art chiefly for distraction, but without really troubling to understand it. Society's preferences in art are distinguished by a "morbid need of arbitrary novelties." [54] The ideal man of fashion, in the Guermantes style, is "good for nothing." And to this man of fashion, Proust prefers even a pedantic old professor like Brichot, whose ponderous academic jokes and heavy paraphernalia of learning would

[51] *The Past Recaptured,* pp. 215, 222.
[52] *The Guermantes Way,* Part 1, p. 377.
[53] *Ibid.,* Part 2, p. 224. [54] *Ibid.*

make him a laughing stock at the home of the Duchesse de Guermantes. But to Proust the Sorbonne scholar, beneath his rough and unappetizing manner, displays the possession of a "well-nourished brain." [55] And that possession might well be envied by some of the thin wits who are so admired in society. The more Proust looked at society the more certain he became that the intellectual world was the sole reality worth bothering about.[56] The Duchesse de Guermantes is representative of the cleverest side of the Faubourg Saint-Germain (a very minute part), and yet even her much admired wit, as Proust shows, is more often than not the simple desire to create a sensation rather than the wish to discover the truth. The character of the Duchesse as it finally emerges in Proust's work is that of one who desperately seeks for notoriety rather than for wisdom. She finds her true intellectual level at the end of the book in the company of actresses.

But if intellectual nullity were the worst charge that could be made against the fashionable world, Proust's judgment of it would not be so harsh. Much worse is its deliberate cruelty, exemplified in a hundred instances. There is, first of all, the insufferable arrogance of the aristocrats, the patronizing condescension which is so painful to the sensitive soul, and is designed to give pain. When the narrator as a young man is walking upon the beach at Balbec in the company of his grandmother, they are introduced for the first time in their lives to "a royalty," the Princesse de Luxembourg, and she makes them both feel like members of a menagerie. This hurt the narrator more for the sake of his gentle grandmother than for himself. The humor with which

[55] *Swann's Way*, p. 328. [56] *Cities of the Plain*, Part 2, p. 378.

he clothes the incident does not rob it of any of its bitterness:

Meanwhile the Princesse de Luxembourg had given us her hand and, now and again, while she conversed with the Marquise, turned to bestow a kindly glance on my grandmother and myself, with that embryonic kiss which we put into our smiles when they are addressed to a baby out with its "Nana." Indeed, in her anxiety not to appear a denizen of a higher sphere than ours, she had probably miscalculated the distance there was indeed between us, for by an error in adjustment she made her eyes beam with such benevolence that I could see the moment approaching when she would put out her hand and stroke us, as if we were two nice beasts who had poked our heads out at her through the bars of our cage in the Gardens. And, immediately, as it happened, this idea of caged animals and the Bois de Boulogne received striking confirmation. It was the time of day at which the beach is crowded by itinerant and clamorous vendors, hawking cakes and sweets and biscuits. Not knowing quite what to do to show her affection for us, the Princesse hailed the next that came by; he had nothing left but one ryecake, of the kind one throws to the ducks. The Princesse took it and said to me: "For your grandmother." And yet it was to me that she held it out, saying with a friendly smile: "You shall give it to her yourself!" thinking that my pleasure would thus be more complete if there were no intermediary between myself and the animals. Other vendors came up; she stuffed my pockets with everything they had, tied up in packets, comfits, sponge-cakes, sugar sticks. "You will eat some yourself," she told me, "and give some to your grandmother," and she had the vendors paid by the little negro page, dressed in red satin, who followed her everywhere and was a ninedays' wonder upon the beach.[57]

Probably the most extensively developed characters for cruelty are given by Proust to the Duchesse de Guermantes and to the successful climber, Mme Verdurin. Basically, the

[57] *Within a Budding Grove,* Part 2, pp. 389–90.

Duchesse is a very unhappy woman, for she is married to a gross and insensitive man who not only does not love her but refines the torture by making his wife accept his discarded mistresses into her society. It is a kind of retirement plan which he has developed for outworn and unwanted mistresses to introduce them to his wife. So the Duchesse pays a tremendous price for having married "the most eligible bachelor" of the Faubourg Saint-Germain, who enables her with his money and title to be one of its first ladies. Like other unhappy people, who assuage their own hurt by hurting others in turn, it is the pleasure of the Duchesse to make her servants share some of her unhappiness. No one stays very long in her employ, for she is a past mistress of inventing the most ingenious and seemingly innocent devices to torture those who serve her. She especially delights in wounding them, as she herself has been wounded in their most susceptible feelings of love. One episode dealing with the frustration of a footman's innocent pleasure is developed with singular clarity.[58]

But the masterpieces of her malice are reserved for her old friend Swann. As he is basically an outsider in society, a rich and witty Jew who has always admired and praised the beauty and wit of the Duchesse, he is peculiarly vulnerable to her. The Duchesse was probably a cold and calculating person to begin with, and her unfortunate marriage has completely frozen her sympathies with humanity. What right did anyone have to be happy when she, Oriane de Guermantes, was not happy? That she has no feeling for the friend whom she has seen daily for almost twenty-five years is shown in her confused reception of the news that his doc-

[58] *The Guermantes Way*, Part 2, pp. 382–84; *ibid.*, pp. 242 ff.

tors have told him he is dying.[59] But if that confusion is the result of a lack of feeling, her refusal to grant Swann's lifelong wish (at no cost to herself) is more deliberate.

Swann's wish was a silly one, to be sure, but just in proportion to its triviality, it meant everything in the world to him. Briefly, it was to introduce his wife Odette and more especially his daughter Gilberte to the Duchesse. He did not even wish that anyone should be present at the meeting or know anything about it. The nature of his ambition itself is enough of a commentary on the seriousness of life in the fashionable world. But as Proust develops it, it is seen to be a perfectly understandable and natural desire in Swann. He had married a demimondaine far below himself in the social scale years after their child had been born. Even middle class friends of his, like the parents of the narrator, snubbed his wife; and so he set out very patiently to conquer a place in society for her. His oldest and he thought his "best" friend was the Duchesse, and, whatever rebuffs he might have expected from others, he had every reason to hope for her sympathy and understanding. But it was just this desire that was destined to be frustrated. The irony is all the greater insofar as the motive for his bad marriage to Odette, or at least one of the chief motives according to Proust, was that Swann hoped to introduce her and their daughter to the Duchesse. We must remember that he marries Odette long after he has fallen out of love with her, and he is chiefly concerned with the welfare of his child.[60] But he did not sufficiently understand the depth of the unhappiness of the Duchesse, nor the store of malice which this had begotten

[59] *Ibid.*, p. 392.

[60] *The Sweet Cheat Gone*, pp. 219–20; *Within a Budding Grove*, Part 1, pp. 59–60.

in her. Nor did he realize that in a crucial moment, it would be upon himself that she would turn for revenge. Her refusal of his innocent request even when she knew that he would be dead in a short time satisfied, in her own mind at least, her desire for domination over him.[61] It makes some of the most painful reading in the book when she expresses her sentiment that it would mean the end of society if one should humor the whims of one's dying friends by allowing introductions which one had previously refused to them!

And so Swann dies "thinking that the ladies would never meet," but the Duchesse relents in her decree of ostracism after his death (without, however, feeling any remorse apparently for her previous actions) and allows the daughter, Gilberte, to call upon her. Gilberte had been brought up to regard the Faubourg Saint-Germain as the topmost pinnacle of the world. She is not satisfied until she has exchanged the fabulous fortune left her by her father and some of his relatives for the title of Marquise de Saint-Loup. Yet, as Proust shows, Gilberte's attitude is by no means a simple one. She deeply resents the snubs and insults which she has been forced to endure all her life. It is the impotent rebelliousness of the slave, however, who murmurs threats in his heart (sometimes without realizing it himself) against the master whom outwardly he serves. Gilberte, after she has secured her own position as a Guermantes, shows her real feelings by undertaking to outrage as many of the aristocratic traditions as she can. But that phase, too, passes with time apparently, for our last glimpse of her in the book shows her as one of the most reliable pillars of the house she has entered, ready to exclude and to insult other unfortunate bourgeois who, like herself, have the temerity to dare

[61] *The Sweet Cheat Gone,* p. 223.

aspire to the Faubourg Saint-Germain. So it is the aristocracy, serene always in its infernal self-assurance, that at last digests the bourgeoisie. Just as Jews (with whose situation Proust often compares that of his climbing bourgeois) are able to enter an anti-Semitic society after sloughing off all real sympathy for their own kind, so it is with the rising member of the middle class. It is not the Hebrews who assimilated the Egyptians by becoming incorporated in their monuments (though some rationalists among them would doubtless have wanted to believe that), nor does the bourgeois in the pages of Proust assimilate the aristocracy, as Wilson, Lemaitre, and other critics have thought. In this connection—as in another main point of dispute among the critics of Proust, namely, the questions revolving about his ethics—the point of view of his latest biographer, Maurois, is basically sound. He writes: "It is inexact to say that his book describes the decadence of the nobility and the triumph of the bourgeoisie. When Madame Verdurin or Gilberte Swann intermarry with the Guermantes, it is the Guermantes who assimilate these foreign elements." [62]

Cruelty and ill-breeding, Proust says in a generalization, are the hallmarks of the aristocracy.[63] Though they have no monopoly of the unsavory aspects of human nature, for we see these qualities in Françoise and in other servants (the elevator operator at Balbec is an especially good example [64]), yet they appear with an exceptional lack of grace in those who make a pretense to gentility and good manners. And it is perfectly clear to Proust whence these obnoxious traits come in the upper classes. Speaking of the meanness of the Verdurins, he says that its cause lay in their "idleness." [65]

[62] Maurois, *Proust: Portrait of a Genius,* p. 284.
[63] *The Captive,* p. 331. [64] *Cities of the Plain,* Part 1, pp. 315–16.
[65] *Ibid.,* Part 2, pp. 64–65.

Lack of serious occupation—that is the great source in Proust of unhappiness in oneself and of brutality to others. A good example of the effect of lack of occupation upon a nature originally much better than that of the Verdurins is afforded by the development of a malicious streak in the character of the invalid Aunt Léonie and its exercise upon her servant Françoise. To Proust it is "a spirit of mischief engendered by the utter idleness of her existence." [66] This mischief takes the form of playing absolute monarch with her dependents.

> A middle aged lady in a small country town, by doing no more than yield to her own irresistible eccentricities . . . could see, without ever having given a thought to Louis XIV, the most trivial occupations of her daily life, her morning toilet, her luncheon, her afternoon nap, assume, by virtue of their despotic singularity, something of the interest that was to be found in what Saint-Simon used to call the "machinery" of life at Versailles; and was able, too, to persuade herself that her silence, a shade of good humor or of arrogance on her features would provide Françoise with matter for a mental commentary as tense with passion and terror, as did the silence, the good humor or the arrogance of the king when a courtier, or even his greatest nobles had presented a petition to him, at the turning of an avenue, at Versailles.[67]

The reverse side of this medal is Proust's extraordinary (though rarely expressed) sensitivity to the existence of the "lower orders." His portrait of Françoise has been universally admired, and yet it is rarely pointed out how vital a part of this picture, without ever becoming cloying or sentimental or patronizing, is Proust's sympathy with the pathos of her "peasant existence." [68] The relations between master and servant are realistically drawn, the frequent nervous abrasions inseparable from close personal contact, the

[66] *Swann's Way*, p. 150. [67] *Ibid.* [68] *Ibid.*, p. 66.

resentments of Françoise which lead her at one time (so he hears indirectly) to say to a friend that he is not worth the price of a rope with which to hang him. But still, there is an immense sympathy at the bottom of the narrator's soul, especially with those born unfortunate enough to have to serve others:

> We do not put ourselves sufficiently in the place of these poor maid-servants . . . we close our hearts to the pathos of the country-side . . . we must learn not to remain unmoved, despite the solemn, menacing fatuity of the things she says, her maternal heritage and the dignity of the family "kailyard," before an old cook draped in the honor of her life and of her ancestry, wielding her broom like a sceptre, donning the tragic buskin, stifling her speech with sobs, drawing herself up with majesty. That afternoon, I remembered or imagined scenes of this sort which I associated with our old servant, and from then onwards, in spite of all the harm she might do to Albertine, I loved Françoise with an affection, intermittent it is true, but of the strongest kind, the kind that is founded upon pity.[69]

He understands her irritations; he excuses them; he even dreams about her with pity; so that, when he awakes, he regrets his frequent impatience with her, his inconsiderateness. It is against this background that we have his resentment of the Duchesse's deliberate abuse of her menials.

The feeling for the poor and downtrodden as a class is even more evident in a passage from the volume *Within a Budding Grove,* in which the narrator sees the poor of Balbec looking in through the windows at those who are dining there,[70] and goes on to speculate as to whether the glass between them will always protect the fish swimming as in a bowl behind it or whether those outside may not some

[69] *Cities of the Plain,* Part 1, pp. 247–48.
[70] *Within a Budding Grove,* Part 1, pp. 363–64.

time break the glass and devour their "betters." I am not saying that Proust is a revolutionary, and in his last volume, he expresses sympathy with the victims of Bolshevism, grand duchesses who suddenly appeared in rags and tatters in the streets of Paris, but he is very sensitive to the causes which might lead to a social overturn. A letter to his friend Sidney Schiff in 1922 is significant in this connection: "I am amazed . . . that people are courageous enough to have published *urbi et orbi* all the dinners, gouters, etc. they eat, while in the next column one learns that hundreds of people (perhaps as interesting as the Shah of Persia) were found dead of starvation in Austria and elsewhere." [71]

In one place in his books [72] he says that he prefers workingmen as a class, with the nobility next, and the professional class (from which he himself sprang) last of all. His democratic inclinations were apparently not altogether pleasing to the narrator's mother with her Combray caste conceptions and old-fashioned ideas of social decorum. He describes her astonishment when finding him at dinner with his chauffeur!

The First World War, in which Proust was too old and too ill to serve, roused his social conscience with more force than anything that had happened to France since the Dreyfus Case. Friends like Mme Scheikévitch have described his untold agony because he could not fight, though he was somewhat consoled by the idea that his disease had for many years inflicted so much pain upon him that it somehow mitigated the moral necessity for his bearing a share of the national suffering at the front. He has written much in his last volume about the war, from the honest point

[71] *Letters of Proust*, ed. by Curtiss, pp. 399–400.
[72] *Cities of the Plain*, Part 2, pp. 237–38.

of view of one who remained behind the lines in Paris. One of his best passages recalls the Balbec episode, for again he sees sufferers outside the lighted windows of a fashionable restaurant where the smart slackers are jostling each other for the best seats in the house. This time the sufferers are soldiers, whom Proust compares to the poor, except that he notes that the suffering of the soldier surpasses any other kind and contains quintessentially the prospect of sudden death which for the others is doled out, in the words of Céline, on "the installment plan." In a letter to Lucien Daudet in 1918, he says that he regrets the death of soldiers more than the destruction of churches, "which were only the recording of an heroic gesture which today is reenacted at every moment." [73]

The world of the Faubourg Saint-Germain, wrapped in a haze of poetry derived from the past which was so attractive to his youthful imagination, is finally revealed as fraudulent in its philosophy and barbarous in its conduct. The Faubourg had vivisected the soul of the noble Swann, who would have done much better to have stayed close to the origins from which he sprang and to which he eventually returned, under the impact of the Dreyfus Case, after wasting the best years of his life in a milieu where basically he did not belong and which showed him by a thousand actions and attitudes and words, both subtle and gross, that it did not want him. The silliness of the ambition to achieve a worldly reputation and status for oneself is underscored heavily in the case of Swann, not only by the inhumanity of some of his aristocratic friends as he is dying, not only by the fact that his dearly loved daughter Gilberte changes her name after his death and her mother's remarriage, but

[73] *Letters of Proust,* ed. by Curtiss, p. 314.

by the success of their combined conspiracy of silence, shame, and distortion, the final stamp of which appears in the last volume when the narrator attends the reception after the war at the new Princesse de Guermantes' and finds Swann, that lofty aesthetic spirit, that wit once beloved of princes, that member of the most exclusive clubs who thought that he was doing the President of the Republic an honor in dining with him, remembered as "an adventurer." [74]

And Proust hints that it may have served Swann right. For there is ingrained in Proust a deep conservative spirit which is his own more sophisticated version of the Combray wisdom. He finds it good and aesthetically satisfying that a man, like a musical composition returning to its original key at the end, should go back to the ancestral sources from which he sprang. That is why he says that it is to the credit of Swann that, at the end of a life which he had spent mostly in vain straying and intruding upon a foreign province, he returns to "the ways of his ancestors." [75] Proust calls this process "recasting."

Curiosity certainly leads us to modulate into strange keys far removed from our basic tonality in the course of our existence ("God has made man upright, but he has found out many inventions"). After long wandering, however, we want to go back home, and they are fortunate who know where their home is, and can find their own way back to it. Proust himself, half-Jewish and half-Gentile, half-man and half-woman in his affective life, was not so lucky as Swann. He remained in suspension to the end, and perhaps we owe his whole great work to that irresolution in his life.

[74] *The Past Recaptured*, p. 299.
[75] *The Guermantes Way*, Part 2, p. 375.

# The Ethics of Proust

*Most critics have reproached him for being immoral and not taking sides.*

REGIS MICHAUD [1]

*Everything is arranged in this life as though we entered it carrying the burden of obligations contracted in a former life. . . . All these obligations which have not their sanction in our present life seem to belong to a different world, founded upon kindness, scrupulosity, self-sacrifice, a world entirely different from this, which we leave in order to be born into this world, before perhaps returning to the other to live once again beneath the sway of those unknown laws which we have obeyed because we bore their precepts in our hearts, knowing not whose hand had traced them there—those laws to which every profound work of the intellect brings us nearer and which are invisible only—and still—to fools.*

MARCEL PROUST [2]

OVER and over again, we hear the view first set in motion by writers like François Mauriac and Ramon Fernandez that Proust is an amoral author, that he lacks "a

[1] Régis Michaud, *Modern Thought and Literature in France,* p. 62.
[2] *The Captive,* pp. 250–51.

hierarchy of values." [3] Mauriac, who, in spite of his ethical reservations, is a great admirer of Proust's art, puts the objection most brilliantly and memorably:

> God is terribly absent from Marcel Proust's work. . . . From the literary point of view alone, it is the weakness of that work and its limitation; the human conscience is absent from it. Not one of the beings who people it is acquainted with moral anxiety, or scruples, or remorse, or desires perfection. Scarcely a one who knows what purity means; or else the pure, like the mother or grandmother of the hero are so without knowing it, as naturally and effortlessly as the other characters who sully themselves. It is not the Christian who judges here; the lack of moral perspective impoverishes the humanity created by Proust, narrows its universe.[4]

It will be my purpose in this chapter to show that, while it is true that certain characters in Proust are as naturally and effortlessly moral as others are the opposite, this is so not because Proust "lacks moral perspective" but because he has a different moral perspective from that of Mauriac. To Proust morality is an instinct, and, as in the case of all instincts, it is stronger in some than in others; in still others, perhaps, it is entirely perverted. Proust says that "the body has a certain instinct for what is wholesome just as *the heart has an instinctive sense of moral duty*." [5] As for the statement that "the human conscience is absent from [Proust's work]" I will try to prove precisely the contrary. I will show that the entire book originated in Proust's own conscience and that one of its great virtues is that it serves to sensitize the dormant conscience of his readers. I feel, in other words, much as Proust's friend Lucien Daudet felt when he wrote one of the first reviews [6] of *Swann's Way* for the newspaper

[3] Ramon Fernandez, *Messages, première série*, p. 147.
[4] Mauriac, *Proust's Way*, pp. 46–47.
[5] Maxim 8, *The Maxims of Marcel Proust*, ed. and trans. by O'Brien.
[6] Marcel Proust, *Lettres à Mme C.*, pp. 209–10.

*Figaro* on November 23, 1913. The younger son of Alphonse Daudet said in that review, and I see no reason for changing our minds about this, that *albeit indirectly* Proust seemed to him to attain to the very loftiest heights of morality. It is the indirection of Proust that seems to have caused a great deal of trouble. Here, as elsewhere in criticism, the first job is to restore to view the artist's original intention, an intention which many readers have grasped, especially those who knew Proust personally, but which, unfortunately, many other readers, and some with the greatest names and critical authority, have not grasped.

In the famous passage from *The Captive* which I have placed at the head of this chapter Proust tells us that the business of the profound intellectual work is to clarify the moral law, which is not simply a compact of convenience among men but has originated in a world unrecognized by positive science, a world "founded upon kindness, scrupulosity, and self-sacrifice." The moral law, futhermore, is not something external to us but has been inscribed in our inmost being—like Kant's categorical imperative. We obey it, not through taste alone, but because we are compelled to by something in ourselves—we are under an "obligation," and a burdensome obligation it is. All this is clear, says Proust, to everyone but fools.

Now this is stated so clearly, so forcefully, and so simply, that it should satisfy even the most implacable critic that Proust was not neutral in questions revolving around the subject of ethics. By his own admission of what constitutes a profound work of the intellect, Proust, if he is not a fool, cannot possibly have constructed his books without "a hierarchy of values." It is for us to discover those values, or to condemn him by his own criterion.

Regardless of how his work appeared to his critics, Proust thought of it apparently as definitely fulfilling that moral intention which he thought inseparable from an intellectual work worthy of the name. When he was originally submitting his manuscript to the *Nouvelle revue française* (the offer which was rejected), he had written that "the work as a whole reflects a metaphysical and moral outlook." [7] It would, indeed, have been strange had it been otherwise. Proust was no longer a child when at twenty in answer to the question "How would you like to die?" he wrote, "A better man than I am, and much beloved." [8] His first writings, as I have indicated in another chapter, reflected his admiration of Tolstoy. One story in particular, "The End of Jealousy," in its ideas of brotherly love and in its rejection of sensuality, seems like a cross between certain portions of *War and Peace* and Tolstoy's novelette *The Kreutzer Sonata.*

In *Remembrance of Things Past,* I see in Proust's very style of writing—that famous, long-breathing, hesitating style, with its endless qualifications, its variable hypotheses about the motives, the actions, the intentions, and the excuses of the people he describes—the result of his immense scruples. In his youth, he had answered a question as to his favorite character in literature with the name Hamlet—and is not Hamlet a man never-endingly tormented by conscientious scruples? What tentativeness and delicacy, what tact Proust employs when he approaches the motivations of his character Swann, for example, who likes to identify the faces he sees around him with those in his favorite paintings:

> Perhaps because he had always regretted, in his heart, that he had confined his attention to the social side of life, had talked, always, rather than acted, he felt that he might find a sort of indulgence

[7] Maurois, *Proust: Portrait of a Genius,* p. 252. [8] *Ibid.,* p. 39.

bestowed upon him by those great artists, in his perception of the fact that they also had regarded with pleasure and had admitted into the canon of their works such types of physiognomy as give those works the strongest possible certificate of reality and trueness to life; a modern, almost a topical savour; perhaps, also, he had so far succumbed to the prevailing frivolity of the world of fashion that he felt the necessity of finding in an old masterpiece some such obvious and refreshing allusion to a person about whom jokes could be made and repeated and enjoyed today. Perhaps, on the other hand, he had retained enough of the artistic temperament to be able to find a genuine satisfaction in watching these individual features take on a more general significance when he saw them, uprooted and disembodied, in the abstract idea of similarity between an historic portrait and a modern original, whom it was not intended to represent.[9]

It is almost as if he gives all his characters the benefit of every doubt, and if he makes up his mind finally and sets a thing down as so and not otherwise, he does this with such great pain and pity for the wickedness and cruelty of mankind that even his most pessimistic conclusions carry an extraordinary weight. The moral reflections which the actions of his character necessarily give rise to are calculated to sensitize the most ethically obtuse. Mankind appears in Proust's work to cut a very poor figure indeed. The vast majority is mean and ungrateful; the little light of goodness or even kindness is a rare exception.[10] Cruelty is widespread, and cowardice hardly less so. Even when men are not busy actively and purposefully tormenting each other, they go their own way and do as they please, indifferent to the hurt which they may incidentally be inflicting. Unawareness of the suffering we cause, says Proust, is "the most usual and lasting form of cruelty." [11]

[9] *Swann's Way,* p. 288. [10] *Cities of the Plain,* Part 2, p. 79.
[11] *Swann's Way,* p. 212.

Only in some few spirits (the narrator's own may be included among them) do the sorrows which they themselves suffer result in a feeling of sympathy for other sufferers.[12] Most men apparently put down their sufferings on the debit side of the ledger of what they think mankind owes them. They are too busy feeling hurt and resentful to become kind. But for those few who have been touched by pity, by compassion, by a real love for the life of others, by a feeling which "might make a man greater than his own trivial life,"[13] there exists a foundation for the strongest tie which can exist between creatures in this world.[14] It is only a man who is capable, at least at moments, of flashes of the greatest moral insight, who could write, as Proust has, that compassion for suffering is a stronger cause of love than the desire for pleasure.[15] So long as his sweetheart Albertine is the mere instrument of physical joy, she can touch the heart of her lover only with a feeling of fierce possessiveness and hatred both for her and his imagined rivals for her favor. But when she appears in his eyes as an agonized human being, like himself, she fills him with such real love for herself that he is ready to forego the superficial sensual excitements for which he has been longing. Even art, which we have seen Proust extol in worth far above the values of society, friendship, or carnal love, yields at last to the power of Proust's ethical concern. If necessary (but what a tragic necessity this is for him!) he is ready, during the war, to consent to the sacrifice of the monuments of the past, in order to preserve

[12] *Cities of the Plain,* Part 1, pp. 234–35.

[13] L. F. Céline, *Voyage au bout de la nuit* (Paris, 1932), pp. 613–14. Translated by John Monk, as *Journey to the End of the Night* (Boston, 1934), p. 501.

[14] *Cities of the Plain,* Part 1, p. 248.

[15] *The Sweet Cheat Gone,* pp. 14–15.

those feelings of spirituality which churches and art masterpieces embodied.[16]

Art and ethics are not separated for Proust any more than they are for Ruskin who was his first major literary enthusiasm. Those critics who either blame him for his supposed dichotomy between art and morals, or else praise him for becoming so purely an aesthete (there are such critics too) in contrast to a tiresome old preacher like Ruskin,[17] are doing no service in clarifying either his intentions or his accomplishment. They are both blaming him and praising him in ways he would have thought equally undeserved.

Proust, it seems to me, would have found highly agreeable, from his own point of view, the following passage from the writings of Wagner on the symphonies of Beethoven: "Their effect upon the hearer is that of setting him free from the sense of guilt, just as their afterthought is a feeling of 'paradise lost,' with which one again turns towards the world of phenomena. Thus these wonderful works preach repentance and atonement in the deepest sense of a divine revelation." [18] Only a very superficial notion of the meaning of morality as it appears in the work of art would readily dismiss this sentiment of Wagner's as too far-fetched. To the most sensitive listener, there are moral lessons to be derived from the most pure and abstract of the arts, music. What tone deafness (or else, what excessive concern with the presence or absence of one particular tone!) must be

[16] *The Past Recaptured,* p. 108.

[17] Arnaud Dandieu, *Marcel Proust: sa révélation psychologique,* p. 111: "La grande différence entre Ruskin et Proust consiste dans le scepticisms de Proust qui l'à defendu contre ce 'Moralisme' qui gate les plus belles pages de 'La Couronne d'Olivier Sauvage.' " In similar vein, Harold March in his *Two Words of Marcel Proust,* p. 91, speaks of "the supple amorality of Proust" in contrast with "Ruskin's didactic morality."

[18] Wagner, *Beethoven,* pp. 55–56.

necessary, then, entirely to miss the ethical aspect of a writer like Proust, who thought that art should be moral, certainly wished his own to be so, and was not bereft of the talents to implement his intentions. It would have been remarkable if he had failed to accomplish what he manifestly set out to do, but we shall see that he did not fail.

"Kindness, scrupulosity, self-sacrifice"—these are the high points of the ethical structure of *Remembrance of Things Past.* The converse qualities, of course, are cruelty, unscrupulousness, selfishness. The positive as well as the negative attributes are illustrated profusely, the lessons are drawn, reinforced, hammered in with the relentlessness of a morality play. Paul Elmer More, the humanist whose steadfast concern with the connection between morality and art ought to constitute him a competent witness in the point at issue, said of Proust that he was "as didactic as Matthew Arnold." [19] His latest biographer draws an interesting distinction: "There could be no greater error than to think of Proust as amoral. Immoral, perhaps, but suffering atrociously on account of his immorality." [20]

Before Proust ever traces any other outlines of a person's appearance, he draws what might be called a moral profile. So, one of the first things we are informed of concerning the grandmother is that "she had brought so foreign a type of mind into my father's family that everyone made a joke of it." [21] This foreign element, we are soon informed, is simply an extraordinary moral endowment:

She was so humble and so sweet that her gentleness towards others, and her continual subordination of herself and of her own troubles, appeared on her face blended in a smile which, unlike those seen

[19] Lindner, *Marcel Proust—Reviews and Estimates,* p. 167.
[20] Maurois, *Proust: Portrait of a Genius,* p. 74.
[21] *Swann's Way,* p. 12.

on a majority of human faces, had no traces in it of irony, save for herself, while for all of us kisses seemed to spring from her eyes, which could not look upon those she loved without yearning to bestow upon them passionate caresses.[22]

In passing, we may note how effective such a method of presenting character is. How much better do we not see that smile when we know the moral ingredients of which it was composed, than if he had described it directly. It is a felicity of the kind noted by Lessing in Homer's indirect method of conveying to us an impression of Helen's beauty.

Shortly after this passage on his grandmother, we are informed of the narrator's own moral physiognomy. We see that he is by no means as pure as his grandmother, though neither is he as insensible as some of his other relatives, his aunt, for instance. His character lies somewhere between the moral extremes. He is neither greatly good nor bad, like Aristotle's tragic hero or like such an alter ego of the satirist as Gulliver. He loves goodness without being quite able to achieve it to his own satisfaction. He is tremulously delicate in his feelings and is moved to tears with almost feminine readiness. He sympathizes with his good grandmother, though in secret, and this secrecy, which he regards as cowardice, excites his shame: "In my cowardice I became at once a man, and did what all we grown men do when face to face with suffering and injustice; I preferred not to see them. I ran up to the top of the house to cry by myself in a little room." [23]

We shall see presently that Proust, when he was a grown man, did not prefer always to turn his eyes away from suffering and injustice. He did not have such morally superior progenitors in vain: "I had inherited from my mother and

[22] *Ibid* [23] *Ibid.*, p. 13.

grandmother their incapacity for resentment." [24] He was to write to Gide later on that, in the interest of a friend, he was capable of complete forgetfulness of himself.[25]

Some of those critics who do not see Proust devoid of moral concern go as far astray in the opposite direction—that is, they regard Proust as being capable of the apocalyptic indignation of a prophet out of the Old Testament.[26] Much as I respect Proust's ethical concerns, they have none of the quality to my mind of a Hebrew prophet. He does not explore those original springs of human nature from which the great rivers of morality flow—as Dostoyevsky does, for example. Proust did not live in a time or place or in a position in society from which such elemental discoveries could be made as are described in *Crime and Punishment* or in *The Brothers Karamazov*. Even as he lived all his life on a family inheritance rather than on what he was able to earn for himself, so he lived by a standard of values which he had inherited, too. Or, if he did not always succeed in *living* by that standard, at least he did always *write* by it.

The conflict between the morality enunciated by a writer in his work and the lack of it in his own life concerned Proust. He discusses it in his book in relation to the character of the novelist Bergotte, in whom this disparity was plainly evident. In the following conversation, the diplomat Norpois—one of the more noisome creatures in Proust's cast of characters—is explaining why he had refused, while stationed abroad, to yield to the pressure of some influential personages who had wanted him to invite the novelist and his mistress to his embassy:

[24] *Within a Budding Grove,* Part 2, p. 61.
[25] Marcel Proust, *Lettres à Gide* (Neuchâtel and Paris, 1949), p. 29.
[26] See, for example, Edmund Wilson excerpt from *Axel's Castle* in Lindner, *Marcel Proust—Reviews and Estimates,* p. 142.

I must admit that there are depths of degradation to which I should hesitate to descend, while these are rendered more repulsive still by the tone, not moral merely—let us be quite frank and say moralizing—that Bergotte takes up in his books, where one finds nothing but perpetual and, between ourselves, somewhat wearisome analyses, torturing scruples, morbid remorse, and all for the merest peccadilloes, the most trivial naughtinesses (as one knows from one's own experience), while all the time he is showing such an utter lack of conscience and so much cynicism in his private life.[27]

Norpois, the hypocrite, who has kept a mistress all his life, simply judges Bergotte on this occasion as a hypocrite also. But Proust, without any apologies, realizes that the case, perhaps, is not so simple—it may be perhaps like his own infinitely complex case, and he expends upon it his most subtle power of analysis, entirely worthy of the character of the great writer he is dealing with:

Perhaps it is only in really vicious lives that the moral problem can arise in all its disquieting strength. And of this problem, the artist finds a solution in the terms not of his own personal life, but of what is for him the true life, a general, a literary solution. . . . Great artists, while being thoroughly wicked, make use of their vices in order to arrive at a conception of the moral law that is binding upon us all.[28]

Whatever Proust's practice was, the theory of conduct enunciated in his books could not have failed, when properly understood, of course, to please his parents. It could not have failed to please them because basically, in all the most important respects, it consisted actually of their own values. The critic F. L. Lucas proves the morality of Proust by the semantic test of comparing his vocabulary with that of his parents.[29] *Proust was a moral* rentier *as well as a financial one. He lived on the accumulated ethical capital of both his*

[27] *Within a Budding Grove,* Part 1, pp. 66–67. [28] *Ibid.,* p. 186.
[29] Lindner, *Marcel Proust—Reviews and Estimates,* pp. 189–90.

*Jewish and Christian ancestors.* That he himself realized this is proved by an extract from one of his writings which remained unpublished until a few years ago—I had written down my own conclusions before becoming aware of this passage which seems so definitely to confirm them:

> Maybe it is typical of the age that its artists should be more conscious of the anguish of sin, yet more hopelessly enslaved to sin, than were those of an earlier time, denying their lives to the world at large, *clinging to the old standards of honor, to the moral landmarks of a period now dead,* from reasons of self-love, and because they honestly regard their own conduct as scandalous.[30]

If he made any additions of his own to the ideas which were his by inheritance, it was to urge the necessity of tolerance and charity in two realms where these virtues are generally neglected—namely, in the relations between Jews and Christians and again in the attitude of normal society towards sexual aberration. And this feeling for tolerance in Proust, because he was the offspring of the marriage of a Christian father to his mother who refused to become converted from the Jewish religion of her parents ("out of respect for them," says Proust), was present in him from his earliest childhood. He was not more than thirteen when, in answer to the question as to which virtue was his favorite, he replied: that virtue which is universal and not particular to any nation. He never changed his mind about that.

Maurois rightly says: "No matter what he might do, he never succeeded in freeing himself from the virtues which he had learned in the bosom of his family." [31] Proust puts the matter very well when he writes:

> Those who not only talk well about certain virtues but even feel their charm and understand them perfectly are often the descend-

[30] Maurois, *Proust: Portrait of a Genius,* p. 135. [31] *Ibid.,* p. 73.

ants of the mute, unpolished and artless generation which practised them. That generation is reflected but not contained in its successors. Instead of the ancestor's character, the descendants have a sensitiveness and an intelligence which do not lead to action.[32]

The aspect of the personality of Proust in which "kindness, scrupulosity, and self sacrifice" were dominant is, I think, nowhere presented so vividly as it is in the *Memoirs* of Léon Daudet. Lucien Daudet, whom I have mentioned before, was the younger son of Alphonse; Léon, the older son, was the founder, with Charles Maurras, of the reactionary political movement of the *Camelots du roi* in France. A professed anti-Semite and a bitter anti-Dreyfusard to his death almost half a century after the Case, Léon Daudet was nevertheless so good and loyal a friend to the half-Jewish Dreyfusard Proust, and so fortunate in distinguishing his literary sensitivities from his political sympathies (a feat much more possible in France than in Anglo-Saxon countries —see, for example, the curiously divided attitude of the bourgeois chemist Homais to Racine in Flaubert's *Madame Bovary*) that he was responsible for the first major recognition of Proust by the public and the first flowering of Proust's fame which came with the award of the Goncourt Prize to him in 1919. Proust recognized his debt for that triumph and repaid it in part with the dedication of *The Guermantes Way* "à l'incomparable ami, Léon Daudet, en temoignage de reconnaissance et d'admiration." The following passage was written by Daudet long before the name of Proust was known to the general public and after only *Swann's Way* had appeared. There is no suspicion attached to this reminiscence as there is to retrospective accounts of

[32] Maxim 54, *Maxims of Marcel Proust,* ed. and trans. by O'Brien.

so many great men, including Proust, that its primary impulse has been journalistic rather than purely literary, and that, in an effort to give the public what it wants or else to astonish and shock it, a confusion has sprung up in the writer's mind between the personality he is drawing as it appeared to him in life, and as it is now more widely known on the printed page, both in the writer's own work and in the memoirs of his other intimate friends. A memorialist needs an extraordinary self-control in order to be faithful to his own untutored and true impressions of his subject, when the light of publicity is beating down upon him. But here we have a sketch in advance of what Proust's whole later work amply fills out in detail.

At the very height of the political conflict in 1901, in other words in the midst of the Dreyfus Case, Proust conceived the idea of giving a dinner party with sixty guests of various shades of opinion. Every piece of china was liable to be smashed. I sat next to a charming young person, looking like a portrait by Nattier or Largillière, who, I afterwards learned, was the daughter of a prominent Jewish banker. Anatole France presided at the next table. The bitterest of enemies ate their chaud-froid within two yards of each other, for the currents of understanding and benevolence in Marcel flowed about the guests and enveloped them in coils. For the space of two hours, the greatest imaginable good-will reigned among the warriors. I doubt if anyone except Proust could have accomplished that feat. As I was complimenting the host on his achievement, he replied modestly: "But, monsieur, really, monsieur, it all depends on the first reaction to each other of the different characters." I gathered that he realized the danger of his experiment and was pleased to see it succeed.[33]

This passage is part of a larger context of description in which the key phrase "currents of understanding and benevolence" is paralleled by the sentiments: "He was clever

[33] Léon Daudet, *The Memoirs of Léon Daudet*, ed. by Arthur Kingsland Griggs (New York, 1925), p. 267.

in finding excuses for his good nature," "He was devoured by ironic scruples," and, in language reminiscent of Proust's own about Bergotte, "the obligations into which his excessive kindness and friendliness would lead him." This was written by Daudet long before the publication of *The Captive.*

That famous dinner party at the time of the Dreyfus Case was something more than a quixotic or isolated gesture on the part of Proust. Daudet's analysis of his friend's good nature has many confirmations from Proust's other friends. Stephen Hudson, for instance, quotes a letter written to him by Proust in which he defines a beautiful book as one which "brings harmony among scattered spirits and peace to troubled hearts." [34] Shakespeare was termed gentle by his contemporaries, and the same adjective I think may apply to Proust as well. He was a man who felt intensely hurt by the spectacle of spiritual conflict, perhaps because the split in his own sex and race disposed him to identify himself with both sides. How could men of good will, all of whom were friends of his, be mortally opposed to each other on the issue of the Dreyfus Case? Was it not due to some terrible misunderstanding which could be cleared up at once if only the antagonists, instead of being left to their own devices among their own parties writing tirades against each other, could somehow be brought out into the open, face to face with each other? That is how Proust must have reasoned in giving that dangerous dinner party at which all the dishes might have been smashed. In troubled times of brutal and irreconcilable conflict, men of extraordinary generosity of spirit have always dreamed such dreams of making peace.

His insatiable desire to bring together bitter foes, who

[34] Lindner, *Marcel Proust—Reviews and Estimates,* pp. 10–11.

were each separately friends of his, in order that they might be able to see their essential unity and agreement with each other, extends even to the dead! He admired the work of both Ruskin and Whistler, who, as we know, were not only at critical odds with each other but at odds in the law courts as well and so, in a letter to Marie Nordlinger, he undertakes to prove that, underneath superficial appearances, the two men had far more in common with each other than they ever realized.[35] In the same vein, it is interesting to read his letter to Robert de Billy in which he says that he knows of Ruskin's dislike of one of his own favorite books, George Eliot's *Mill on the Floss*, "but I reconcile all of these warring deities in the Pantheon of my admiration." [36] He, who was so little given to boasting or self-display, nevertheless boasted to Gide on one occasion of his almost magical power of reconciling estranged friends and making peace among the most formidable adversaries—namely, those who are lovers! [37]

I don't think that it has ever been properly noted in Proustian criticism before that his sense of loss during the First World War, that almost unbearable pain in him to which Lucien Daudet, Mme Scheikévitch, and other intimate friends have testified, was due to this fact above all—that the war conclusively demonstrated to him what the Dreyfus Case had already made him suspect: certain conflicts between men, though irrational in origin (or, perhaps we ought to say just because they are not of rational origin), are unavoidable and can apparently only be settled by a

[35] *Letters of Proust,* ed. by Curtiss. See letter to Marie Nordlinger in 1903, p. 93, and to the same correspondent in 1905, p. 104.

[36] *Cahiers de Marcel Proust* (Paris, 1927), I, 32.

[37] Marcel Proust, *Lettres à Gide,* p. 28. In the same vein, see also Louis de Robert, *De Loti à Proust* (Paris, 1928), pp. 176–77.

resort to violence. It was a shocking solution for Proust to have to admit, for if there were irreconcilable antagonisms in the world, perhaps there were some also in the individual. Proust hated the idea of conflict with an uncommon strength, but he also felt it to be his duty to endure it when it came against his will. He did not try to maintain a neutral pose above the battle between good and evil. It was his boast to the end of his life that he had been one of the first Dreyfusards, and this in spite of his social ambitions which such a view did not help, and, more important from a personal angle, that his father did not share his views—in *Remembrance of Things Past,* the father of the narrator did not speak to his son for a week after finding out that he had signed a petition asking for a reopening of the case.

To his friend Montesquiou, Proust wrote at this time: "I did not answer the question you asked me yesterday about the Jews. The reason is very simple; while I am Catholic like my father and brother, my mother is, on the contrary, Jewish." [38] For Montesquiou apparently, Proust was tainted in the purity of his French patriotism, as he would have been for the character Charlus in his story, by belonging to the Jewish *nation* on his mother's side. His answer to Montesquiou is certainly the reflection of something that is deeply true for himself. His answer, by which he confined himself to the question of religion, was not perhaps the one which Montesquiou was seeking, but it was the only one which Proust thought he had a right to expect. Yet we must be clear about one thing—if Proust became a partisan of Dreyfus, it was not out of respect for his Jewish mother, but out of his respect for the truth. That Mme Proust, who was born Mlle Weil, reproduced herself very strongly in her older son,

[38] *Letters of Proust,* ed. by Curtiss, p. 45.

every writer on the subject admits. It is this which leads to the ambiguity of his sex as well as to his sensitivity relating to everything concerning the Jews. Proust regularly visited the graves of his ancestors who were buried in the old Jewish cemetery, and when he became so ill that he could no longer do so, he expressed regret that no one would be left to perform this act of filial devotion.[39] Apparently, then, his brother Robert, who was always the healthier one and survived Marcel by many years, did not take part in these excursions. It was from a letter to Mme de Noailles that I quoted Proust's phrase about his mother earlier—a very interesting and important letter in which he tells his friend that "when she married father, [she] did not change from the Jewish religion because in it she saw a refinement of respect for her parents." [40]

It was Proust's misfortune as a man and his good fortune as a moralist that he was born out of a Jewish-Christian marriage into a generation when these two parts of the world around him as well as of his own personality were in the most bitter opposition to each other. He attempted to solve his problem not as stronger and perhaps more ruthless people do, by forcibly subordinating one of the recalcitrant factions to the other, but by doing his best to reconcile them and to make peace between them, and, if unable to do that, at least to find a tolerable modus vivendi. In 1917, Proust could say with a clear conscience that his friend Montesquiou is "perhaps the only person towards whom *my will to peace* fails." [41]

When a man acts on the assumption that the world is only

[39] That Proust regularly visited the graves of his Jewish ancestors is one of the significant facts about him noted by Maurois.

[40] *Letters of Proust,* ed. by Curtiss, p. 132. [41] *Ibid.,* p. 299. Italics mine.

a larger edition of himself, he is only doing what is natural. Proust is part of a long tradition when he tries to break down a large social entity like the nation into its component individual parts. He was himself a man torn asunder by conflicts (which would be quite sufficient to explain why, as Léon Daudet wrote, he was "always tired"), very much troubled by his mixed origin and his confused sex. In the novel, the narrator is always desiring to be what he is not and where he is not—a romantic in the sense in which Lawrence defined the term as one who was "homesick for somewhere else." Proust insists upon the necessity of evaluating each man for what he is in himself instead of arbitrarily treating him as a simple unit of a social group, a certain nation or class.

In his books, the Dreyfus Case serves Proust as a prism with which to break down the complex and undifferentiated light of French society into the chromatic nuances of an immense collection of unique individuals. How deeply disturbed Proust was by the famous case is shown vividly in his letter to Mme Straus in 1906 in which he writes: "To think that this could have happened a few years ago in France and not among the apaches. The contrast that exists on the one hand between the culture, the intellectual distinction, and even the glitter of the uniforms of these people and their moral infamy on the other is frightening." [42] Not only does he show how French society as a whole is refracted into the groupings of Jews and Gentiles, Dreyfusards and anti-Dreyfusards (it is not repetitive to use the two sets of terms, for, as I shall show, they were not necessarily synonymous), but he shows how these groups themselves are fur-

[42] *Ibid.*, p. 146.

ther broken down into persons who are almost as far removed from each other spiritually as they are from the units of the opposing side.

Proust exhaustively treats all the variations of his subject. He shows us Jews who are rabid anti-Semites on one occasion and hysterically defensive about their Jewish heritage on another occasion. He shows us anti-Semites who are nevertheless Dreyfusards—in which, as I shall demonstrate, he was only borrowing from the endless contradictions of life itself.

Swann, Bloch, and Rachel are the most minutely portrayed of Proust's Jewish characters, and the three are very different from each other. Swann, the son of a very rich stockbroker, is, when we first see him at the beginning of the book, an aesthete of infinite delicacy of taste and tact. He is a member of the Jockey Club, the most exclusive aristocratic club in Paris, and a frequenter of the most brilliant society. His artistic tastes center about painting, and particularly about the Dutch painter Vermeer. Swann is a recognized authority on the art as well as a patron of it. We are told indirectly that he is consulted by museums about the authenticity of certain masterpieces and that his name appears in the newspapers (where it is noticed by the narrator's family) as the donor of pictures from his private collection to public exhibitions. At the beginning of the novel, neither he nor anyone else seems to be particularly conscious of the fact that he is a Jew at all. Even the narrator's grandfather, who, we are informed, used to resent the fact that his grandson had a special predilection for choosing Jewish friends, does not seem to think of "young Swann" as a Jew. The grandfather of the narrator seems to have been the friend of Swann's father, about whom he likes to tell stories. Evidently we have in Swann the picture of a French Jew whose family is so old and assimilated to French culture that not even those people ordinarily conscious of differences would make a distinction between him and any other Frenchmen. One of the other characters in the book, though we are left uncertain as to how reliable her information is, says that Swann is a convert and the son and grandson of converts, but these Jews, she adds, as everyone knows, are "the worst of all." [43]

If Swann is one of Proust's most sympathetic and agreeable characters, Bloch, on the contrary, is made offensive to us from the moment of his first appearance on the scene. He is a malicious gossip, a show-off, an insincere and affected pedant. He does not seem at the beginning to be self-consciously Jewish, but he arouses the suspicions and hostility of the narrator's grandfather at once. One of the most comic scenes of the book occurs at Balbec during a walk taken by the narrator and his friend Saint-Loup. They are shocked to overhear a virulent anti-Semitic tirade coming from an unseen person indoors. They await the emergence of the ferocious Jew-eater, and it turns out to be Bloch, who is now shown to us in the midst of a very compact and standoffish group of Jews—his family and their friends. Bloch is evidently not as much assimilated to French culture as Swann, though he wants to be, because it is French and classical culture, rather than anything specifically Jewish, which interests him most. His anti-Semitic sentiments, of course, are not really sincere; they are part of his whole awkward pattern of trying to identify himself with the dominant social group to which he aspires eventually to belong as unmistakably as Swann does.

[43] *Swann's Way*, pp. 433–34.

The third character, Rachel, who is nicknamed by the narrator in the manner of his grandfather "When from the Lord" after the famous aria from *La Juive,* is Jewish too, but much more important to an understanding of her actions are the facts that she is both a prostitute and an actress. As a specimen of humanity, in other words, Rachel stands very low indeed. She puts success in her art above every consideration of morality in life; she even puts it above money or social position. She appears to be a monomaniac with fame as her obsession. It is not because she has any genuine convictions but because she is really wicked that she makes a Dreyfusard out of her lover, Saint-Loup, estranges him from his aristocratic family, introduces him into the bohemian circles she is a part of where, because of his background, he is treated with contempt, and finally, after having almost ruined him financially and in every other way, abandons him.

Of these three, Swann, who is by far the noblest and the furthest removed from his own Jewish source, is the hardest hit by the Dreyfus Case. Something very deep within him is touched, though Proust emphasizes that it is not his sense of justice. From the extreme of not being conscious of any anti-Semitism at all in society, he goes to the opposite extreme of seeing it everywhere. He makes the blanket generalization to the narrator that the whole Faubourg Saint-Germain is against Dreyfus, because it is and always has been completely anti-Semitic, and he says this in spite of the most signal exceptions (such as that of the Prince de Guermantes of whom I shall speak later on) which obtrude themselves on his notice. Now in making such a false generalization, Swann, in the eyes of Proust and of his reader, is acting no differently from an anti-

Semite like Charlus, who says that all Jews are for Dreyfus because they always stick together and are a separate and alien nation in the midst of France. It is Charlus, we remember, who announces the precious discovery that Dreyfus *couldn't* have committed treason, as he was charged with doing, because it was Judea that was really his nation; towards France, he was guilty at most of a "breach of hospitality." [44] This kind of perverted humor is perfectly characteristic of Charlus, who, as in all other things, is capable of raising his antipathies to the heights of satirical fantasies.

Swann seems to suffer from a sudden, almost inexplicable reaction. Proust, as he reveals on many occasions in his book, believed almost mystically in the importance of heredity, and in Swann he seems to discover a belated return to his Hebraic ancestors. Swann is punished for the long suppression of the truth about himself by the heart-rending discovery that some of his best friends in life have been anti-Semites all the while. Even Odette, Swann's wife, is an anti-Dreyfusard and owes her rise into society principally, it seems, to this qualification, for she lacks any other.

Proust shows that most Frenchmen, like Swann, lined up on one side of the Case or the other, because, as he puts it, there are "unsuspected depths" (unsuspected, that is, even to those who have these qualities) of "Jewish patriotism" and of "Christian atavism." [45] He knew human nature well enough to recognize that the ordinary man was too lazy, too much a creature of habit and herd organization, too little conscientious and scrupulously truthful, to investigate such a specific and important question as Dreyfus presented for

[44] *The Guermantes Way,* Part 1, pp. 396 ff.
[45] *Within a Budding Grove,* Part 2, p. 266.

himself. Each man went along with his crowd—he was either liberal or reactionary, Catholic or anticlerical—and few were brave or adequate enough morally to make a deliberate effort to judge the facts for themselves and to adhere strictly to their independent findings. The worst example of conformity represented in the book is that of the most brutal character who can be found in its pages, the Duc de Guermantes. On the other hand, to show us how close extremes lie to each other, the most independent and conscientious attitude in the book is to be found in the Duc's brother, the Prince de Guermantes.

The Duc is automatically against Dreyfus, because he feels that that is what his position in society requires of him. He does not investigate the issues, he does not hesitate for a moment, he has no sensitivity to the question of justice. What he is capable of in human relations is revealed clearly in his callous reception of Swann's casual announcement of his fatal disease. The Duc torments his wife with his innumerable infidelities. He is, generally speaking, more common than a donkey driver. His only absorbing interest in life seems to be women. The final irony about him, such as only Proust seems capable of inventing, is that eventually, he too becomes a Dreyfusard! Not because of the promptings of conscience, but because, at a well-known watering place to which he had gone for his health, he met three noble ladies, who were all Dreyfusards. This coincidence convinces him, by the irrefutable arguments of both social rank and sex, that Dreyfusism, which he had previously regarded as an opinion held jointly by Jews and the riffraff of society, is in reality not merely a respectable opinion but even a smart one! Neither in his anti-Dreyfusism nor in his change-over did it occur to the Duc that he might think for himself, or think of the individual man, who might have become the victim of injustice.

The Prince de Guermantes, on the other hand, is one who neither makes up his mind by the expectations of his social class, nor perversely moves against it. It does not occur to him that certain views in such a matter are or are not *smart*. He strives instead to arrive conscientiously at a decision based on the truth according to his light. He regrets that he cannot agree with other members of his family and with most of his friends that Dreyfus is guilty. Scruples keep the Prince awake all night thinking about the case and lead him to ask his priest (who is himself, by the way, secretly convinced of the innocence of Dreyfus) to say Masses for the innocent prisoner and his unhappy family.[46] Caught between his class and his conscience, he keeps his unorthodox opinions to himself and reveals them (aside from his confessor) to only one other person, his friend at school, Swann, who, according to the malicious society gossip of those unaware of the Prince's real feelings, is being turned like a dog out of the house. There is an ironic note ending the Prince's story too. He has concealed his views (as I have indicated) even from his family, from his own wife, only to discover by accident eventually that she, too, being evidently a match for her husband, has been subscribing secretly to *L'Aurore*, the Dreyfusard paper, and has been afraid to worry him by sharing her convictions with him! So we see Proust weaving his ethical commentary together with strands of ironic humor, all of which seem to have one purpose—to reveal the existence of conscientious people

[46] *Cities of the Plain*, Part 1, pp. 151 ff.

and of conscienceless ones, to show the sharp contrast of the thoughtful and the thoughtless, the sensitive and the insensitive.

The Prince de Guermantes seems essentially more admirable than Swann, because he alone has made up his mind on the basis of the truth. Swann had been motivated by his outraged Jewish feelings, and had been precipitated into all sorts of conclusions, which, in their own way, were as absurd as those of the anti-Semites.

Even stranger than the case of the Prince is that of Mme Sazerat, the Combray neighbor of the narrator's family, who is at the same time an anti-Semite and a Dreyfusard! [47] If it is objected that this is simply too wild a fiction of Proust's, let us turn to the actual story of the French novelist, Octave Mirbeau. That bitter satirist, the author of *The Diary of a Chambermaid,* was, as Léon Daudet describes him, an anti-Semite; but he was also, it seems, a conscientious man, and when he was confronted with an indictment not of the Jews in general but of one in particular, and that on the obviously hypocritical ground that he was a German spy, Mirbeau's conscience rebelled. And he became a Dreyfusard, says Daudet, without ceasing to be an anti-Semite, and was absolutely furious to find himself ranged on the side of so many Jews. The heat of the time in politics is conveyed clearly by a brief exchange that took place between Daudet and Mirbeau at the height of the tension in which Mirbeau said to him simply: "A Nationalist is a murderer!" Such anti-Semitic feelings as we find in Mme Sazerat or in Mirbeau or in the narrator's own grandfather must have led Proust to think of anti-Semitism as a foible, "one of those little weaknesses, one of those irrational preju-

[47] *The Guermantes Way,* Part 1, pp. 397 ff.

dices, that one so often finds in upright and noble-minded persons—in fact, more often in them than in others." [48] But Proust finally rejected this passage from the pages of the novel itself, perhaps because he did not wish to extenuate a feeling which he certainly did not condone.

The great virtue of Proust seems to me to be that he shows us how complex such social issues as that which the Dreyfus Case presented really are, how painfully difficult it is to arrive at the truth. Blanket judgments of groups are bound to be coarse and incorrect. And politics, as has been noted often before by others, makes the strangest bedfellows. Each individual, says Proust, must be judged for what he is in himself, and not simply by the company which he keeps—the company is often deceptive as a key to the individual. Still less reliable is a judgment based upon the company into which a man was born, or, for various reasons, may be forced to cultivate.

The Dreyfus Case is an ideal symbol of the value of tolerance in arriving at the truth. At its heart is an individual who was accused of a definite crime, not of belonging to a certain group. He protests his personal innocence but is not believed. Even the weightiest evidence on his side is ignored until it must become evident to objective observers (but how many are there of these?) that the original accusation was not meant seriously, that the real indictment was based on facts kept carefully concealed—perhaps even by the judges from themselves! Here, in a word, is a classic instance of the evil bound to arise from a blanket judgment based upon intolerance.

According to Proust's line of reasoning, Dreyfus as an individual might have been guilty as charged. Certainly

[48] Maurois, *Proust: Portrait of a Genius,* p. 152.

he discovers meanness, weakness, and corruption enough among the Jews he analyzes (he could have agreed with Mark Twain, who said that the Jews were *human*, which was the worst thing that anyone could say of them!), yet this does not answer the question as to whether Dreyfus, the individual, *is* in actual fact guilty. Investigation of the facts made Proust himself a Dreyfusard. In his novel, he says that Joseph Reinach, during the Dreyfus Case, won "the most astonishing victory for rational policy . . . the world has ever seen." [49] And in a letter to Mme Straus, he says of Reinach that he is "the most enviable man I know for the good he has desired and achieved." [50] But this did not blind him to the faults of his own side as well as those of the other. On both sides, he saw men who made up their minds on the basis of irrelevant and irrational prejudices, the Dreyfusards could perhaps claim a factual correctness, but many of them were not any more moral (that is to say, scrupulously truthful) than their adversaries.

Certainly Bloch's Dreyfusism is not any better than the Duc de Guermantes' opposing views, because both of these men loved themselves most of all. They were concerned with their own comforts more than they were with the truth. Ultimately, it is only the love of truth that is admirable to Proust. A party member or a nationalist may be on the side of truth at a given moment when it suits his political convenience, but he cannot be trusted, by such a criterion, because his motivations are not pure.

Bloch, during the Case, along with other young intellectuals, spent whole days in the courtroom, bringing lunch, and in the evening adjourned to the café where they could

[49] *The Guermantes Way*, Part 1, p. 406.
[50] *Letters of Proust*, ed. by Curtiss, p. 154.

relive every moment of the trial. When it comes to such a mean, graceless, and unprincipled character as Bloch, the reader feels sure that the agreement of his views with the truth is entirely accidental. The Case simply presents to him an opportunity to better his intellectual fortunes, to reverse the whole social order perhaps. The last thing in the world that Bloch is concerned with is that which is most troublesome to the conscientious Prince de Guermantes—namely, the personal fate of Dreyfus and the human sufferings of his family. Proust shows us in the Dreyfus Case and later on in the war how social misfortunes are the lucky harvest seasons of the selfish and unscrupulous. To Mme Verdurin, for example, the importance of a Dreyfus Case or of a war is measured by the additions it can make to the brilliance of her drawing room. To Rachel, as I've pointed out before, the Dreyfus Case was only another means of tormenting her lover, Saint-Loup, by taunting him with the unenlightened and supposedly "cruel" views of his mother, Mme de Marsantes. Rachel might well have been an authority on cruelty. Her taking the side of Dreyfus is simply the consequence of her presence in an intellectual milieu where such a view is fashionable and perhaps of her being born a Jewess, but she cancels out any moral credit she might have had for being on the side of the truth by the way she uses that truth as a weapon against her unfortunate lover.

An interesting example of Proust's meticulous consideration of his characters as individuals is afforded by the delineation of Charlus. The anti-Semitism and anti-Dreyfusism of Charlus are by no means the same as the qualities we see in the Duc de Guermantes. If the views of the Duc were the result of callousness, in Charlus they were the result of perhaps excessive sensitivity perversely expressed. Charlus is so much a pariah himself because of his abnormal sexual tastes that he is very happy to find another pariah on whom he can vent his spite. This is not creditable morally in Proust's eyes, to be sure, but it is understandable and insofar as it is understandable a little forgivable.

Proust, I would say, is Jewish to the extent to which he stresses the sacred importance of the individual against the group, but he is Christian in that respect too, for, as regards individualism, Jewish and Christian ethics merge with each other. What he definitely is not, in his moral outlook, is statistically scientific in any characteristic modern manner. When the sages of the Talmud forbade the conviction upon circumstantial evidence alone of a man covered with blood who is seen coming out of a cellar containing a dead body, they were concerned with letting ninety-nine guilty murderers go free rather than make one poor innocent suffer. But modern social systems which are prepared to destroy a hundred individuals for the sake of punishing only a single guilty one among them proceed on another assumption—namely, that the welfare of the group is everything and the rights of the individual nothing. And in this view, they are more up-to-date and efficient, it must be admitted, than the sages of the Talmud or than Proust. We must judge all people as individuals and all issues on the basis of truth—that is the simple and old-fashioned morality which I find in Proust. When, later on, the Dreyfusards, flushed with victory, began to attack the Church as a whole, Proust rose to its defense in very much the same spirit as he had risen to defend Dreyfus. He remained extraordinarily clear-sighted and truth-seeking in the most confused and difficult circumstances. He was without feeling for any particular party, but always took the side of tolerance and of truth.

Here is how he answered, in a letter, the anticlerical arguments of his friend Georges de Lauris:

> In the first place, it is only too clear that everything we find detestable about clericalism—first of all, antisemitism, or, for that matter, clericalism itself—is wholly distinct from Catholic dogma and Catholic faith. Alphonse Humbert, Cavaignac, radical antisemites, seem to me a breed that must not be allowed to multiply. And the priests, not necessarily the Dreyfusards but the tolerant ones, seem to me tolerable only insofar as they themselves are tolerant.[51]

Toleration is, of course, a time-honored position to take with reference to the Jews since the Enlightenment. It will be difficult for the ordinary reader, however, to follow Proust when he extends his discussion to cover the subject of sexual deviation. And there is no doubt that there is a hint of special pleading in the rhetorical devices by which Proust assimilates the situation of the homosexual to that of the Jew. Both are to him members of a despised race. They are both born that way—Proust affirms this many times—and they are punished by the majority for being what they cannot help being. The stigma upon the homosexual imposes upon him the characteristics of the pariah, no matter what other qualities or social advantages he may possess. When the narrator sees the Baron de Charlus eyeing him furtively while pretending to read a sign in a railway station, he takes the illustrious nobleman to be a burglar.

The importance of this aspect of Proust's work can hardly be overestimated. It is literally and figuratively very close to his heart. It has in fact been shown that the genesis of the immense work lay in his resolve to write an article for *Figaro* in 1907, dealing with a recently exposed scandal in

[51] *Ibid.*, pp. 77–78.

the court of the Emperor Wilhelm II about the abnormal tastes of some prominent men there.

There is no doubt that Proust was very worried about the reception of his frank discussion, and he thought it likely that he would offend the homosexuals themselves as much as he did the rest of society. The homosexuals would accuse him of excessive objectivity, detachment, and perhaps roguish satire, while the majority would find him guilty of partiality and self-defensive rationalizations. He briefly introduced the theme of homosexuality in the first volume of the work (though the brevity did not prevent him from receiving some frightened and outraged religious protests), but he postponed the full exposition of that theme as long as he could, and after finally venturing upon it in the volumes which are translated into English as *Cities of the Plain,* he did not survive their publication by a year and left the rest of his work to be published from his rough drafts after his death. He was worried, too, towards the end for much the same reasons about the coming publication of the posthumous memoirs of his patron, Robert de Montesquiou (though these memoirs which might have provoked a major scandal proved to be a dud).

Proust was certainly not exaggerating in his fear of the average reader's reaction to the discussion of such a subject as homosexuality when he felt that it was likely to be as instinctive, as irrational, and as uncomprehending as his reaction to any other foreign element in his environment. The unprepared reader may utterly fail to respond, in his first shock at the revelation of Proust's subject, to the poignant cry for understanding which is uttered in his pages. Proust's attitude towards some of the greatest sufferers in our civilization (namely, those who suffer from some cruel form of sexual maladjustment—I have always thought Krafft-Ebing the modern equivalent of Dante's *Inferno*) is very complex, but certainly one of its chief components is such a pity as has come to seem unsophisticated and unfashionable in this age. So that Proust himself, conscious of the desert of feeling about him, clothes his pity in humor and irony, but in spite of these disguises it comes home strongly to our heart. The rolling periods of his invocation of justice and fellow-feeling almost have the tone of an ancient bard, Proust being much more primitive in his artistry than he generally is:

Race upon which a curse weighs and which must live amid falsehood and perjury, because it knows the world to regard as a punishable and a scandalous, as an inadmissible thing, its desire, that which constitutes for every human creature the greatest happiness in life, which must deny its God, since even Christians, when at the bar of justice they appear and are arraigned, must before Christ and in his Name defend themselves, as from a calumny, from the charge of what to them is life itself; sons without a mother, to whom they are obliged to lie all her life long and even in the hour when they close her dying eyes, friends without friendships, despite all those which their charm, frequently recognized, inspires, and their hearts, often generous, would gladly feel; but can we describe as friendship those relations which flourish only by virtue of a lie and from which the first outburst of confidence and sincerity in which they might be tempted to indulge would make them expelled with disgust, unless they are dealing with an impartial, that is to say a sympathetic mind, which however in that case, misled with regard to them by a conventional psychology, will suppose to spring from the vice confessed the very affection that is most alien to it, just as certain judges assume and are more inclined to pardon murder in inverts and treason in Jews for reasons derived from original sin and racial predestination.[52]

Proust distinguishes almost as many different varieties of homosexuals as he had Jews. And he makes us aware how,

[52] *Cities of the Plain,* Part 1, pp. 20 ff.

in both groups, it is the pressures which the world has exerted upon them that has made them very largely as we find them. Homosexuals are caricatures of normal lovers. The difficulty has arisen from the vindictiveness of a majority against a minority.

So great is Proust's pity that those who come upon it for the first time must think it somewhat melodramatic, hysterical, overstated, almost a little satirical. But though there is undoubtedly irony in Proust's description, it is as much at the expense of the world as of those who are at odds with it—more, if anything, at the expense of the world; for the world is large and comfortable and self-confident, while its victims feel themselves small, persecuted, and easily confounded and abashed. Dante felt compassion even for some of the undoubted sinners of the underworld, but Proust feels uncertain as to whether the tortures visited upon these aberrant lovers are indeed a just retribution for their vices. He never uses the word "vice" in connection with homosexuality without the equivalent of quotation marks or of italics, without gratifying it and softening its sting by adding some such parenthetical expression as "if we can call it such" or "we use the term for convenience only." In other words, while making no explicit apologies for his inverted characters, and perhaps implicitly condemning them by the use of the names of Sodom and Gomorrah to describe their society, Proust makes the world ashamed for the harm it has done to those people who, if they are not completely harmless, are at least defenseless.

Their honor precarious, their liberty provisional, lasting only until the discovery of their crime, their position unstable, like that of the poet who one day was feasted at every table, applauded in every theater in London, and on the next was driven from every lodging, unable to find a pillow upon which to lay his head . . . excluded even, save on the day of general disaster when the majority rally round the victim as the Jews rallied round Dreyfus, from the sympathy—at times from the society—of their fellows, in whom they inspire only disgust at seeing themselves as they are . . . like the Jews again (save some who will associate only with others of their race and have always on their lips ritual words and consecrated pleasantries), shunning one another, seeking out those who are most directly their opposite, who do not desire their company, pardoning their rebuffs, moved to ecstasy by their condescension; but also brought into the company of their own kind by the ostracism that strikes them, the opprobrium under which they have fallen, having finally been invested, by a persecution similar to that of Israel, with the physical and moral characteristics of a race, sometimes beautiful, often hideous . . .[53]

Just as Proust had differentiated between the character of a Jew like Bloch on the one hand and that of Swann on the other, so he shows us sharp contrasts in the characters of his inverts too. On one side of the picture we have people like Legrandin and Morel, on the other side, Charlus and Jupien. As important in the personality of Legrandin as his homosexuality is his snobbery, which, from the very beginning, repels the narrator's mother. More important to an understanding of Morel than his obvious vice is the fact that, like Rachel, he is a careerist, cruel and ungrateful to anyone who stands in his way. As for Jupien, he is, in spite of his "profession" of tailoring, so educated and gentle a man that he draws the commendation of the narrator's grandmother, who is the exemplar and criterion of all virtue in the book. Finally, Charlus tries indeed to give to the uninitiated the impression of harshness and cruelty, but beneath this guise, as the narrator observes, he is all kindness and considerateness. So that, though there is a strong in-

[53] *Ibid.*, p. 21.

fusion of irony in the following remark which Françoise makes about Charlus, we feel that basically her judgment of him is not awry: "Oh, he's such a good man, the Baron, such a well-behaved, religious, proper sort of man. If I had a daughter to marry and was one of the rich myself, I would give her to the Baron with my eyes shut." [54] At that point of the story, the reader remembers that, though Mme Charlus is a legend throughout the book, her husband had been good to her while she was alive, and had enshrined her memory after her death. Charlus says in one place: "I have lost my wife, who was the loveliest, the noblest, the most perfect creature that one could dream of seeing." [55] We hear of his visiting her grave every day! For apparently the Baron, like most of the other homosexuals in the book, did not know of his "vocation" from the beginning. He is *caught* in it by Proust's narrative, as by a candid camera, but he may have taken as long to come to a full realization of his own nature as his nephew Saint-Loup does in the course of the narrative. "For no one," says Proust, "can tell at first that he is an invert or a poet or a snob or a scoundrel." [56]

There are two morals which can be drawn from this ignorance. The first is that no one can be really sure of his own nature, and consequently he ought to treat others as he himself would like to be treated if he were in their place.[57] If only Saint-Loup had felt this way, he would not have been

[54] *Ibid.*, p. 43. [55] *The Guermantes Way*, Part 1, p. 400.

[56] *Cities of the Plain*, Part 1, p. 33.

[57] Charlus invents some seemingly strange statistics on the prevalence of inversion in society. According to him, all but 30 per cent of the population is tainted one way or another by this vice (*The Captive*, p. 402). Brichot is amazed by this and says that even if the Baron's figures were reversed—that is to say if only 30 per cent of society instead of 70 per cent was homosexual, the Baron would still rank as a great scientific discoverer and force us to revise all of our estimates upwards. The latter figure (30 per cent) is actually that of Kinsey!

so ready to beat those unfortunate young men who, while he himself was still in normal relations with Rachel, were attracted by his beauty and made proposals to him which he regarded as deliberate insults.

The other moral to be read is that, though a man is more than one thing at one time, we must not assume that there is a causal connection between his different characters. One who is ready to make prejudiced, hasty, and unjustified generalizations may find a homosexual who is a scoundrel, or a Jew like Bloch who is base, and he will conclude that these different characteristics are part of a single pattern. Proust, therefore, shows us members of each group who are base and who are noble, who are scoundrels and who are honorable men.

It may be said that in general Proust fragments those vast terms which society adopts for mnemonic convenience, and displays the minute, disparate, sometimes contradictory particles of which the large and seemingly unified entities are actually composed. In this sense, he is like the oculist to whom Gide compared him (a comparison which Proust found so satisfactory, it seems, that he incorporated it into the last volume of his own work) who, by his treatment, enabled a patient to see for the first time the tiny pebbles of which the courtyard was actually composed, she having assumed until then that it was made of large blocks of uniform stone.

He shows us homosexuals who are proud of themselves and wear bracelets and rouge and take pleasure in outraging the feelings of conventional people and who try to win over others to their own practice with a kind of missionary zeal. Far from recognizing their own state as unredeemed, they think that there is something especially beautiful and redemptive about it. What the rest regard as a brand of infamy is to them the mark of an elite. He shows us other homosexuals who are ashamed of themselves and do their best to disguise their tastes, who go to the trouble of changing the sex of their beloved in ordinary conversation, in order to bring themselves into line with accepted usage, who would deny under torture that they are what they are. He shows us homosexuals who form little societies like music clubs and yachting clubs, while others retire into the solitude of the desert as soon as they discover themselves. Proust calls homosexuality an "incurable malady,"[58] and therefore seems to think them entitled, like other invalids, if not to our respect then at least to our sympathy.

And, in truth, Proust has done, I think, an enormous amount of good in bringing about a greater understanding and consequently a greater forgiveness (if, that is, we are so bold as to think that those who are different from ourselves are in need of *our* forgiveness) into the consideration of this subject which, barely half a century ago in most of the world and still, to this day, in many parts of the world, is regarded as being in the province of the law rather than of medicine. Proust has done more for the toleration of the outcast group than did Gide, who was a confessed member of it himself. A confession like Gide's arouses emotions, while a reasonable and sympathetic analysis like Proust's appeals to the heart through the intellect.

Proust's analytic scalpel enables him to find goodness under the appearance of evil, and real evil, on the contrary, under the appearance of goodness. Mlle Vinteuil and Charlus are better than they seem, Bloch and Legrandin not nearly so good. The theme of homosexuality is introduced

[58] *Cities of the Plain*, Part 1, p. 22.

in a few startling pages of the opening volume, though it is not greatly developed until much later in the book. The narrator, while still a boy, accidentally witnesses a shameful scene between a neighbor, Mlle Vinteuil, and her Lesbian friend. It is as sadistic, as shocking, and as melodramatic a scene as can be imagined, and some religious admirers of Proust, like the poet Francis Jammes, begged him to cut it out of his book—which was like asking him to remove one of its corner stones, for that scene has a most important role to play in the architecture of the work as a whole, as he pointed out to his well-meaning critics. After the death of her great father, which was due perhaps in part at least to the anguish which she caused him, Mlle Vinteuil lives in unconcealed intimacy with her female friend, and, since she can no longer abuse her dead father directly, she vindictively pursues his image. As part of the erotic ritual, her friend has to take down a picture of Mlle Vinteuil's father and outrage it. The boy who witnesses the scene is struck with horror: "I knew now what was the reward that M. Vinteuil, in return for all the suffering he had endured in his lifetime, on account of his daughter, had received from her after his death." [59]

But just where an inferior moralist would have stopped, Proust doubles back upon his own track and exposes the superficiality of the picture he has composed: "And yet I have since reflected that if Vinteuil had been able to be present at this scene, he might still, and in spite of everything, have continued to believe in his daughter's soundness of heart, and that he might even, in so doing, not have been altogether wrong." [60]

Proust continues this discussion with what is really a

[59] *Swann's Way*, p. 210. [60] *Ibid.*

remarkable insight into the connection between an excessively repressed, Puritanical upbringing and the appearance of perversion later in life. Puritanism and perversion are to Proust different sides of the same medal:

> "Sadists" of Mlle. Vinteuil's sort are creatures so purely sentimental, so virtuous by nature, that even sensual pleasure appears to them as something bad, a privilege reserved for the wicked. And when they allow themselves for a moment to enjoy it they endeavor to impersonate, to assume all the outward appearance of wicked people, for themselves and their partners in guilt, so as to gain the momentary illusion of having escaped beyond the control of their own gentle and scrupulous natures into the inhuman world of pleasure.[61]

The same reflection essentially occurs when Proust writes concerning his character Bergotte: "There may be vice arising from supersensitiveness just as much as from lack of it." [62]

Turning the idea he had gotten while speaking of Mlle Vinteuil about and about, as is his habit, Proust sees ever new lights glancing off from it:

> It was not evil that gave her the idea of pleasure, that seemed to her attractive, it was pleasure, rather, that seemed evil. And as, every time she indulged in it, pleasure came to her attended by evil thoughts such as, ordinarily, had no place in her virtuous mind, she came at length to see in pleasure itself something diabolical, to identify it with Evil.[63]

The contradictions of appearance and reality are still further complicated for the moralist by the innumerable contradictions within the character himself—that is to say, no one can be considered wholly good or bad, and not only must people be evaluated individually, but even their in-

[61] *Ibid.*, p. 211. [62] *Within a Budding Grove*, Part 2, p. 186.
[63] *Swann's Way*, p. 212.

dividual actions must be weighed in themselves. A basically vicious character in Proust's pages is capable of one magnificently virtuous action which, even if it does not destroy the memory of what has gone before, still has to be adequately credited.

The most remarkable inconsistency of this kind which occurs to me is in the character of the Verdurins. They had never been remarkable for their disinterestedness or generosity. Quite the contrary. They had tried once to break up the love affair between Swann and Odette; later, they actually succeeded in destroying that of Charlus and Morel. The Verdurins are ruthless to whoever stands in the way of their social ambitions. But nowhere does their inherent coarseness appear more blatantly than in their attitude towards their relative Saniette. They conspire with the most insensitive of their guests, like Forcheville, to humiliate the already humble Saniette, to persecute him with their miserable jests, to disconcert him on occasion to the point of tears. They even encourage the servants to be rude to him. And Saniette is helpless before them; he is too gentle himself to retaliate or to reproach them tacitly even by refusing to return for more punishment. Later on in the story, however, Saniette loses his fortune, and then the narrator learns accidentally (for to their good deed has been added the virtue of silence about it) that the Verdurins have relieved his want and settled a sufficient income upon him. Certainly this compensation does not completely relieve them of their burden of guilt towards him. In fact, it is this ray of light which makes the rest of their darkness visible. But the light is genuine. Proust thinks that this is an important part of his reading of life. It is a part of his brilliant analysis which begins by breaking down society as a whole into smaller groups, breaks these groups down in turn to the individuals who compose them, and finally reduces the individuals themselves to series of actions, which are sometimes of opposite import to each other. Proust continually is destroying our complacency about our understanding of other people or even of ourselves.

It is probably his very notion of the instability of social groups as well as of the individual personality that makes Proust value so highly a principled consistency of conduct and to ground this consistency upon the secure base of habit. In the opening scenes of the work, the mother and grandmother of the narrator are contrasted with the father, because their relations to the child are governed by plan and principle and, no matter how much it hurts them to carry out the plan or to adhere to the principle, they do so consistently. They represent a concept of law in human relations, while the father of the narrator, less sensitive than the women, allows himself to be governed by his impulses and whims in relation to the child. And Proust apparently blames the father's inconsistency of attitude and behavior for the development of the child's neurosis. He is convinced that the mother and grandmother are both wise and good in trying to undo by adherence to a strict code the harm which the father unconsciously does all the time by his whimsical, inexplicable injunctions and indulgences. Having no rule to govern him, the father is on occasion too lenient and on occasion too harsh.

So the child becomes "spoiled," which, as Proust analyzes the concept (or rather, enables us to analyze it for ourselves), consists simply in acting according to the transports of emotion, "the intermittences of the heart" as Proust calls them, that carry us momentarily away with themselves, instead of acting according to fixed rule, law, right principles which are confirmed by habitual obedience. For Proust, as for Aristotle, the secure base of the moral life is in habit. A bad man is a man of bad habits, and though he may be moved on occasion to be good, yet his "intermittences of the heart" are not to be relied on. The human heart, of which Proust is so consummate an analyst, is anarchic in its motions. It is not to be trusted. The real tragedy of most of the characters in the book, including the narrator's own, is that they do not realize this, or realize it too late, or are unable to act on their realization of it. Bloch first arouses the opposition of the narrator's family to him because, though he exhibits some extraordinarily generous impulses, he does so spasmodically, carried away for the moment, or, as we say sometimes, "in spite of himself." [64] The family's judgment upon Bloch, however arbitrary it seemed at the time to young Marcel, is eventually proved to be the correct one. Habit, which is the bad angel of the artistic process because it is inimical to our fresh perception of the world, is the safest guardian of our moral life. On one occasion, however, Proust makes a parallel between the role of habit in both aesthetics and ethics:

> No less than a man's character, habit makes the writer's style; and the author who has often been satisfied to achieve a certain charm of expression of his thought sets once and for all the limits of his talent just as by often yielding to pleasure, to sloth, to the fear of suffering, one sketches for oneself the outline of one's vices and the limit of one's virtue.[65]

Proust seems to say that he has proved this negatively as well as positively by living so badly, in defiance of all rule and regulation.

He is the plaything of his heart. Peripheral trifles arouse

[64] *Ibid.*, pp. 112 ff.
[65] Maxim 389, *Maxims of Marcel Proust*, ed. and trans. by O'Brien.

him or annoy him. He reacts eccentrically to the most ordinary human experiences. Thus, the death of his beloved grandmother does not come home really to his consciousness until long afterwards when, bending down once to untie the laces of his shoes, he is reminded of how she once did it for him as a child. She is present then to his feelings, and the springs of adequate grief are at last unlocked within him. But those critics who do not see that Proust, far from feeling complacent off the beaten path of the experience of mankind, tries continually to break out of the constricting bonds of his peculiarities, are unaware of what is going on in his work. Proust deals with the abnormal in order to find his way to a concept of normality. He does not set up any personal vagaries as universal laws and new principles of conduct. He is only too aware of his own shortcomings, and if he relies on the same principle of the moral life as Aristotle, that is neither accident nor irony. Beginning from an extremity of disease and dislocation, he gradually found his way back to a classic conception and definition of moral health, and that is more than his own age or the age following his has done.

An anecdote by Harold Nicolson about Proust and the Marquis de Chaumont reveals that until the very end of his life Proust was regarded even by some of his intimate friends of the Faubourg Saint-Germain as, first of all, a Jew,[66] and the gossip which mushroomed around him in the years of his fame and in those following his death in 1922 indicates how widespread was the knowledge of the true state of his private life. Why, then, did Proust deal with the questions of Judaism and homosexuality as if his concern with them sprang from no personal interest but from an

[66] Lindner, *Marcel Proust—Reviews and Estimates*, p. 159.

impersonal curiosity? Why, in short, did he suppress the identifications of Jew and invert from the person of the narrator of his books? I think he did so, because he was primarily concerned with establishing objective laws about human behavior, and this effort might have become hopelessly entangled by the intrusion of a purely confessional element into his story. The first person singular is always explosive. Proust feels himself too threatened by narcissism not to be aware of its dangers; hence his friendly advice to Gide to admit nothing in his books so far as the first person was concerned.

It may be noted that it is the greatest egotists precisely who are most impelled to escape from the toils of egotism. It is not more modest historians but Julius Caesar in his *Gallic Wars* and Leon Trotsky in his *History of the Russian Revolution* who adopt the third person singular in writing the narrative of their own deeds. Proust's narrator resembles the author very much indeed, and he goes so far as to assume that Albertine may have addressed him with the name "Marcel" and yet, as I have pointed out earlier, the two differ in a few vital respects. These differences enable Proust to satisfy the same need of objectivity which impels the historian to write of himself in the third person. To some readers, no doubt, Caesar and Trotsky will appear to be more egotistical rather than less because of their adoption of this device, and to them Proust may appear to be hypocritical because of his pretense of impersonal interest in matters which affected him very intimately. Yet his need to escape from himself, if only in his work, seems to me at least to be a very sympathetic motivation. He did not wish his morals as well as his art to become too soon a matter of controversy; they became so soon enough in any case after his death. His elimination of personal identification has not emasculated his work of its controversial elements. Judaism and homosexuality have continued to be, in our generation as they were earlier, sore and troublesome subjects of literature: the Jew as a person who tests the conscience of the community and the homosexual as one who challenges the complacency of its emphasis upon conformity. But Proust went beyond these particular concerns of his own into the more troubled area of exploring the ground for a general morality to govern mankind. No modern writer seems to me to have produced more telling arguments for tolerance and an individual appreciation of men and their actions. No writer has so consistently held justice, charity, and benevolence up for our admiration. Or denigrated cruelty and insensibility. That he has done so without any clear and unequivocal belief in the religious sanctions of morality is no argument, as some critics seem to believe, for the lack of the existence of the morality itself. I don't think that Proust, who was so great an admirer of Plato, would have been one of those poets whom the philosopher so regretfully excluded from his ideal Republic. A careful reading and understanding of Proust, it seems to me, can only make men better and more reasonable creatures. If this is not the greatest recommendation of his art, it is also certainly no objection to it—especially in a time when, even more than in other times, men seem to be so much in need of understanding and compassion.

"Everything is arranged in this life as though we entered it carrying the burden of obligations contracted in a former life." I should like now to suggest another meaning than the obvious one for this passage. Perhaps unknown even to Proust himself, the "former life" he speaks of may not be a life in another sphere than our own, but *the life of his parents and ancestors.* The moral life of these antecedent generations of Proust seems indeed not to have its "sanction in our present life"—that is, the life of our hedonistic civilization—and "to belong to a world different from our own." But Proust obeyed—or if he did not obey them himself, then at least he did the next best thing, which was to present them in the pages of his work in a winning light—"those unknown laws" of "kindness, scrupulosity, and self-sacrifice" which were traced by he knew not "whose hand." The hand, I suggest, was that of his parents and ancestors, both Jews and Christians, for we see how, in spite of the turbulence of their meeting during the Dreyfus Case, the two streams finally flow together harmoniously in his work. Proust was wise enough to realize that no new moral discoveries were to be made in a time such as his, and so he decided to live on his inherited morality. In certain respects, he attempts to refine some of its applications, but in basic essentials he leaves it untouched. The spiritual desert in which Proust found himself and the background which his accomplishment must ultimately be judged against is almost startlingly delineated, I think, by both the tone and content of the apology for the Bible which he was compelled to write in one of his articles:

> I would, by means of a quotation from Ruskin, make you realize that whatever your beliefs, the Bible is something real and actual, that we should set ourselves to find in it something other than the savor of the past, or the mere satisfaction of our curiosity.[67]

I do not see in Proust the evidence of that decadence and amorality which many of his critics have found in him. He was too busy emphasizing the best qualities which he discovered in the world around him to be charged with responsibility for corrupting it.

[67] Marcel Proust, *Selections from His Miscellaneous Writings*, p. 39.

# Conclusion

*Thought is hidden in verse, like the nutritive value in fruit. A fruit is nourishment but it seems to be nothing but pure delight. One perceives only pleasure but one receives a substance. Enchantment veils the imperceptible nourishment it brings with it.*

PAUL VALERY

THE German critic Ernst Curtius informs us that Schlegel once called the novel a modern form of the Socratic dialogue. "In this free form," wrote Schlegel, "has found refuge the wisdom which has fled the philosophers." [1]

The statement is suggestive in more ways than one. Proust must always be the despair of excessively formalistic critics, not because he has no form but because his form is (like Whitman's in this respect) "free"—that is to say, original, *sui generis,* of his own invention, obedient to deeper laws than have yet been formulated. By an excessively formalistic critic I mean one who waylays every new work that comes along with a little Procrustean bed constructed out of all his previous experiences of art. He is the keeper with the strait jacket for whatever in the least de-

[1] Curtius, *Proust,* p. 138.

viates from the conventional. He is an ostrich carrying his own sand with him wherever he goes to avoid shock at the presence of any new or surprising or unclassified creatures in his travels. Chances are that if he came across a real centaur or unicorn, he would strenuously deny the evidence of his senses rather than admit the textbooks may be wrong in saying that such creatures are figments of mere imagination. He is the very converse of the poetic reader, who is always looking for centaurs and unicorns and often convinces himself that he sees them where in fact they are not. Nowadays, the excessively rigid formalist is likely to call himself an "Aristotelian," though Aristotle might shudder at the sight of his paralytic disciples, since there seems to be at least as much difference between true analysis of form and what I have called formalism as there is between liberty and license. Aristotle was a biologist among other things, who studied form as the inevitable manifestation of the development of living organisms, but "Aristotelians" often seem to think of form as if it were a compass measure of deadwood.

Alarmed by the presence of stirring life which wonderfully refuses to conform itself to deductive "rules," such critics must be simply infuriated at the nerve of Proust in daring to exist. For here is a writer so eccentric in his deviation from the convenient pigeonholes in which literature can be filed away forever and forgotten that he carelessly refers to his *monstrous* offspring as if it were at the same time a novel, a history, and an autobiography. It is almost as if he were mimicking Polonius's cross-breeding of dramatic forms: "comical-tragical-historical-pastoral." Shakespeare, too, had apparently not suffered the pedants easily, though light in his satire of them. More seriously, Proust provided his critics with a mystery rather than a mystification. By saying that his work may be taken to be so many things at once, he was really denying that it belonged to any of the accepted classifications. Spoiled child that he is, he demands that we make definitions to suit his living work, rather than that we force his work to suit our ready-made definitions. The artist has done his work sufficiently well when he has given it birth. The rest is up to us. Hairs or heads may be split because of his provocative form, but he denies the responsibility.

Some of the critics, at least, have apparently recognized that Proust's books are not a *pure* example of anything save Proust himself. One of these has written:

> *Remembrance of Things Past* is no more a pure novel than it is pure autobiography, pure psychology, or pure philosophy. Incorporating every aspect of the author's physical, emotional, and intellectual life, it portrays probably a more vivid and a more comprehensive picture of a growing and developing consciousness and personality than any other novel that has yet appeared.[2]

The Socratic dialogue to which Schlegel compared the modern novel is itself an example of just such a "free" form. Is it drama? Is it philosophy? Whatever it is or is not, pure or otherwise, it is at any rate Plato! And that has been enough for the world, it seems. Plato, like Proust, is a leisurely author, who is often given to sportive digressions and inconclusiveness (in *Theaetetus* Socrates suggests that only slaves are worried about departing from the main thread of their discussion). Above all, Plato is unsystematic. He denied that anyone would ever reduce his teaching to a system, for he himself could not. He is, like the stream of life itself, continually flashing and flowing, with here and

[2] Derrick Leon, quoted in Lindner's *Marcel Proust—Reviews and Estimates,* p. 283.

there marked places (like the cave allegory) of almost unsoundable depth.

The comparison with Plato would have pleased Proust, who exclaimed enthusiastically in reply to André Chénier's famous remark that after three thousand years Homer was still young: "But how much younger yet is Plato!" [3] What could be more essentially Platonic in tone (for though Plato may not have a system, that doesn't prevent him from having a personal key) than Proust's passage: "Swann had regarded musical motifs as actual ideas, of another world, of another order, ideas veiled in shadows, unknown, impenetrable by the human mind, which none the less were perfectly distinct one from another, unequal among themselves in value and in significance." [4]

There is even a parallel between the irony with which the Socratic dialogues are salted (as a preservative of their freshness?) and the humor which is so often found in Proust. This humor is not in an anemic vein; it approaches so close to hilarity at times that some critics have invoked the name of robust Dickens for comparison. Humor is the honey with which Proust, following the classical prescription of Lucretius, rubs the edge of his cup of philosophical wormwood, the dregs of which have changed neither in their extreme bitterness nor in their salutary effect since the time of Ecclesiastes.

Nietzsche remarks somewhere in *Zarathustra* that he should not be able to believe in a god who did not dance. It would also be hard to take with the utmost seriousness a

[3] Marcel Proust, *Chroniques*, p. 227. Logan Pearsall Smith (*Marcel Proust: an English Tribute*) discovers Platonism even in Proust's earliest work. Van Meter Ames (*Proust and Santayana: the Aesthetic Way of Life*) writes: "Following the poets who followed Plato, he fell back upon the reminiscence of another world to explain the spell of art."

[4] *Swann's Way*, pp. 451 ff.

writer who did not condescend now and then to make his reader laugh. Proust presents no difficulties upon this score. He wants to enrich, but also to entertain. The recently discovered *Jean Santeuil* is filled with perfectly characteristic Proustian nougats—for example, the society woman who, upon hearing that her famous dinner guest is feeling a little ill, can't help wishing for a moment that he might drop dead in order to make of her house a historical shrine. In his masterpiece, there are innumerable touches of that kind. One that comes to mind is Swann's story about the unfortunate Mme Blatin, who was inspired to address a Cingalese native in the Jardin d'Acclimatation with a salutation which she thought perfectly proper: "Good morning, nigger," whereupon, as Swann tells it, " 'Me nigger,' he shouted (quite furious, don't you know), to Madame Blatin, 'me nigger; you, old cow.' " [5]

An incident from the schooldays of Jean Santeuil which had to be sacrificed from *Remembrance of Things Past* because the latter did not provide room for that side of the narrator's career, is, indeed, an excellent example of what Proust at his best is capable of doing along these lines: [6]

Without pretending to foretell in advance Jean's future development, we can say that while at school he had become exceedingly vain. When he received an invitation on one occasion to dine at the headmaster's house, the ignorance of his schoolmates concerning this favor was more than he could bear. There was among them one particularly who, rich and well-born, played billiards and, despite his youth, already wore long trousers, played the races and was a monarchist, excited the envy and admiration of Jean whom he wished to impress by this piece of news. After hesitating an entire hour between the various ways of informing him, while the teacher was elucidating for the class the text in Livy describing

[5] *Within a Budding Grove,* Part 1, p. 153. [6] *Jean Santeuil,* I, 116–17.

Hannibal's return across the Alps, Jean suddenly leaned across to his neighbor and, becoming as bright red as a cherry, whispered abruptly: "You know, I've been dining at the headmaster's." Fernay, after an hour of total silence on the part of Jean, was unprepared for this information and leaped into the air, exclaiming loudly: "What's that?" The teacher, of course, made them both come up front and, under penalty of keeping them after class, demanded to know what they had been talking about to each other, and so, while Jean thought that he would die of embarrassment and pride, Fernay confessed: "It's Santeuil who's been telling me he had dined at the headmaster's."

A backward glance over these pages will show that the postulate underlying my reading of everything in Proust is that literature is required, in the language of Horace and Sir Philip Sidney among others, to "delight and instruct." The *delight* comes first because without it, as Sidney pointed out, there cannot be much profitable *instruction.* Perhaps, though, these terms sound needlessly harsh, old-fashioned, and autocratic to the sensitivities of the ears of our contemporaries. Perhaps they ought to be altered slightly without affecting their basic import. We might call the characteristic qualities of literature *liveliness* and *disturbance.* It is the liveliness of the author's manner which I've been talking about here and which brings with it pleasure. Yet liveliness in itself is not a sufficient recommendation of a writer, or else every juggler and clown would be a great writer. A great writer is something other than a vaudeville entertainer (though not necessarily on occasion above acrobatics and clowning). If he is to appeal to more than ephemeral tastes, he must be troubled by the ideas which he expresses so neatly. The reader must be moved to sympathy by his evident concern. Pascal's phrase "chercher en gémissant" expresses a writer's ideal relation to his material—a relation which makes his feelings immediately infectious. The educator should be primarily a self-educator. Socrates denies being a teacher at all, perhaps because being a teacher means no more than to be a student or learner, a little more eager and capable than the rest, and he that forgets this soon becomes a pedant. Least of all, art can afford to become pedantic.

I shall risk the observation that imaginative literature is a form of social thought. In it, first of all for his own clarification, a writer poses more sharply the questions already posed by the conflict between human ideals and practices. The more important the problem which the author sets himself and the closer his quest comes to a durable solution, the more affecting will be his work. If there is to be any hierarchy of values among literary works, it must be based on some such criterion.

Matthew Arnold, in defining literature as a criticism of life, was already toning down the moral emphasis a little bit, I feel—the most sophisticated Victorians, a generation after Romanticism, were self-conscious of what the young thought a tendency to stuffiness. Yet books seem to me much more than passive criticisms of life. They are active directives and incentives to life. Our lives, in all sorts of ways, as La Rochefoucauld implied, are the results of our reading. When Oscar Wilde said that life is an imitation of art, he was coining a paradox which brilliantly inverted the Aristotelian formula, but the piquancy of the phrase is supplied by the large measure of truth in it.

A more profound though less inviting paradox than Wilde's is that the literature from which we learn the most is that which was created with the least direct intention of teaching us. De Quincey was right to emphasize the *moving* qualities of imaginative literature as distinguished from the instructive ones, but it must be added that the best instruction is that received from what has first of all been a moving experience. Poets, just as Plato with paternal care insisted, must not be allowed to become merely the cause of wanton and irresponsible movements of the soul.

It has been my view throughout that the imaginative writer is, to adopt some of Sidney's words, the "right popular" moralist—not in the sense that he takes any advantage of a sudden access of popularity for morals, and still less in the sense that he waters down morality to the taste of the populace, but that he uses his powers first to delight and then to discipline the pleasure-seeking palates of mankind. From the authors whom we read, we hope to learn something about those eternal questions which "tease us out of thought." How shall we live? What shall we live for? Is it worthwhile to live at all? Those of us whom it "hurts to think" (that is, if I may be allowed to interpret Housman's line, not those who find it difficult to think, but those who find it only too easy) read to discover some "momentary stay against confusion," as Frost once phrased the purpose of poetry—though if its effect is only momentary it remains minor in our memory.

But what is it that we learn from good authors? Nothing perhaps that we did not know before. They do not preach, they attract us into the acceptance of the moral thesis to which preachers have failed to reconcile us. To be good, we perceive with astonishment, is something very beautiful. The way to the soul lies through aesthetic admiration.

When one has been long in communion with a writer's work, it is hard to say in exactly how many ways one has been affected by it. It is the measure of his importance that the reader never quite sees the world in the same light that he did before. Consider, for example, Proust's development of the theme of *occupation* in his work. After the most miserable and confused wanderings—wanderings on occasion diverted as were those of Odysseus by entertainments and magic but which finally proved meaningless or absurd, painful or boring—the narrator of the story finds *himself.* He finds the clue to his own significance, which turns out to be nothing else than his artistic occupation. All the evil and suffering, with which Proust's pages are filled, arise, if we will only think about it, either from lack of occupation or from false occupation. Because occupation in Proust is not to be confused with the work which one is forced to do for a living. Occupation is service to the divine; it is the work which Kafka so beautifully called prayer. Working for a living is only servitude, and the servants in Proust are hardly more admirable than the frivolous creatures whom they serve and whose occupation consists of gossip, lovemaking, and snobbish schemes involving incredible exertions. Nor is occupation to be confused with the occasional practice of an inadequately mastered art, undertaken as an escape from the ennui of doing nothing at all. This is simply dilettantism and the characters who are dilettantes are to Proust only abortive suggestions of the real thing.

Occupation, as Proust conceives of it, is a compulsive activity which ends only with life itself. It arises perhaps only where there has been an excess of suffering, and while all other activities in life seem inevitably to lead to the hurt and betrayal of someone, such occupation alone is harmless and recreative. The whole last volume of Proust is one long hymn to the glory of finding a true and transcendent occupation. For occupation is that which lies wholly within a man's own power. It does not depend upon anyone else's whims. Spinoza advises us if we would be happy to fix our love on that which is eternal. Occupation is that which is eternal in man. It is what he was especially brought into the world to do. Not what he is compelled to do by urgent material needs, nor what he chooses to do for trivial social reasons, but what he must do because he was born to do it. Occupation, in Proust, is like memory—it is insignificant when it is merely a voluntary affair. It cannot be arrived at by the Will or by taking thought about it. It is the talent given to man, as grace is given, in compensation for he knows not what merit of his own.

With Stoic austerity, Proust rejected ease and pleasure as the aims of life. The happiness of being able to face ourselves in a moral mirror for a single moment without flinching is worth years of insipid and empty "pleasures." Happiness, he says in one place referring to the Duchess de Guermantes, is impossible to achieve when one does nothing else than seek it. It is something indirect. It enters the mind through the corner of an eye, like the light of those stars which remain invisible so long as we turn our gaze directly on them.

An indirect yet powerful testimony to the importance of the moral element in art is supplied by the curious fact that those "aesthetes" and sterile dabblers, whom Proust satirized as nature's unfinished sketches of the artist, seem invariably to fasten for their spiritual nourishment on the works of the most religious, the most positively *believing* of artists—El Greco in painting, Bach and Palestrina in music, Dante and Dostoyevsky in literature. At those seasons of the year when the great masterpieces of religious song are to be heard, the churches are filled with the sensitive who think they have come for the music and not for the doctrine there. On a conscious level, such people often discount and even deprecate the existence of "impure" admixtures with their art. They think that they can abstract the aesthetic element alone from it. But why is it, then, that they are forced so often to find their greatest pleasure where it can be said with the least chance of contradiction that the artist was as concerned with the purity of his faith as he was with the purity of his art (these did not seem to conflict or get in each other's way in former times)? To ask this question, as it appears to me, is to answer it. There is more than just perverseness involved (though perverseness explains a great deal, especially in such people). A particular affinity for devotional art in many unbelievers is, I think, unknown to themselves, a shamefaced and left-handed way of satisfying certain neglected spiritual needs. Surely art in our time has come "to assume the burden which has dropped from the shoulders of the priests" (to use an idea of Yeats), but those who benefit from its ministry are not often aware of it and are sometimes ungrateful. Proust was not one of these. He had learned well from his own master Ruskin (some of whose works he rendered into the French language) to credit the original well-spring of religious faith as the true source of inspiration in much of the art that he loved, and he always speaks reverently of the moral fervor which had produced so many glorious works, even when he feels deprived of the ability to imitate it.

Without this dimension, Proust's work, whatever its technical merits, would be not that of a *seer* but only of the *voyeur*, which some of his most uncomprehending or uncharitable critics think they have discerned in him.[7] The

[7] Charles Briand, *Le Secret de Marcel Proust* (Paris, 1950).

failure to recognize the life-giving importance of morality in art, or a too great narrowness in the conception of what the moral message should be—both result from a deficiency in the critic's own equipment which he tends to blame his subject for. The complete Proust, like the complete Socrates, is something greater than what he is usually credited as being. Rationalist philosophers, who pretend that Socrates was nothing more than one of themselves, must drop from their memories the meaning of the Socratic daimon and of the religious reassurances in the *Phaedo* concerning the immortality of the soul. Just so, it seems to me, do those critics who do not admit in Proust that which raises him above the power of the voyeur to that of the seer. For though the common course of his faithless time makes him *see* only as if truth shone with a fitful and intermittent phosphorescence and not with the brightest and steadiest clarity, still what distinguishes him from the rest is that he does *see* at times, even through the milky membrane of a vision impaired for him by the accepted science of his generation, the light that is there eternally to be seen, the light which was seen by Socrates, and the outline shapes of higher ideas thus revealed.

### PROUST'S STATUS AMONG THE CLASSICS

The clue as to what constitutes a classic in literature is, for me, contained in the magnificent tribute paid by Samuel Johnson to Shakespeare:

> The effects of favor and competition are at an end; the tradition of his friendships and his enmities has perished; his works support no opinion with arguments nor supply any faction with invectives; they can neither indulge vanity nor gratify malignity; but are read without any other reason than the desire of pleasure,

> and are therefore praised only as pleasure is obtained; yet thus unassisted by interest or passion, they have past through variations of taste and changes of manners, and as they devolved from one generation to another, have received new honors at every transmission.

This was written more than a century after Shakespeare's death. It seems to me to indicate how hopeless it is to try to arrive at any definitive conclusion about a writer's genius before a period of at least one hundred years has passed after his death. There is such a thing as literary politics, and evaluation by those living too close to the author himself often becomes confused with personalities. Before the required time has passed and the ground haze of fashion and prejudice finally clears, no writer, however powerful, can honestly be viewed as other than a candidate for immortality. Of course, we can't help feeling, much sooner, that certain authors who seem to be making a very good run of it will still be there in the same position when the race is over, but conservative considerations based upon the experience of the past caution us against any premature commitments. Proust is still a probationer, though he seems likely to some of us to become something more with time.

But it should be said at once that popularity or lack of it seems to have very little if anything to do with the question of permanence. Proust himself was forced to subsidize the publication of what is at this moment probably the most universally recognized and admired example of contemporary literature. Except by a scattered handful of devotees, he was ignored at first by the public. Even Léon Daudet, personal friend that he was to Proust, could still write in 1916, three years *after* the appearance of *Du côté de chez Swann*, as if Proust were only a beginner in letters: "If he can manage to guide his steps, to control himself, to establish firmly his literary point of view, he will one of these days write on the margin of life itself something quite extraordinary." [8] In another passage from the same essay, the wonder of which is not that it underestimated Proust but that it dared to discuss him at all at a time when he was almost completely unknown, Daudet writes: "He was the author of an original, rather mad book, full of promise, called *Du côté de chez Swann.*" And then, gradually at first and with tremendous momentum after the award of the Goncourt Prize to him in 1919 at the urging of Daudet, Proust's reputation spread from the inner circle of his friends to increasingly remote circles of readers all over the world. By the time of the Second World War, Proust's material had become so proverbial that a German officer quartered in France after 1940, in an effort to show his breeding to his hosts, is quoted by the Princess Marthe Bibesco as describing somebody as "du côté de chez Guermantes," expecting the expression to call up a perfectly definite picture, as indeed it does to anyone familiar with Proust.

Popular works, as distinguished from the classics, are like communicable diseases. They are very infectious; they cause a high fever and then subside. But some of the great works built to last often seem to surprise and antagonize their earliest readers with a kind of peculiarity or novelty that is taken at first to be no more than eccentricity of vision. The public, like a fish, goes after the minimally curved hook and the most obvious bait, but it gets off the flattering device as easily as it catches on. The lure of permanence, on the other hand, is more subtly contrived. The

[8] *The Memoirs of Léon Daudet,* ed. by Griggs, p. 258.

public swims round it skeptically, quite often for a great while. But the meat there is good and the hook of the classic when it catches never lets go. Not one year or ten years or a lifetime set any limit to its hold. It is unforgettable. The book that is merely popular has to be calculated for a certain moment; it must have split-second timing or be left forever in the shallows. But the true classic is not dependent on the wave of the present; it waits patiently to find its own depth in time.

Great writers are those whom, not by any accident, everyone interested in literature eventually agrees to talk about. As one works his way through the undelectable mountains of criticism, one becomes aware that in this constant babble about the great suns of literature, there is an extraordinary amount of repetition, vanity, triviality, perversity, and general wrong-headedness. And as in all other things, very little sensitivity, straightforwardness, and simple truth are to be found. Criticism, with its confusing and contradictory noises, gradually begins to resemble a stock exchange of literature, and it is a great wonder to the spectator that out of these amazingly complex transactions the right figures do manage at last to emerge. Though it takes the world a long time on occasion to get around to quality, it invariably does. The brokers loud on the floor of the Bourse often succeed in attracting attention to themselves and to their poor clients. But the more sober and discreet tones of those with substantial intellectual fortunes at their disposal, though sometimes drowned out and scarcely noticed at the beginning of the auction,[9] eventually carry off all the prizes at the end.

The critic's account with his reader is an accumulation of

[9] The figure of speech is Emily Dickinson's, of course: "Publication is the auction / Of the mind of man."

first-hand perceptions of the quality of art, just as the artist's is an awareness of nature and social life. These are necessarily simplified formulas, to be sure, but I mean them to indicate that a good critic's relation to his subject is no less difficult to achieve than the artist's is to his material. Gide has written the most sensitive criticism of Proust that I have ever read—he has managed to do so by entirely subordinating himself to his subject and allowing his mind to act as the transparent medium between the work and the world. But much of criticism, like much of art, is not so modest. It is not a description of fresh experiences but a defensive rationalization of personal taste. The critic too often is trying to shield his self-esteem, instead of trying to make his subject transparently clear to his reader, possibly at the cost of his self-esteem, as in the case of Boswell and Johnson.

It is not much more helpful to appeal for the meaning of art from the critic to the artist himself. Though it is true that artists have often had some very pregnant things to say about art in general and their own particularly, yet Plato's view in *Ion* is basically correct—creation seems to be the result of a happy inspiration which need not be accompanied by the ability intellectually to elucidate it. He who can understand cannot always create, while he who can create cannot always explain. To expect the artist to be the wisest critic of his own work is something like asking of a mother that she also be the best pediatrician and child psychologist.

The problem in criticism is to dig below the crust of the conventional response to where the true impressions made by art lie hidden. Proust is right in making a contrast between factual erudition about art (which requires comparatively little feeling for art itself) and what might perhaps be called depth analysis of art—that is to say true criticism which, involving as it inevitably does all of the critic's own personality and experience as well as his intellectual powers of penetration, succeeds at last in laying bare the foundations of the work itself. The difference between mere scholarship and scholarly criticism which it is so easy to confound with each other, is nowhere brought out more clearly than in Proust's last volume where he writes:

> The slight groove that a musical phrase or the sight of a church made in our consciousness we find it too difficult to try to comprehend. But we play the symphony again and again or keep returning to look at the church, until, in this running away from our own life which we have not the courage to face—they call this "erudition"—we come to know them as well, and in the same manner, as the most learned lover of music or archaeology.[10]

Erudition serves an important purpose in the great writer. It is a kind of dam which he makes use of to stem the flood of his natural feelings in order eventually to derive the maximum force from their expression. The obstacle which education and study present to "the spontaneous overflow of powerful feelings" itself becomes in time the source of a new and unmatched strength. The Classics are the Boulder Dams of Literature. Learning kills off little artists and makes great ones greater. Naive folk literature, however natural and fresh and lovely it is, has I think been much overestimated in value by romantic primitivists. Folk productions are like the lucid, softly humming stream, and though there are sometimes rapids in nature too which surpass the artifice of man, nevertheless the virtue of the natural for the most part lies in its charm rather than in its power. In every sphere, strength is added to nature by art—that is by the self-conscious utilization of definite strategies,

[10] *The Past Recaptured,* p. 220.

machinery and restraints. A great writer absorbs all the relevant information available to him in his time—not only, it is clear, by way of the schools but also by private application and study.

In Proust's work, as in the work of those contemporaries of his who by the general consensus of qualified criticism most nearly approach to his worth as an artist—Thomas Mann and James Joyce and T. S. Eliot and André Gide—the reader is aware at all times of the extraordinary amount of factual knowledge which went into its making. Proust knows not only all the great artists of the very old culture in which he does his work, a culture which crosses all the boundaries of European languages, but an astonishing number of those of secondary and tertiary magnitude as well. In this connection, it is interesting to recall that in a letter to a friend of his mother's after the latter's death, Proust says that he and his mother were always agreed that if he had ever been forced by the decline of the family fortunes to work for a living he would have made a very good teacher:

> I have always been in agreement with Mama on this one point—that there was only one thing in life I could do well (though that was something of which both of us thought so highly that it is saying a great deal) and that was to be an excellent professor. And the consequence has been that to be held in the esteem of professors is very precious to me.[11]

And, of course, that is what he has become now, if only we agree to look upon great writers in their proper light, as the teachers of teachers. I think that underneath the cloak of Marxian terminology in the early Edmund Wilson, the feeling for the extent and depth of Proust's cultivation which I am trying to express is the same as that found in

[11] Marcel Proust, *Lettres à Mme C.*, p. 205.

the following sentences: "[Proust] comes at the close of an era and sums up the whole situation. . . . [He] is perhaps the last great historian of the loves, the society, the intelligence, the diplomacy, the literature and the art of the Heartbreak House of capitalist culture." [12] This is one good reader's testimony as to how much a great writer appears to know. He can only speak as if he were the medium for the expression of a whole culture, a society, and an epoch.

Art is not nature merely or the natural production of a noble savage. It is nature modified in a distinctive and purposeful way. The simply natural—that is to say, so often (as in Nurse's wonderful speeches in *Romeo and Juliet*) the inconsequential, the repetitious, and the banal! The ideal in art is always to be found in an exquisite balance between the too great restraint of an arthritic form and no restraint at all which issues in a kind of logorrhoea. Art begins where nature leaves off, though nature goes a long, long way (no artist, to use Jonson's distinction, can possibly be *made* who is not born with inspiration). Art is the indirect rather than the direct. It is in large part a calculated effect. The calculation may take place, in the case of long artistic training and sufficiently powerful impulses, below the threshold of consciousness; it is none the less there.

It is the indirectness characteristic of an advanced tradition in art which enables writers from Keats to Proust to regard their art as a refuge from reality. The romantic attitude, dominant since the beginning of the nineteenth century in a number of European countries, has done so much firmly to establish this point of view that it is easy to forget that there is something parochial about it and that art was not always regarded by the artist as an escape from

[12] *Axel's Castle* (New York, 1931).

the world. Art has always been a sanctuary for the artist, but there is a great difference between regarding a sacred grove as an asylum where alone it is possible to save one's life or sanity and regarding it as a place of peaceful worship. For Bach, we like to remember, music served the glory of God but was at the same time "a very pleasant recreation." He did not regard his art, as so many moderns regard theirs, as a last ditch defense against the intrusion of murderous reality. But Bach was working in a community in which the place of the artist was recognized and secure, while moderns have often created in a situation in which the very meaning of the word community is hard to understand. An artist like Van Gogh, for example, expended as much of his energy in attempting vainly to forge a *community* (and not of all kinds of workers but of artists only) as he did in painting. This lack of community in the contemporary world, this painful feeling of separateness which divides individual persons from each other "as if they were so many houses," is undoubtedly responsible in part for the particular quality of pessimism which we find in Proust. It is one of the causes, though not the only one because his chronic illness, the prospect of an early death before he could complete his work (an anticipation realized in fact), and the human situation itself which has always supplied the deepest roots of pessimism—all contributed to Proust's elegiac tone.

For all these reasons Proust was not very much attached to his contemporary world. For whatever it is worth and with no vulgarly optimistic overtones, he seems to sense in the future the locus of his ultimate triumph. One of the more strange and curious passages of his work is the one in which he speaks of "the United States of the World"—"The ancients were no less strongly attached to the group of humanity to which they devoted themselves because it did not exceed the limits of their city, nor are men of today to their country than will be those who in the future love the United States of the World." [13] The last phrase was certainly not chosen haphazardly. All of Proust's references to the United States of America, springing from his ideals of universal tolerance as well as from his gratitude for the help extended by America to France in the First World War, are full of friendliness and benevolent warmth, and these seem to me a legitimate addition to other more compelling reasons for the interest and honors which both America and Americans have extended to Proust's work almost from the very beginning. If Proust should rank indisputably some day with the great classics and the political union of the world actually take place under some such favorable auspices as his striking phrase envisages, the passage about "the United States of the World," which has hardly been noticed or commented on as yet, may become as celebrated for its prophetic quality as that famous passage in the Fourth Eclogue of Virgil which was supposed, by followers of the struggling new religion, to have forecast the coming of the Christian era.

### LAST WORDS

What has been regarded by some social-minded critics as a defect of Proust is to my mind his outstanding virtue as an artist—namely, his ability to portray eccentric human beings in such a way that they no longer seem strange to any of us. It was Proust's discovery (or perhaps rediscovery is the better word, for Shakespeare and Dostoyevsky share in the same knowledge) that it is not the eccentric who is out-

[13] *The Captive,* p. 435.

side the herd called humanity, but that humanity itself is thoroughly composed of eccentrics in varying degrees. The closer we come to the average face in the crowd and the more we are able to sympathize with its expressions and the impulses recorded there, the more aware we become, along with the greatest writers, of a matchless individuality in the creation of nature. Only in the grossest, most superficial and least important aspect of social behavior, does the personality yield to the pressures of the necessity to conform. And even so, a man like Proust suspects most people of being such complete mavericks beneath the guise of their conventional exterior, that their private lives and invisible personal histories, if honestly told, might well bring them the attentions of psychiatrists or the police, if only because of mistaken identities and intentions misunderstood. That is what happens in fact to the narrator of the book once, when he is summoned to appear before a police inspector in response to a complaint lodged against him by the suspicious parents of a very young girl to whom he has turned for companionship, in the terrible vacuum of loneliness which he suffers after the precipitate flight of Albertine, though he has done her no harm at all.[14]

The really basic thing in this world is that individuality which makes every leaf of a tree different from every other leaf but which few writers have the patience to see or the delicacy to draw. The label which is put for convenience on the stubborn core and essence of each personality has as much relation with it as does the uniform with the prisoner. It is a mnemonic aid to busy people, but more important to a consideration of the individual are the variations which each succeeds in embroidering upon the common theme of exist-

[14] *The Sweet Cheat Gone*, pp. 36 ff.

ence. The servant may be only a servant in her official capacity, with a conventional attire and things that she is habitually compelled to do or say, but to a writer like Proust she is also the inimitable Françoise, a neurotic, poetic, feudal old woman, who has as many foibles as the Baron de Charlus, though infinitely less leisure in which to let such foibles grow.

His ability to draw eccentric characters convincingly was accompanied, as a similar gift was in the case of Dickens, with a phenomenal talent for mimicry, which led to his first reputation on a purely local scale in French high society and literary circles. His "singeries" were applied with equal success to the styles of the classics and the mannerisms of his friends. He was able to "hit off" the *points* of certain well-known literary men in a way that won him his earliest celebrity with *aficionados* of the craft. Léon Daudet wrote of these parodies: "Proust has an ultra-refined taste in literature. He has explored the authors of the seventeenth, eighteenth, and nineteenth centuries down to their foundations. He can write Michelet that is better than Michelet and turn out Bossuet by the yard." [15] Proust himself quite rightly valued these pastiches, and he not only collected some of them into a separate volume but included one of the manner of the Goncourt Brothers in the last volume of *Remembrance of Things Past.*[16]

The basis of these imitations was that faculty of intense concentration possessed to so extraordinary a degree by Proust. Reynaldo Hahn, the composer who was one of Proust's oldest and most intimate friends, contributed a

[15] *The Memoirs of Léon Daudet,* ed. by Griggs, p. 267.
[16] *The Past Recaptured,* pp. 14 ff.

famous page to the first collection of tributes paid to him after his death[17] in which he recalled a scene of Proust losing himself in the contemplation of a Bengal rose bush, which they were walking past together one day, so that he interrupted their conversation, stopped absolutely still, and fell for a long time into what seemed to be almost a cataleptic trance. I remember no parallel to this spiritual state in literature unless it is that in Plato's *Symposium* which describes the absent fits to which Socrates was subject. Proust relates the inner content of such a session, I believe, in this striking passage:[18]

How often in Paris, during the May of the following year, was I to bring home a branch of apple blossom from the florist, and to stay all night long before its flowers in which bloomed the same creamy essence that powdered besides and whitened the green unfolding leaves, flowers between whose snowy cups it seemed almost as though it had been the salesman who had, in his generosity towards myself, out of his wealth of invention too and as an effective contrast, added on either side the supplement of a becoming crimson bud: I sat gazing at them, I grouped them in the light of my lamp—for so long that I was often still there when the dawn brought to their whiteness the same flush with which it must at that moment have been tingeing their sisters on the Balbec road—and I sought to carry them back in my imagination to that roadside, to multiply them, to spread them out, so as to fill the frame prepared for them, on the canvas, all ready, of those closes the outline of which I knew by heart, which I so longed to see—which one day I must see again, at the moment when, with the exquisite fervor of genius, spring was covering their canvas with its colours.

The objects which engrossed him at such hours, as we can see here, afterwards made their reappearance in his

[17] *Les Cahiers de Marcel Proust I* (Paris, 1927), pp. 33–34.
[18] *Within a Budding Grove,* Part 2, pp. 5–6.

writing. His descriptions of nature at Combray and elsewhere, which together are among the most notable things in his book, owe their almost hallucinatory vividness to an absorption and study seldom if ever matched by any other writer. Proust was willing to drive himself to the extreme limits of organic endurance (he even speaks somewhere of experimenting with drugs in order to study the dreams which they induced) in order to bring out of the last obscurity every vestige of the precious store of his talent. This eagerness to endure the worst pains associated with creation is itself not the least impressive part of his equipment.

But when we speak of his talent, how can we avoid, too, the thought of his preternatural memory? Memory is the key to Proust's creation, as he himself emphasizes in different ways, beginning with the title he gave to his work. His example comes nearest to being a satisfactory explanation of the significant myth recorded in Hesiod thousands of years ago which makes Memory the mother of all the muses. "Memory, you have the key!" is the message of the earliest as well as of the latest poets. It is also what is significant in Wordsworth's formula: "emotion recollected in tranquility." It has long been evident that the excitement inseparable from the immediacy of experience is not conducive to a reflective process like composition. It has been observed that many of the greatest war stories, for instance, have appeared not during or directly after a conflict, but only when many years have passed. The reason for this was given by Hemingway when he told how for the first ten years after the First World War, it was too painful for him to think about it at all—he wrote *Farewell to Arms* in the eleventh year after the war. The pattern of suffering requires a period of peace and quiet in which to settle most enduringly. Yet in spite of everything, it remains Proust who adumbrates most clearly for us the actual role which memory plays in the process of creation.

He succeeds in communicating to us the very feeling of Time itself as a palpable medium which gives an iridescence to the most commonplace experiences immersed in it, somewhat after the way which the earth itself has of transforming into colorful and arresting objects any ordinary bits of glass that have been buried in it for thousands of years—as those can say who have been delighted by the sight of glassware excavated from the remains of the ancient world. The wonder of the traveler at old Roman household articles, which Time itself has covered over completely with earth colors resembling all the most beautiful, rare and precious stones of the world, seems akin to the wonder inspired in an artist like Proust when he beheld once more in palpitating recollection his early childhood and youth and indeed his whole past life. These memories had lain undisturbed in the depths of his mind for a certain necessary gestative period of time, when they were delivered fresh and unretouched to the surface by a strong sensory impression like that made upon the narrator by the taste of the little madeleine dipped into a cup of tea, out of which, like the goddess Venus, Combray sprang in full bloom. Commonplace experiences and memories recalled after many years had passed were commonplace no longer. Something magical had happened to them. They were transmuted as if by alchemy, and, simply from having lain imbedded for so long in the mysterious caves and recesses of the mind, they came forth once more into the light of an unfading day, completely emblazoned and covered over with the golden imagery of his genius.

In the seventh of the Epistles which have (perhaps fallaciously) been attributed to Plato, the great philosopher is made to say of his philosophy that "the subject does not admit, as the sciences in general do, of exposition. *It is only after long association in the great business itself and a shared life that a light breaks out in the soul, kindled, so to say, by a leaping flame, and thereafter feeds itself.*"

Something like that should also probably be said about the "system" of Proust. It is there, to be sure, as the inevitable condition of the consistency of his thought, but it is not the kind of thing that can be "summed up" or "digested." Art like philosophy demands to be lived with in order to be really understood. Yet if the light were not already a part of us, it could not come to us wholly from the outside. The vision communicated by art is not imprinted as a picture on a passive retina—it is rather ignited in us as if we had always been filled with an airy, illuminating medium awaiting this moment of explosive revelation.

Proust is a writer who has done more than add his work to literature. He is one of those who has contributed "the figure of himself." This figure is not the one conjured up by scabrous gossip and surmises. It is the figure created by a man who was capable of representing something. In the secluded hermitage of his chamber to which he voluntarily withdrew for the best part of his life, he was being neither idle nor irresponsible. For what he chose to do with complete devotion and, as becomes increasingly apparent, complete success was to represent ourselves.

# *Selected Bibliography*


Abatangel, Louis. Marcel Proust et la musique. Paris, 1939.

Adelson, Dorothy. Article on Proust and music in the London magazine *Music and Letters* (July, 1942), pp. 228 ff.

Alden, Douglas W. Marcel Proust and His French Critics. Los Angeles, 1947.

Aristotle. The Poetics (Butcher translation) and Nicomachean Ethics.

Arnold, Matthew. Essays. London, 1914.

Bell, Clive. Proust. New York, 1929.

Bergson, Henri. Matter and Memory. London, 1911.

Bibesco, Princess Marthe. The Veiled Wanderer. London, 1949.

Briand, Charles. La Secret de Marcel Proust. Paris, 1950.

Cahiers de Marcel Proust, Les. Paris, 1927. A collection of tributes and criticisms by French men of letters which is paralleled by Marcel Proust: an English Tribute, London, 1923.

Cattaui, Georges. "Proust and the Jews," *Jewish Review* (1932), No. 3, pp. 66–75.

Clermont-Tonnerre, E. de. Robert de Montesquiou et Marcel Proust. Paris, 1925.

Curtius, Ernst. Proust. Paris, 1928.

Dandieu, Arnaud. Marcel Proust: sa révélation psychologique. Paris, 1936.

Daudet, Léon. Memoirs of Léon Daudet. Edited by Arthur Kingsland Griggs. New York, 1925.

Dostoyevsky, Feodor. The Brothers Karamazov and Crime and Punishment.

Dreyfus, Robert. Souvenirs sur Marcel Proust. Paris, 1926.

Eliot, T. S. Selected Essays. New York, 1932.
Fernandez, Ramon. Messages: première série. Paris, 1926.
Feuillerat, Albert. Comment Marcel Proust à composé son roman. New Haven, 1936.
Flores, Angel. "Marcel Proust in Review," *The Bookman,* LXVII, 272–73.
Fowlie, Wallace. "Swann and Hamlet," *Partisan Review,* IX, 195 ff.
Freud, Sigmund. Introductory Lectures to Psychoanalysis.
Green, F. C. The Mind of Proust. Cambridge, 1949.
Hier, Florence. La Musique dans l'oeuvre de Marcel Proust. New York, 1933.
Hindus, Milton. "Proust and Society," *New Republic,* CV (December 8, 1941), 780 ff.
—— "The Pattern of Proustian Love," *New Mexico Quarterly,* XXI (Winter, 1951), 389 ff.
—— "Proust's Ethics and the Jews," *The Chicago Jewish Forum,* XI (Fall, 1952), 31 ff.
Kieve, Rudolph. "Marcel Proust, Correspondent," *New Mexico Quarterly* (Spring, 1950), pp. 96 ff.
Krutch, Joseph Wood. Five Masters. New York, 1930.
Lavrin, Jacob. "Proust and Dostoyevsky," an essay in Studies in European Literature. London, 1929.
Lemaitre, Georges. Four French Novelists. London, 1938.
Lindner, Gladys Dudley, compiler. Marcel Proust—Reviews and Estimates in English. Stanford University, 1942.
March, Harold. The Two Worlds of Marcel Proust. Philadelphia, 1948.
Mauriac, François. Proust's Way. New York, 1950.
Maurois, André. Proust: Portrait of a Genius. New York, 1950.
Michaud, Régis. Modern Thought and Literature in France. New York, 1934.
Pierhal, Armand. "Sur la composition wagnérienne de l'oeuvre de Proust," Bibliothèque universelle et revue de Genève (Juin, 1929).
Pierre-Quint, Léon. Marcel Proust, sa vie, son oeuvre. Paris, 1925.
Plato. Ion, The Symposium, Phaedrus, The Republic (all in the Jowett translation).

Proust, Marcel. Remembrance of Things Past. Translated by C. K. Scott-Moncrieff with the exception of the last volume, The Past Recaptured, which was done by Frederick Blossom. Introduction by Joseph Wood Krutch. New York, 1934.

—— Selections from His Miscellaneous Writings. London, n.d.

—— Chroniques. A collection of his occasional pieces selected by his brother, Dr. Robert Proust. Paris, 1927.

—— Lettres à Mme C. Janin, 1946.

—— Pleasures and Regrets. A translation by Louise Varèse of large sections but not the whole of Proust's first published volume, Les Plaisirs et les jours. New York, 1948.

—— The Maxims of Marcel Proust. Edited and translated by Justin O'Brien. New York, 1948.

—— Lettres à André Gide. Neuchâtel and Paris, 1949.

—— Letters to a Friend. London, 1949.

—— Letters of Proust. Edited and translated by Mina Curtiss. With an Introduction by Harry Levin. New York, 1949.

—— Jean Santeuil. Paris, 1952.

Ransom, John Crowe. The World's Body. New York, 1938.

Rivane, Georges. Influence de l'asthme sur l'oeuvre de Marcel Proust. Paris, 1945.

Robert, Louis de. De Loti à Proust. Paris, 1928.

Saint-Simon, Louis de Rouvroy, duc de. The Memoirs of Saint-Simon. 3 vols. London, 1906.

Scheikévitch, Marie. Time Past. New York, 1935.

Schopenhauer, Arthur. The World as Will and Idea. 3 vols. London, 1909.

Shakespeare, William. Hamlet.

Souza, Sybil de. La Philosophie de Marcel Proust. Paris, 1939.

Spagnioli, John. The Social Attitude of Marcel Proust. New York, 1936.

Turquet-Milnes, G. From Pascal to Proust. London, 1926.

Vigneron, Robert. "Genèse de *Swann*," Revue d'Histoire de la Philosophie et d'Histoire générale de la civilization (January 15, 1937), pp. 67 ff.

Wagner, Richard. Beethoven. London, 1880.

Wilson, Edmund. Axel's Castle. New York, 1931.

# Index

*A la recherche du temps perdu,* see *Remembrance of Things Past*
Albertine (character), 39 f., 55, 103, 104, 126, 129, 133, 139 f., 150
Antagonisms, irreconcilability of, 221
Anti-Semitism, Proust's literary treatment of, 225 ff.
Anxiety, the moving force of love, 140
Appearance and reality, 244 f.
*Arabian Nights,* 171
Aristocracy: its literary value for Proust, 190 f.; cruelty and ill-breeding of, 199
Aristocracy, French: improbability of its revival, 170; Proust's debunking of, 191 ff.
Aristotle, 253; applicability of his categories to Proust's work, 4 ff.
Arnold, Matthew, 258
Art: Proust's theory of its antagonism to life, 29 f.; Proust's theory of, 33 ff.; interpreters of, 36 ff.; Proust's attitude towards, 63; its subjectivity emphasized by Proust, 66 ff.; Proust's belief in its indestructibility, 109; the artist's refuge, 270 f.; society preferences, 193; allied to ethics, 210 f.
Art, devotional, 262
Art, modern, Proust's optimism concerning, 66
Artistic creation, painfulness of, 72 ff.
Art simile: Proust's use of, 47 ff.; as a comic device, 51

Bach, Johann Sebastian, 271
Beauty, unrelated to love, 140
Beethoven, Ludwig van, 46, 211
Bell, Clive, 110
Bergotte (character), 31, 34 f., 36 f., 129, 214
Berma (character), 36 f.
Bible, Proust's apology for, 251
Blatin, Mme (character), 256
Bloch (character), 91, 225, 232 f.
Boredom, the enemy of the socialites, 193
Brichot (character), 98

Cambremer, Mme de (character), 128, 185
*Cantos* (Pound), Proust's work compared to, 54
*Captive, The,* poetic imagination exemplified in, 57 f.
Caste point of view, Proust's literary use of, 172 ff.
Causality, Proust's attitude towards, 116
Cervantes Saavedra, Miguel de, 20
Cézanne, Paul, 60
Character, *see* Personality
Charlus (character), 124, 188, 190 f., 227, 233, 239 f.
Church, Proust's defense of the, 234 f.
Circumstantial evidence, Talmud's forbiddance of, 234
Classic literature, characteristics of, 265 f.
Clericalism, Proust's views on, 235
Clermont-Tonnerre, E. de, 182
Combray, church of, Proust's description of, 48 f.

Combray caste, 180
Compassion, *see* Sympathy
Concentration, Proust's powers of, 274 ff.
Conduct, principled consistency of, 246
Cottard, Dr. (character), 164, 187
Criticism, literary, 266 ff.
Curtius, Ernst, 110, 118

Dandieu, Arnaud, quoted, 116, 211*n*
Daudet, Léon, 129, 223; quoted, 217 f., 264 f., 274
Daudet, Lucien, 182; belief in Proust's morality, 206 f.
Death, Proust's nonresistance to, 103
Devotional art, *see* Art, devotional
Dickinson, Emily, quoted, 15, 266*n*
Dinner party, given by Proust, 219
Doctors, Proust's derogatory attitude towards, 117, 164
Dogmatism, Proust's rejection of, 120
Domestic scenes, Proust's ability to transform, 60
Dreams, Proust's evaluation of, 70 f.
Dreyfus Case, 176, 220, 221, 223, 226 ff.; Proust's interest in, 53; role played by graphology, 128 f.; effect upon Swann, 203
Drunkenness, Proust's analysis of, 114
Dutch painters, Proust's fondness for, 59

Eccentrics, Proust's portrayal of, 272 ff.
Ecclesiastes, contempt for women, 93; danger of knowledge cited, 98
Einstein, Albert, 112 f.
Eliot, T. S., 269
Elstir (character), 34 f., 60
Erudition, 268
*Eve of Saint Agnes, The* (Keats), Proust's prose compared with, 61

Fashionable world, *see* Society
Faubourg Saint-Germain, *see* Saint-Germain-en-Laye
Figures of speech, Proust's use of, 25 ff.
First person singular, literary use of, 249
First World War: Proust's inability to serve in, 202 f.; painful effect upon Proust, 220 f.
Force, Physical, *see* Physical force
Formalism, 253
France, Anatole, quotations from Proust's letters to, 119
Franck, César, 47
Françoise (character), 51 f., 123, 151, 190, 274
Freud, Sigmund: Proust's similarities to, 159 ff.; point of difference from Proust, 163 f.
Friendship, Proust's rejection of, 158
Frost, Robert, quoted, 259

Genealogy, importance of, 189 f.
Genius, Proust's definition of, 36
Gide, André, 181, 249, 267, 269
Gilberte (character), 126 f., 131, 150, 198 f.
Gogh, Vincent van, 271
Goncourt Prize, awarded to Proust, 217, 265
Goya y Lucientes, Francisco José de, 191
Graphology, *see* Handwriting
Guermantes, Duchesse de (character), 194 ff.
Guermantes, Duc de (character), 228 f.
Guermantes, Prince de (character), 228 ff.
Guermantes family, 189
Gunther, John, 185

Habit: anaesthetic characteristics of, 68 ff.; the enemy of art, 71; opinions formed by, 227 f.; literary style affected by, 247; moral life based on, 247
Hahn, Reynaldo, 274 f.
Handwriting, the psychological importance of, 126 f.
Hawthorne, Nathaniel, quoted, 15
Homosexuals: Proust's defense of, 235 ff.; contrasts between, 239, 241 f.

Hudson, Stephen, 219
Human personality, *see* Personality
Humor, Proust's use of, 254 ff.

Idleness: a cause of mischief, 101; effect on the aristocracy, 199 f.
Imagery, Proust's use of, 56 ff.
Imagination, Proust's literary use of, 167 ff.
Imagination, poetic, *see* Poetic imagination
Imaginative literature, *see* Literature
Immortality, Proust's attitude towards, 104 ff.
Inferiority, plebeians harmed by, 170
Institutions, instability of, 134
Intellectual world, *see* Scholarship
Intolerance, cultural, 62

Jealousy: its role in Proust's fiction, 137; its inseparability from love, 156
*Jean Santeuil,* 3 ff., 256; themes developed in *A la recherche du temps perdu,* 29
Jews: Proust's sensitivity concerning, 222 ff.; literary use of, 224 ff.
Johnson, Samuel, quoted, 263 f.
Jonson, Ben, quoted, 24
Joyce, James, 269
Jupien (character), 124, 239
Juvenal, contempt for women, 93

Keats, John, *The Eve of Saint Agnes,* Proust's prose compared to, 61
Krafft-Ebing, Richard von, 237

La Bruyère, Jean de, 142
Lauris, Georges de, 235; quoted, 107, 110
Legrandin (character), 124 f., 239
Leon, Derrick, quoted, 97
Léonie, Aunt (character), 88, 123, 155, 200
Leroi, Mme (character), 184
Literary criticism, *see* Criticism, literary
Literature: society perpetuated by, 184; the characteristic qualities of, 257; a form of social thought, 258
Love: Proust's theory of, 32; Proust's analysis of, 136 ff.; subjective nature of, 138; Proust's reference to it as a disease, 140; uncertain nature of, 144 f.; relation of guilt to, 145 ff.; painful nature of, 145 ff.; the inspiration of art, 149; consent necessary for, 151; the ultimate test of life, 154; war compared to, 154; nonreciprocity in, 154 f.; Proust's clinical treatment of, 155; worthlessness of its objects, 156; origin of, 157; Proust's rejection of, 158; enigmatic character of, 159; analogy with parental relationships, 160
"Lower orders," Proust's sensitivity to, 200 ff.
Lucas, F. L., 215; quoted, 159*n*
Luxembourg, Princesse de (character), 195
Lyly, John, 22

Mankind, Proust's poor opinion of, 209
Mann, Thomas, 269
Marcel (character), 159
Marriage, mundane motivation of, 192 f.
Martin-Chauffier, Louis, Proust's appreciation of, 55 f.
Marx, Karl, weakness of, 169
Maugham, William Somerset, *Of Human Bondage,* compared to *Swann's Way,* 44
Mauriac, François, quoted, 27 f., 206
Maurois, André, quoted, 199, 212, 216
Medicine, Proust's derogatory attitude towards, 117, 164
*Memoirs of Saint-Simon,* 171 f.
Memory, the key to Proust's creation, 276 f.
Men, opinions formed by habit, 227 f.
Mirbeau, Octave, 230
Mobility, social, *see* Social mobility
Mohammed II, 95
Montesquiou, Robert de, 129, 221, 222, 236

Morality: Proust's reflections on, 32; Proust's advocacy of, 250 f.
Moral law, Proust's interpretation of, 207, 215
Moral life, affected by habit, 247
Moral profiles, Proust's literary use of, 212 f.
More, Paul Elmer, quoted, 101, 212
Moreau, Gustave, Proust's remarks about, 8 f.
Morel (character), 36 ff., 124, 239
Music: Proust's exaltation of, 40 ff.; moral lessons to be learned from, 211
Music, modern, Proust's optimism concerning, 66
Mutability, Proust's observations on, 90 ff.

Nature, Proust's subordination to art, 50
Nicolson, Harold, 248
Nietzsche, Friedrich Wilhelm, 255
Nirvana, Proust's goal of, 100
Nobility, *see* Aristocracy
Nordlinger, Marie, quoted, 109
Norpois (character), 214 f.

Occupation, Proust's development of the theme, 260 f.
Odette (character), 127 f., 227
*Of Human Bondage* (Maugham), compared to *Swann's Way*, 44
Old age, Proust's realization of its meaning, 99 f.
Optimism, the tendency of modern thought, 112

Personality: instability of, 132; Proust's theory of, 133; individual variations in, 273
Physical force, insignificance of, 170
Physicians, *see* Doctors
Place names, significance of Brichot's lectures on, 98
*Plaisirs et les jours, Les* (Proust), 78 ff.
Plato: theory of the relation of poets to their work, 9; Proust compared to, 252, 254 f.; quoted, 278
Pleasure, its identification with evil, 244
Plot, importance of, 4
Plutarch, 85
Poetic imagination: as exemplified in *Swann's Way*, 59; as exemplified in *The Captive*, 57 f.
Politics, Proust's attitude towards, 175
Pope, Alexander, quoted, 24
Pound, Ezra, *Cantos*, Proust's work compared to, 54
Prepossessions, our opinion of character influenced by, 124 f.
Principles, the proper rules of conduct, 246 f.
Proust, Marcel: evolution of, as a creative artist, 3 ff.; relation of his life to his work, 10 ff.; style of, 20 ff.; adherence of language of, to meaning, 23 ff.; use of figures of speech by, 25 ff.; theories of, on love, 32; aesthetics of, 33 ff.; Wagner's influence upon, 40 ff.; irony of, 51; image-making ability of, 56 ff.; poetic imagination of, 57 ff.; answer of, to his critics, 64; philosophy of, 78 ff.; pessimism of, 81, 84 ff., 101 ff.; observations of, on transitoriness and mutability, 90 ff.; homosexuality of, 94*n*; similarity of his work to that of Schopenhauer, 96; individualistic philosophy of, 101; effect of his constitutional defects upon his philosophy, 111 f.; relativism of, 112 ff.; rejection of a rigid dogmatism by, 120; understanding of psychology by, 122 ff.; accidental nature of his psychological enlightenment, 124; similarities of, to Freud, 160 ff.; Freud's point of difference from, 163 f.; pessimism of, 164; sociological aspects of his work, 165 ff.; imaginative aspect of his work, 168; literary use of the caste point of view by, 172 ff.; dynamism of his social outlook, 175; accused of snobbishness, 181; mother's influence upon, 183*n*; preference of,

for workingmen, 202; distress of, at inability to fight in the First World War, 202; the irresolution in his life, 204; conservatism of, 204; ethics of, 205 ff.; moral qualities of, 213 f.; inherited personality traits of, 215 f.; Jewish ancestry of, 216 f., 221, 222; desire of, for harmony, 219 f.; distress of, over the Dreyfus Case, 223; personality conflicts of, 223; individual judgments stressed by, 231 f.; need of, to escape from himself, 249; objectivity of, 249; morality advocated by, 250 f.; analysis of his work, 252 ff.; status of, in literature, 263 ff.; recent recognition of, 264 f.; pessimism of, 271; ability of, to draw eccentric characters, 272 ff.; faculty of, for concentration, 274 ff.; imitative skill of, 274; the preternatural memory of, 276 f.; devotion of, to self-analysis, 278
Proust, Robert, 222
Proustian irony, 51
Psychology, Proust's understanding of, 122 ff.
Puritanism, its relation to homosexuality, 244

Rabelais, François, quoted, 170
Rachel (character), 36 ff., 226, 233, 239
Realism, Proust's opinion of, 65 f.
"Recasting," Proust's belief in, 204
Reinach, Joseph, 232
Relativity, Proust's belief in, 112 ff.
Religious art, *see* Devotional art
*Remembrance of Things Past,* 3 ff.; its immensity compared to that of Wagner's *The Ring,* 45; attitude of critics towards, 68
Resignation, Proust's belief in, 102
Rimbaud, Arthur, 139
Roman Catholic Church, *see* Church
Royalists, *see* Saint-Germain-en-Laye
Ruskin, John, 220; Marie Nordlinger's remarks about, 109; Proust's first major literary enthusiasm, 211
Saint-Germain-en-Laye, 167 ff.; symbolism of, 181 ff.; poetry of, 188; fraudulence of, 203
Saint-Loup (character), 62, 97, 131, 139, 143, 240 f.
Saint-Simon, Louis de Rouvroy, duc de, *Memoirs,* 171 f.
Saniette (character), 245
Santeuil, Jean (character), 31 f.
Sazerat, Mme (character), 230
Schlegel, A. W. von, quoted, 252
Scholarship, Proust's respect for, 194 f.
Schopenhauer, Arthur, 30 f., 66, 113; influence on Proust, 82 ff.; reference to his *Metaphysics of Love between the Sexes,* 94
Science, Proust's dependence upon, 112
Scott-Moncrieff, C. K., 20
Sea, Proust's literary use of, 135
Seurat, Georges, 132
Self-analysis, Proust's devotion to, 278
Sexual perversion, *see* Homosexuality
Shakespeare, William, quoted, 110; Samuel Johnson's evaluation of, 263 f.
Sidney, Sir Philip, 257; quoted, 259
Snobbery, 167 f.; Proust accused of, 181; Proust exonerated from, 182; the unforgivable sin, 186 f.; poetry of, 188
Social life, *see* Society
Social misfortunes, exploited by the selfish and the unscrupulous, 233
Social mobility, Proust's belief in, 177
Social weather, one of Proust's favorite topics, 176
Society: Proust's rejection of, 158; stability of, 174; power of literature over, 184; futility of, 187; intellectual nullity of, 193 f.; cruelty of, 194
"Society writer," appellation resented by Proust, 193
Sociology, Proust's relation to, 165 ff.
Socrates, 263

Socratic dialogue, novel compared to, 252, 254 f.
Sollier, 163
Spagnioli, John, 167, 182
Straus, Mme, 129
Style, literary, 252 f.; affected by habit, 247
Suffering: Proust's emphasis upon, 72 ff.; the goal of lovers, 137 f.; advantages of, 148 ff.
Swann (character), 39, 143, 144, 152 f., 196 ff., 208 f., 224 f.
*Swann's Way:* second half a novelette, 43 f.; poetic imagination exemplified in, 59
Swift, Jonathan: attitude towards style, 24; contempt for women, 93
Sympathy, importance of, 210

Thibaudet, Albert, 166; notice of Proust in *Encyclopaedia Britannica,* 64
Third person singular, literary use of, 249
Tolstoy, Leo, 208
Transitoriness, Proust's observations on, 90 ff.
Translations, disadvantages of, 20 f.
Truth: Proust's search for, 116 ff.; inaccessibility of, 125; unpalatability of, 125; Proust's love of, 232; Proust's devotion to, 234 f.
Twain, Mark, quoted, 232

*Ulysses* (Joyce), Proust's work compared to, 54
Unattainable, the luster of the, 166
"United States of the World," Proust's reference to, 271 f.

Valéry, Paul, 44*n*
Van Gogh, Vincent, *see* Gogh, Vincent van
Verdurin, Mme (character), 195, 233
Verdurin family (characters), 245
Vermeer, Jan, 59
Vettard, Camille, 112*n*
Villeparisis, Marquise de (character), 184
Vinteuil, Mlle (character), 34 f., 124, 243
Voice, significance of, 129 f.

Wagner, Richard: influence upon Proust, 40 ff.; quoted, 211
War: Proust's attitude towards, 97 f.; inevitability of, 220 f.
*Wasteland* (Eliot), Proust's work compared to, 54
Watteau, Antoine, 191
*Weltanschauung,* 78
Whitman, Walt, 64
Wilde, Oscar, 258; quoted, 14
Will, importance of, 95 f.
Wilson, Edmund, 83, 180; quoted, 112*n*, 269 f.
Women: Proust's attitude towards, 92 ff.; attitude towards love, 141 f.; attractive qualities of, 150 f.
Work, a source of happiness, 101 f.
Workingmen, preferred by Proust, 202
Worldly ambition, silliness of, 203 f.

Yeats, William Butler, quoted, 262